A Writer Teaches Writing

W9-BRH-986

A Writer Teaches Writing

Revised Second Edition

DONALD M. MURRAY

University of New Hampshire, Emeritus

THOMSON

━━━━✦━━━━ ™

HEINLE

Australia Canada Mexico Singapore Spain United Kingdom United States

A Writer Teaches Writing, Revised Second Edition
Donald Murray

Publisher: Michael Rosenberg
Acquisitions Editor: Dickson Musslewhite
Development Editor: Stephen Marsi
Production Editor: Matt Drapeau
Marketing Manager: Katrina Byrd

Director of Marketing: Lisa Kimball
Manufacturing Manager: Marcia Locke
Compositor: Pre-Press Co., Inc.
Cover Designer: Matt Drapeau
Printer: Webcom Limited

Copyright © 2004 by Heinle, a part of the Thomson Corporation. Heinle, Thomson and the Thomson logo are trademarks used herein under license.

All rights reserved. No part of this work covered by the copyright hereon may be reproduced or used in any form or by any means—graphic, electronic, or mechanical, including photocopying, recording, taping, Web distribution or information storage and retrieval systems—without the written permission of the publisher.

Printed in Canada.
1 2 3 4 5 6 7 8 9 10   07 06 05 04 03

For more information contact Heinle, 25 Thomson Place, Boston, Massachusetts 02210 USA, or you can visit our Internet site at http://www.heinle.com

For permission to use material from this text or product contact us:

Tel	1-800-730-2214
Fax	1-800-730-2215
Web	www.thomsonrights.com

ISBN: 0-7593-9829-1

For
RICHARD GOODMAN
who is responsible for my becoming
involved in the teaching of teachers

and

DONALD H. GRAVES
who is a constant companion
as we continue to learn to write
and teach teachers so their students
will hear the voices they have never heard

Contents

Preface

Books are like children who have a life of their own and I am surprised and honored that a manuscript I delivered with secret pride and public apprehension 36 years ago is now considered a historical document.

The first edition of *A Writer Teaches Writing* was published in 1968 when the protest against the Vietnam War ignited social and political challenges to all our mores and institutions including what was taught and how it was taught in our schools from kindergarten to graduate school.

Looking back I am astonished by my chutzpah. I had only become a teacher four years earlier at the age of 39 and now I was publishing a book on how writers wrote and how teachers could use this knowledge in their classrooms. I did not at the time connect *A Writer Teaches Writing* with the political and social changes that were reinvigorating our educational system. Many teachers, however, welcomed an approach to the teaching of composition that encouraged individual student writing and individual instructor and peer response. The process approach to writing, as it came to be called by others, respected the student's potential and delighted in diversity of both student and teacher. If not a product of that time, it was the climate of the Sixties that allowed its publication and acceptance.

The second edition, which is reprinted here, came out in 1984 and it was a different book. I was now an experienced teacher who had worked with both students and teachers across the country and in Canada. I had extended my investigations into how published writers created their drafts and how that information could be shared with students. In addition, I had been joined by many other teacher-researchers who were exploring the same territory and instructing each other.

The 1984 edition of *A Writer Teaches Writing* was still in some ways an evangelical book and it was still radical to many in the educational establishment, but now there was an extensive community of teachers who were using the process approach, researching it, and publishing their own accounts and interpretations of what had become an established approach to the teaching of writing in elementary, middle, and secondary schools as well as in many college undergraduate and graduate courses.

To me, however, *A Writer Teaches Writing* will always be an autobiographical document, the narrative of one writer who attempted to become a teacher of writing in mid-life. I was a thirty-nine year old full time writer of books and magazine articles when I returned to the University of New Hampshire to establish a journalism program. That first semester I was also assigned a section of Freshman English and a course for prospective English teachers which I did not know was not staffed because of the traditional snobbery of my literature and writing colleagues toward education majors.

I arrived back in Durham on July 1, 1963 and began studying the writing texts available for students and teachers. I was often impressed by their critical examinations of the writing product, but the instruction contradicted what I practiced as a publishing writer. If I followed this formal rhetorical approach the books advocated, I would be producing unreadable and unpublishable writing in my second life outside the academic world.

Not finding a textbook I felt I could teach, I used the students' evolving drafts as the basic text of the writing courses and began to develop my own handouts on how writing was made. In 1939, as a ninth grader doing badly in school but determined to become a writer, I explored the stacks of the Thomas Crane Library in Quincy, Massachusetts, where I found an autobiography by Burton Rascoe, a Chicago newspaperman, about his life as a reporter and then discovered other books on writing by writers in the low 800 numbers of the Dewey Decimal system. I swallowed writers' biographies and autobiographies, collections of their correspondence and published journals, and the books, essays and interviews on writing by published writers. Only 15 years old, I started compiling a commonplace book of quotations on how writers wrote years before I heard the term "commonplace book."

When I began teaching I turned to that commonplace book which soon grew to 24 three-inch thick notebooks of quotations from writers describing how they wrote. I did not, however, know how to organize what writers said about their craft in a manner that would be helpful to students.

In October of my first semester, I paraded my news writing class to a new classroom and told them, "If you forget how I have screwed up, I will forget how you have screwed up."

As a magazine reporter I had researched intercontinental missile stories just before I came to the university. The engineers saw the weapons as three separate parts: a guidance system, a weapon system, and a propulsion system. The system engineers had to connect these into an overall system and in describing their work, they referred to black boxes. They didn't know just what happened in the black boxes but if they worked, they didn't need to know. This terrified me as a human being, but now gave me a way to look at writing and the teaching of writing.

My most mysterious black box was the writing itself, the making of text, so I left that until last. I had done 30 drafts of each magazine article so, in the pre-computer age I had kite-tails of cut-apart and glued-together and marked up drafts to examine. I could study the black box of revision. When I felt I had some understanding of the black box of revision, I moved to the black box of prewriting where I had notes and outlines and charts and journals to examine. And last, I speculated on what went on in the black box of writing when the first draft was completed.

Dr. Richard Goodman, who was superintendent of schools in Hollis and Milford, New Hampshire, invited me to give an evening lecture that was funded by a local corporation. Afterwards he kept me in a car without a heater in midwinter New Hampshire until I agreed to work with an English teacher, the late Bill Sims, at Hollis High School.

Soon Dick Goodman became executive secretary of the New England School Development Council (NESDC), an organization of school superintendents in New England. He persuaded them to make writing first priority. I adapted my handouts for a series of workshops for English teachers on the writing process, emphasizing their own writing and their discovery of writing what they did not expect on the page. Writing was not completed thought written down but a process of finding out what you had to say and how to say it.

NESDEC established a summer writing workshop at Bowdoin College that lasted four years in the Sixties. I assembled a collection of writers' quotes and my class handouts in blue bindings. Each year it grew larger and others started showing it to publishers who praised and rejected it. My favorite rejection note said that the manuscript was so well written that "teachers would read it for enjoyment, not instruction."

A Houghton Mifflin editor told Dick Goodman he wanted to consider the bound handouts as a textbook for teachers. Dick asked for permission and, wise to the surreal nature of publishing, I didn't mention that Houghton Mifflin had already rejected it. This editor bought it and it was published by Houghton Mifflin in 1968, five years after I had started teaching.

I am honored by Heinle's publication of *A Writer Teaches Writing* but I am still apprenticed to the writer's craft. Each morning I come to my writing desk and write what I do not expect in ways I had not planned. My adventures with the writing process have not yet come to an end.

Donald M. Murray   January, 2003

The Author

Donald M. Murray, Professor Emeritus of English at the University of New Hampshire, has distinguished himself as a teacher of writing for the past half century. In addition to serving as chair of New Hampshire's English department and director of the freshman English program, Murray left an indelible mark on the university by inaugurating a journalism program and helping pioneer a graduate program in composition studies. He has twice won awards for his teaching, and has been awarded three honorary doctorates.

Murray established himself as a successful textbook author throughout his teaching career. *A Writer Teaches Writing* first published in 1968, and has since been a defining work of scholarship for generations of teachers. Its second edition printed in 1984. Murray's texts published by Heinle include *Write to Learn*, Seventh Edition (2002), and *The Craft of Revision*, Fifth Edition (2003).

Also an award-winning journalist, Murray earned the Pulitzer Prize for editorial writing at the *Boston Herald* in 1954. He has conducted workshops for corporations and served as a writing consultant for several newspapers, including the *Providence Journal* and the *Boston Globe*. He has been a prolific contributor to the *Globe*, with his popular column "Now and Then" appearing weekly since 1987. Murray's weekly reflections on the joyfulness and hardships of life over the age of 60 have received numerous accolades, and were recently compiled into an autobiography, *My Twice Lived Life*.

His most recent work, *The Lively Shadow: Dealing With the Death of a Child*, will be released in February 2003.

He lives in Durham, New Hampshire with his wife of 51 years, Minnie Mae.

A Writer Teaches Writing

1 Learning to Allow Learning

It is time to give away the secret: teaching writing is fun.

For decades composition teachers have hidden behind the wailing wall created by literature faculties which have complained about the burdens and frustrations of teaching composition. Their complaints are understandable. They have been trained to teach the best writing of the centuries and then are assigned, without special training, to teach beginning students who do not even want to write.

Even today the majority of composition courses in the country are taught by teachers who do not write, do not know how effective writing is made, and do not know how to teach writing. Of course they are ineffective and discouraged. They expect failure, and they get it.

But in the past twenty-five years the profession of composition teachers has grown to be a self-confident, lively profession that combines research and practice, philosophical inquiry and pedagogy, historical traditions and the new technology. The Conference on College Composition and Communication alone has grown from 1,214 members in 1959 to 6,439 in 1984, and its journal has increased its subscription list from 1,230 to 9,383 during the same years.

Increasing numbers of doctoral programs train researchers, teachers of teachers, and as one person put it, teachers of teachers of teachers. The Bay Area Writing Projects across the country and hundreds of other regional conferences and programs are directed by people who feel confident about the teaching of composition. They publish their articles in many new journals, and there is a constant flow of books on the teaching of composition. Many of these resources are listed in the Appendix. But for all the scholarly apparatus there is a mood unusual in education: most of the scholars in this field delight not only in their scholarship but also in their students. They accept and even seek students who are uneducated; students who are slotted in remedial programs; students who do not know they have anything to say and a voice in which to say it; students who are making their second, or third, or fourth attempt at an education; students who are anxious and unsure; students who do not fit normal academic patterns. Of course the new composition discipline and its understanding of how writing is made and its discoveries of how that understanding can be communicated to students has a powerful impact on the best students. But the composition profession — to its enormous credit — does not focus its energy on the elite but on those students who have often been ignored in educational systems.

The reason is selfish as much as altruistic. Composition teachers all know the thrill of hearing — with a student — that student's voice for the first time. Experienced composition teachers are able to help students find, in scattered fragments of unfinished prose, their own style. They are able to help students see meaning in their own experience. They are skillful at giving the student the opportunity of an audience.

Professional composition teachers do not look at teaching Freshman English, advanced composition, or even remedial writing as a chore, but as an opportunity. They know what to try, and they know that what they try may fail. But they have other things to try. The teaching of writing, like writing itself, is always experimental. Failure comes with the territory; failure is something to be expected, experienced, shared, laughed at, and used.

This does not mean lowered standards, but raised standards. The defenders of standards, like my former colleague who would say in department meetings, "We are the defenders of the humanistic faith, and we should withhold our knowledge until there is a generation worthy of it," do not raise standards; they simply abandon students who are not pretaught or who do not instantly learn. The new composition teachers bring to each individual student knowledge of extensive research on how people learn to write more effectively; they have an inventory of pedagogical strategies with which to attempt to draw learning out of the student.

These new composition teachers certainly do not have all of the answers. The discipline of composition theory continues to grow and expand. It is increasingly drawing on the knowledge of the past, and it has at last begun to integrate what we know about the teaching of reading and the teaching of literature, so that the profession can enrich itself with a new integration between the subdisciplines of English.

Those who choose to become teachers of composition have a marvelous opportunity. I backed into teaching composition when I joined the faculty as a writer and was assigned, partly against my will, to teach Freshman English and to teach a course for teachers in the teaching of composition. I did not know that the course for teachers had never been taught. It was given to me because everyone else had turned it down. I became a teacher of composition and a teacher of teachers of composition by accident.

I found myself part of a dedicated group of people who were looking at the magic of writing from many points of view. There were scholars and scientists and therapists and creative writers and intuitive teachers — and they all seemed to share a commitment to students and a belief that writing was important both to the individual who wrote and to the society which received the writing.

I have been proud to be part of this increasing profession, and I welcome you to it. I hope that you will add to the glorious babble of questioning and challenging, experimentation and failure to which we are all contributing.

This book does not describe *the* way to write and *the* way to teach writing. It is simply a book that attempts to describe *a* way of writing and *a* way of teaching writing. It is a book by a writer who is still learning to write and a teacher who is still learning to teach.

I hope that the book will share some tricks of the trade from an old pro. I hope that it will give an approach that beginning teachers may find helpful.

Assumptions

I think it is important for teachers — and students — to know the assumptions and beliefs on which their teaching is based. Several key assumptions underlie this book.

Writing Is Thinking

Meaning is not thought up and then written down. The act of writing is an act of thought. This is the principal reason writing should be taught in the academy, yet, ironically, it is this concept that is most often misunderstood by academicians. They give writing assignments based on the assumption that writing begins after the thinking is concluded, and they respond to those assignments as if the etiquette of language were more important than the thinking represented by language.

Writing is not superficial to the intellectual life but central to it; writing is one of the most disciplined ways of making meaning and one of the most effective methods we can use to monitor our own thinking.

We write to think — to be surprised by what appears on the page; to explore our world with language; to discover meaning that teaches us and that may be worth sharing with others. We do *not* know what we want to say before we say it; we write to know what we want to say.

Writing Is a Process

Writing is a craft before it is an art; writing may appear magic, but it is our responsibility to take our students backstage to watch the pigeons being tucked up the magician's sleeve. The process of writing can be studied and understood. We can re-create most of what a student or professional writer does to produce effective writing.

The process is not linear, but recursive. The writer passes through the process once, or many times, emphasizing different stages during each passage.

There is not one process, but many. The process varies with the personality or cognitive style of the writer, the experience of the writer, and the nature of the writing task.

Effective Teaching Is Responsive

We learn best — at least in the study of composition — when we are *not* told in the abstract what to do and then commanded to do it, but are encouraged to write and then have the opportunity to examine what we have done with an experienced writer, who can help us discover what worked and what needs work.

This method of instruction allows the student to learn how to read each draft so that future drafts — on this subject and others — may be improved. The student, when responsive teaching is effective, becomes the student's best teacher.

Writing Is an Interaction of the Global and the Particular

Traditional writing instruction usually works on the assumption that students need to learn the parts so they can eventually construct a meaningful whole. Traditionally, emphasis is first on vocabulary, spelling, usage, mechanics, and the conventions of manuscript presentation and later on organization, style, and appeals to an audience. Usually the subject is supplied by the instructor since the students do not know anything "substantial." It is logical, but it doesn't work for most students; the particulars are not abstractly significant to students who cannot understand their purpose or importance until they use them to make their own meaning.

Non-traditional composition teaching usually reverses the process and emphasizes personal content and personal voice first, working backwards from global concerns to the particulars of language and manuscript presentation. I voted with that caucus for many years, and if forced to choose between the two positions I would again. Writing is not, however, that simple.

Writing is a product of the interaction of the global and the particular. We use a word to catch a vague idea and it becomes less vague, and so we work back and forth from whole to part and part to whole, each influencing the other, each strand helping the writer weave a pattern of meaning.

There Is No One Way

We do not teach writing effectively if we try to make all students and all writing the same. We must seek, nurture, develop and reward difference. The rich diversity of our students is to our advantage. There is no single kind of person to teach, no one reason to write, no one message to deliver, no one way to write, no single standard of good writing.

Neither is there one way of teaching. I am delighted by the differences in teaching style and methods of the effective writing teachers with whom I work. I would hate it if they all taught as I do or if I were forced to teach as any of them do. Our individuality as students and teachers should be central to all that we do.

The world is complex and diverse, and writing can thrive in such ever-changing and ever-varying soil. We should not just accept diversity but also seek it and make use of it in our writing and our teaching.

I hope this book will help teachers take advantage of diversity and begin to see how to learn to teach less, so that their students can learn more. Our greatest challenge in developing the craft and the art of teaching is to learn how to allow learning, how to get out of the way of our students, so that we can run after them, supporting them when they need support, encouraging them when they've earned it, and kicking tail when they need to get going.

The title of this book, *A Writer Teaches Writing*, implies a personal book by a single writer, but I hope that each reader will become, through the experience of writing and teaching, the writer in the title; that each of us individually and differently will use the book and depart from it as we learn from our own pages and our own students.

This book is not the end for me, but another beginning. I have learned from writing it, and having written it I will learn how to depart from it. It is the sum of what I know today, but fortunately it is not the sum of what I will know at the end of the next semester or the next year or the next years of writing and teaching.

If you accept this profession — this calling, this vocation — you have apprenticed yourself to a lifetime of learning. Neither you nor your students will learn to write. You will use writing as a way of learning, a way of discovering and exploring, of finding what you may have to say and finding ways in which you may say it.

The same is true of teaching. Each semester your students are new, and you are new too. Together you will share the frustrations, the satisfactions, the difficulties, the failures, the successes, the despair, the joy of writing. And you will discover in your own way the secret that all effective composition teachers share: teaching writing is fun.

2 Cultivating Surprise: The Process Theory of Writing

Why write?

To be surprised.

That's the answer from writers who spend their lives returning morning after morning to the lonely discipline of the writer's desk. They write to find out what they will say. Peter Taylor says, "Writing is how you discover what you think." Maxine Kumin states, "I write a poem to find out what it is I want to say. It's a burrowing inward." Ruth Prawer Jhabvala adds, "I just sit down at ten in the morning and write until one and it slowly evolves. I have no idea what's going to happen." Bernard Malamud, who has said, "Writing teaches the writer," explains: "A familiar voice asks: Who am I, and how can I say what I have to? He reads his sentences to see if they answer the question. Thus the writer may tell his fortune."

Writing for Discovery

The writer sits down intending to say one thing and hears the writing saying something more, or less, or completely different. The writing surprises, instructs, receives, questions, tells its own story, and the writer becomes the reader wondering what will happen next.

This is the writer's addiction: we write because we surprise ourselves, educate ourselves, entertain ourselves. Writing, we see more, feel more, think more, understand more than when we are not writing in our head or on the page. As an administrator I felt a strange emotion I had not felt since high school, before I became a writer. I was bored. Writers are not bored. It is in their nature to make use of their world, to observe, to question, to doubt, to wonder, to connect. Our students must share this addiction with discovery and surprise because it is the greatest motivator for writing. It is what keeps writers — and writing students — writing.

Why Write?

Why write? To learn, to describe and therefore see, to speak and therefore hear, to entertain, to inform, to persuade, to celebrate, to attack, to call attention, to think, to make money, to promote, to advocate, to connect, to relate, to make, to share. But always behind each writing purpose is the secret excitement of discovery: the word, the line, the sentence, the page that achieves its own life and its own meaning.

The first responsibility of the writing teacher is to experience this essential surprise. You can't teach what you don't know. It is unfortunate that students can pass through twelve years of instruction in reading, writing and language without having their writing come alive — a metaphor that is a reality for the writer. The students can go on to be English majors in college and even to earn graduate degrees in English or English education without ever having felt language dance out of control on the page and lead the writer to an unexpected meaning.

If you or your students haven't had this experience, sit down immediately and write. Suspend your critical judgment. Don't let anybody look over your shoulder — not the ghost of a parent, a teacher, an editor, or a colleague who once pounced on an early draft and killed it before it had a chance to grow into a mature piece of writing.

Just write. Hard, fast. Make mistakes. Lose control. As Guy de Maupassant said, "Get black on white." See what happens. Let it run. Stand back. Plunge in again. Steal a phrase or a line or an idea or a feeling from what you've just written and try it again.

Study Peter Elbow, the master of free writing, if you want to know more about the techniques of letting your drafts and your students' drafts move towards potential. His books are full of free-writing ideas and such techniques as looping, in which the student grabs a phrase or a line and runs with it, then loops back again and again until a subject is ready to be developed.

Encourage Failure

Look back at the writing you have done. It's probably a failure. It doesn't work as a piece of writing, not yet. Good. It doesn't need to. We don't learn from finished, polished, completed published writing. We learn from the instructive failures of early drafts.

All writing is experimental in the beginning. It is an attempt to solve a problem, to find a meaning, to discover its own way towards meaning. We must learn, to teach writing, the necessity of failure and the advantage of failure. We are afraid to fail; our students are terrified by failure. They have been taught, by teachers and parents, the press, and their own instinct, that everything must be done perfectly the first time. They are inhibited, constipated, frightened — in no condition to produce good writing.

Why This Process

I never lost the excitement I must have felt, as every child does, at making a mark on paper. That squiggle is me, I made it. It is my meaning. But as I got older I found writing harder and harder. I started searching for the writing process under the illusion I could find a way to make writing easy — the sword would come right out of the stone. I didn't realize then that the importance of writing lies in the fact that it is not easy, and should not be. The writer should be exploring new territory with writing, seeking important meanings that are beyond the glib, easy sentence the writer has already mastered.

By the time I was in fourth grade I was publishing a newspaper, using a sickly yellow gelatin spread out on a cookie sheet with purple ink. In junior high I was reading about writers, fascinated at how they made up stories. Ever since then I have been reading about writers, collecting what they have to say about writing, observing them when I can, listening to them, trying to understand how language creates worlds that are more real than the one in which we live, how language creates and communicates ideas, how language keeps surprising me at my desk.

I was lucky years later, when I found myself teaching teachers as well as teaching writers. I needed to understand how writing was made so that I could share the writing process both with student writers and student teachers.

I used my own experience as a writer and all the study I had done since junior high on how writers write to construct a model of the writing process. Through the years I have created a number of other models — or guesses — of how the writing process works. Those models have been adapted and tested and revised by many people, including myself. I have not been restricted by any need for consistency. What I have sought is a clearer understanding of how writing is made, and through the years I have begun to learn that the search is more important, in a sense, than what is found. This book presents my latest model of the writing process, the one that includes all that I know now. It may seem to contradict my last book and it may seem to be contradicted in my next book; it most certainly should be contradicted by you as you confront your own writing, your own research, your own reading of the research of others, your own observations of your colleagues and your students.

A Model of the Writing Process

The process model we will develop and examine in this chapter is:

COLLECT

PLAN

DEVELOP

Remember:

○ This is not *the* model of the writing process, only a model that may help us understand how writing is made.

○ The model will vary according to the writing task. For example, an assignment may cause the writer to plan, then collect, replan and develop.

○ The model will vary according to the cognitive style of the writer. Some students will naturally write faster than others. There's nothing wrong with fast or slow, as long as the deadline is met.

○ The model will vary according to the experiences of the writer. Many beginning writers who have to free-write a first draft and develop it through many revisions will move towards more planning and less revision when they become experienced with a specific writing task.

The process model is still helpful, for it gives teacher and student a common way of looking at writing, a logical procedure which can be adapted to the needs of the student once it is understood. The rest of this chapter and the next will develop the process with a great variety of writing activities that you and your students can use to find surprise in their writing and make disciplined use of it.

Collect

You can't write writing. Effective writing is produced from an abundance of specific information. The writer needs an inventory of facts, observations, details, images, quotations, statistics — all sorts of forms of information — from which to choose when building an effective piece of writing.

It is also information that breeds ideas. Specifics make contact with each other and become an idea. Two and two, in writing, add up to seven. The writer, however, will not have ideas if the writer is not collecting specific information. Students do not realize the importance of the specific in getting ideas and, in general, do not understand how writers discover their subjects.

Where Do Writers Get Ideas?

Many writers, and I am one of them, do not have to seek ideas for writing. Topics rise from within in a constant flow, and there is no need to think of ideas or to stimulate more ideas. The problem is to deal with the ones that demand attention.

Some of the ideas come from the deepest psychological concerns of the writer. Writing is my way of achieving moments of sanity or understanding. I came from a background that was filled with sin, guilt, and threats of Hell and damnation. I was brought up with a grandmother who was paralyzed when I was young, and it was my job when I woke up early in the morning to see if she was still alive. I was a sickly, only child in a world filled with the threat of disease and death, punishment and retribution, and much of my writing is a psychological necessity.

Do not envy my pathological self-absorption. It is not necessary to be a neurotic to be a writer. Many writers find ideas in the world around them. And so do I. Not all of my ideas are the result of Scottish toilet training. Ideas about writing and teaching writing come to me from my own experience in writing, from studying or reading about the experiences of others, from my teaching, from the reports of others' teaching, from my students, from my reading. All we see or hear connects with something else, passing through our unconscious and conscious until it ripens into a subject that is ready to write.

Most writers are exceptionally aware of the world around them. They may be poets lying in wait behind a mask of good fellowship at a cocktail party, journalists asking discomforting questions, researchers quarrying libraries. Writers have many ways of extending their awareness and connecting what they learn with the past, the present, and the future. They gather far more information than they will ever use, never knowing when a stray piece of information will brush another piece of information and spark an idea.

There are also ideas that come entirely from outside the writer, and there are writers who completely depend on external ideas from editors and still are productive. All writers have people who present ideas to them, who are offered assignments from editors, or who simply decide without any conscious internal need that they want to write on a particular subject.

In school this is unfortunately normal. Most ideas come from outside the student — children are given story starters, old students have topics given to them, and assignments made for them. I also am given topics by editors or people inviting me to speak. I usually choose topics on which I have already been making notes or topics I have avoided but which I am challenged to explore. In fact, this is such a common practice that at times, in working with teachers and in working with journalists, I have put "idea" rather than "collect" as the starting point of the writing process. But I have not done that recently, or done it in this book, because I don't really think it is the starting point for writers.

Writers are writing all the time. They are collecting information that may help them in the future. Students need to know how to collect information and connect it so that they can develop their own ideas out of their own material in answer to their own needs. They need to be freed from a dependence on external assignments and made aware of how writers collect information, so that they begin to collect the raw material of writing and have it stacked up, like cordwood in the backyard, ready to fulfill an assignment.

Collecting information is an essential part of the writing process. Information is the resource from which all writing is built, and the resource to which writers return at every stage of the writing process. When the writer receives an idea from someone else, the writer does something that few students do — the writer turns the idea around, internalizes it, and makes it the writer's own. The writer searches through the information that has been collected consciously and unconsciously in the past to see what can be used to make the idea the writer's own. If the writer is given an idea, or if the writer simply decides to write on a specific topic, then the writer begins by collecting the information that will fulfill the idea.

How to Recognize a Good Idea

There are two questions that can be used to test an idea. They are:

- *Does it ask a question you — and a reader — want answered?* The good idea has its own demand. It responds to an itch on the part of the writer and a reader. Writing is a way of exploring a world. It may be a world of experience or a world of ideas, or a world of feeling or a combination of different worlds. But an idea that is worth pursuing is exploratory; it probes; it studies; it questions; it learns; it answers. It has a purpose and a need.

- *Can it be answered?* The effective idea has the possibility of completion. There are many good ideas that we don't know how to develop.

We have to be able to find information that answers the question and to fit it into a form that develops and shapes that information. Each writer has to learn his or her own ground rules for squinting at the territory ahead to see if there is information available and to see if that information has the possibility of being constructed into a meaningful answer. Many times writers have to start down a road before they can know if this topic or idea must be abandoned for the present. The good ideas are usually those in which the question connects with information the writer has already collected. There may be a lot more collection to do, but the writer knows that an answer is available and knows where to seek that answer.

These are six ways writers collect information that produces ideas.

Awareness

The writer is a receiver of information. The writer must develop the ability to lie in wait, to be alert with every sense to what is going on. The writer is a spy on life, looking inattentive while paying close attention, overhearing what is being said, noticing what is not being done, experiencing the taste of fear, the smell of death, the feel of pavement moving under a jogger's feet.

One of the most exciting things about writing is that writing helps us remember what we did not see or hear or feel or touch or taste. Our brain, if we do not clog it with busyness, records much more than we know, and the more we use what is recorded in our writing, the more the brain seems to record.

Observation

The writer must not only receive information but seek it. The writer is not only looking for information from which to build a particular piece of writing, but also collecting information against the day when it may reveal a subject.

Sometimes writing instructors think that description is too simple for college students, and I have colleagues who feel description does not even belong in the freshman composition class. To the writer, however, description is deceptively simple, and the ability to observe details in life is closely allied with observing details in the text, through the microscope or in the management study of a supermarket operation.

Writing is constructed from concrete, accurate, sturdy bits of information, and so is good thinking. Thinking and writing depend on the abundance and the quality of information.

Recall

Writers know how to rummage through the attics of their minds to find what they didn't know they knew and to connect information in new patterns. Writers are well aware that our brains record far more than we are aware of recording and that there are ways to call that information up, dust it off and put it to use.

Brainstorming

An excellent way to recall what is stored in your brain is to suspend critical judgment and simply list anything that comes into your head, whether it seems to relate to the subject or not. Don't worry about sentences, and feel free to use code words or fragments that have meaning only to you. Be silly, be ridiculous. Just list anything that comes to mind.

When you've run dry go back to the list and circle anything that surprises you. Then draw arrows connecting items on the list which relate to each other.

This exercise will stimulate your memory, and you'll find that you are remembering other things when you are away from the list and when you are writing. The items that surprise you or that connect are usually most powerful, and they may point the way to a piece of writing.

Mapping

Put a word in a circle in the middle of a page, and then draw lines out to other words that seem to grow out from that. Usually one word will make you think of other words or specific details related to the first one, and so you draw more lines representing branches from that subject. When you have nothing more to add on that particular topic, you go to another one and keep moving around until the page is filled with branches.

When you have finished stand back and do the same thing that you did with brainstorming: see what surprises and what connects.

Some feminists believe that this is a right-brain activity more productive for women than linear brainstorming. Whether that is true or not, I am fascinated by the fact that I come up with quite different material on the same subject when I brainstorm and map.

Exploration Drafts

We write more than we know we know when we write fast for short periods of time, letting whatever happens to come into our heads flow onto the page. It is a strange and sometimes frightening experience to have words running out of control, to be saying what you do not expect to hear yourself saying. As in brainstorming and mapping, you have to allow yourself to be uncritical, to let language lead you towards a potential meaning, not worrying about the traditions of spelling or usage or mechanics, just letting the writing explore the subject.

When you are done you can stand back to see what surprises you and what connects. This activity, like the others, is both a stimulus to the brain and a potential source of good writing ideas. Writers use these techniques to recall information about a subject they have been assigned by others or themselves, and they also use the techniques when they have nothing assigned as a means of finding out what subjects are getting ready to be written.

Empathy

Writers have the ability to put on someone else's skin, to think and feel like another person. This is a powerful way to collect information, and most people can learn to do it by thinking of a specific person who is different from them but similar in background or experience. This person might be old or young, liberal or conservative, rich or poor. When the writer becomes that person, the writer puts on a movie in the brain and discovers how this person the writer has become will feel and act and speak and respond in a series of dramatic situations. The writer who becomes expert at being empathetic with those for whom he or she has some natural understanding or sympathy may then be able to expand and crawl into the skins of people alien to the writer's background and in doing so make them less alien.

Interviewing

Writers need to learn how to collect information from live sources. Research, for the writer, includes people as much as books and records.

Beginning writers are often understandably shy about interviewing, feeling that it is difficult to meet a new person and an imposition to ask that person questions. I am still shy about interviewing strangers. What experienced writers learn, however, is that the interview boosts the ego of the person being interviewed. Each interview says, by implication, "You are the authority on a subject I'm interested in, you have information I need to know." Most subjects respond to this flattery by saying, "Of course I am, and this is what I know."

Writers discover it's usually a good idea to go to the top to ask questions of the person who, by experience and position, best knows the subject. Going to the top, of course, may mean interviewing the secretary to the dean rather than the dean. You have to speak to the person who really knows what's going on.

I like to prepare the five questions (sometimes there are four, sometimes there are six) the reader needs to have answered. Preparing the questions helps me avoid those that can be answered yes or no — "Did you think the team would win?" — and develop those which may yield more material — "What play told you the team would win?"

I spend time preparing these questions, although I won't follow them rigidly. When the President says, "I just shot my wife," I do not turn to question three about the budget. Good interviewers listen — listen carefully and follow up with questions spun out of what they have just heard.

As I do a series of interviews on the same story I will adapt the questions to what I'm finding out, but it is important for me to have some idea of what I want to get from the interview, and it's important to share that goal with the person I'm interviewing.

I take notes by hand, and my technique is to take a lot of notes so I don't suddenly swoop down on the notebook and frighten the interviewee when the subject gets interesting. People are comfortable with tape recorders these days, but it's still a good idea to take notes, because the tape recorder may not work, and it can make you lazy and not pay close attention to what is really happening. You also need to take notes on how the subject looks and the subject's surroundings, the colorful details that the tape recorder can't get for you.

Interviews on the telephone, or even by mail, are possible, but it's much better to see the person in person to be able to read the gestures, expressions, pauses, behavior of the person who's being interviewed.

Library Research

The search for specific, accurate information is at the center of the intellectual life. The writer needs a personal library and access to a library, or many libraries. The science writer, for example, will need to know how to take advantage of libraries specializing in one branch of science; the medical writer needs to know how to use the medical libraries in each hospital; legal or government writers must know how to get information from their specialized resource centers. (The Appendix reveals something of my own professional library.)

Fortunately, librarians are dedicated to serving the public. Most college and university libraries have programs to educate us in the effective use of the research tools we need on a particular project, and writers make great use of librarians' compulsion to help.

Plan

The most important writing usually takes place before there is writing — at least what we usually think of as writing: the production of a running draft. Writers write before they write.

I had the strange experience of being a laboratory rat in a writing study by Dr. Carol Berkenkotter of Michigan Technological University. ("Decisions and Revisions: The Planning Strategies of a Publishing Writer," Carol Berkenkotter, and "Response of a Laboratory Rat — or, Being Protocoled," Donald M. Murray, *College Composition and Communication*, vol. 34, no. 2, May 1983, pp. 156–172. Note: the word "not" should be stricken from 6. on page 171.) She studied my writing over a two-and-a-half-month period, focusing on two academic articles and a newspaper editorial I wrote during that time, although I did work on other projects, including fiction and poetry. She had me tape-record what I was doing while I wrote as well as keep every note and every draft. Then she studied the 122 ninety-minute tapes and the drafts. She also interviewed me and observed me writing.

The most important discovery, for me, was that I spent three-fifths of my time — or more — collecting information and planning my writing. Most of my rewriting turned out to be, in fact, planning. On occasion, I spent 90 percent of my writing time planning. Dr. Berkenkotter's research and my own observations of my most effective writing students and colleagues led me to the model of the writing process presented in this book.

Inexperienced writers often write too soon. I can hear the reader saying, "But you suggested we start the writing course by having our students plunge in and write." This is one of the contradictions I can never fully resolve in my own teaching. My beginning students need to write immediately so that they experience the territory of writing for surprise. When they know what it is to write, then they can start to learn to write more effectively. Writing is a skill, and students need to mess around with paints before they learn to paint, plunk at a piano before they are taught scales, fool around with a basketball, getting the feel of it, before they are put through a formal practice. Writing, unlike art, music and sports, has not been a matter of play for our students — at least not since the earliest grades of school. They have to write to reexperience that essential play. When they are in the game, we can begin to help them plan so they will write before they write.

Much of the bad writing we read from inexperienced writers is the direct result of writing before they are ready to write. Effective planning doesn't discourage discovery as long as it is open-ended and experimental and the writer understands what John Fowles says, "Follow the accident, fear the fixed plan — that is the rule." But that does not mean the writer should not plan. Planning, in writing, encourages the kind of accidents Fowles — and every other writer — needs. Planning takes the place of the many drafts that are usually necessary without adequate planning.

Focus

An effective piece of writing says one dominant thing. As Kurt Vonnegut, Jr., says, "Don't put anything in a story that does not advance the action." The same thing can be said for argument, memo, technical writing or poetry. Every element in the text supports and advances the main point. Planning starts with the search for that dominant meaning.

There are a number of techniques that help the writer discover the focus of a piece of writing — before it is written. But the writer should never forget that the act of writing itself is an act of discovery. The focus is not found, then kept unchanged. The writing will refine the focus, qualify it, adapt it, and many times cause it to change completely.

The writer does not arrive at the final destination before taking the trip, but the writer still has to have an idea of the destination before starting out. Pointless wandering is not very productive. Significant discoveries in chemistry are not made in the literature class. The writer needs to have some idea of what may happen during the expedition towards meaning.

Here are some ways the writer finds the potential focus in a piece of writing.

The Focal Point

Painters and photographers direct the viewer's eye to a single spot from which the picture can be understood. It may be helpful to study paintings or photographs to learn visually what we need to do with words.

The writer should learn the power of a single point to energize an entire draft. I like to look for an organizing specific — a quotation, statistic, concept, scene — that will draw all the material together. I find it helpful to seek a revealing detail, a significant fragment that will expose an author's style, a failure in a law, a character's weakness. Many times a single image will spark or organize a piece of writing.

William Faulkner explained, *"The Sound and the Fury* began with a mental picture. . . . The picture was of the muddy seat of a little girl's drawers in a pear tree, where she could see through a window where her grandmother's funeral was taking place and report what was happening to her brothers on the ground below." Non-fiction, as well as fiction or poetry, often begins with an image that contains, in a sense, the whole story — the acorn that contains an oak.

What words or phrases have special meaning to me as I work on a piece of writing? Often a rather ordinary word. We all have such code words in our life: the names of our family, the name of our hometown, the title of a special song. Sometimes such words or phrases provide a focus.

To find the focal point, the writer often starts by simply standing back from all the research, closing the notebook, pushing the file drawer shut, and sitting back with a pad of paper and trying to put down the most important thing the writer has learned from all the material the writer has collected.

Writers sometimes find it helpful to stand back and answer, sometimes in a paragraph, usually in a sentence, often in a phrase or a word, such questions as:

- What surprised me the most?
- What organizing specific will help me control material?
- What is the most revealing detail I have discovered or can remember?
- What image sticks in my mind's eye and seems to symbolize the entire subject?
- What person, or face, do I remember from doing the research?
- What idea kept coming back to me during the time I was collecting material?
- What code words have special meaning to me now?
- What is the most important single fact I have learned?
- What is the most significant quotation I heard or read?
- What is the one thing my reader needs to know most of all?
- What do I remember in greatest detail?
- What event is central to what happened?
- What statistic sticks in my head?
- What did I think when I was doing the research?
- What did I feel when I was doing the research?
- What person impressed me the most?
- What story or anecdote do I remember?
- What pattern or order did I begin to see?

Framing

Another way to develop focus is to frame the subject. This is, of course, another word for the traditional counsel of achieving unity. But unity for most beginning writers implies a finished kind of interwoven completeness they cannot conceive. It is more helpful to think of framing the subject or building a fence around it.

Most of us need to start by excluding rather than including. It is very hard to leave out material you have collected — but necessary.

Distancing

Establishing the most effective distance from which to write and, therefore, read a piece of writing is one of the most important planning activities, yet it is rarely taught. When working with professionals on newspapers and magazines it is a concept that surprises, interests, and helps professionals as much as anything else I teach them.

Like most good ideas, it is obvious. And the way to understand the concept of distancing is to think of photography. Photographers work with wide-angle lenses that include the entire mountain range, and with telephoto and close-up lenses that zero in on a cliff or a tiny alpine flower.

The writer has the same range of options, and much ineffective writing is the result of a writer using a close-up lens when the subject should be narrowed.

Distance, of course, implies detachment or involvement. The writer has an entire range of distances that may be created between the subject and the writer. The writer can stand back and view the issue of pollution with scientific detachment, and that very objectivity may be most effective in persuading the reader that something should be done. The writer's professional objectivity gives the writer a special authority. But the writer may also choose to move in close and show the reader the importance of the issue by spending a day with an industrial worker who is dying from the effects of pollution. The close-up may allow the reader to experience the way he, and his family, feel.

Point of View

When the photographer focuses on the subject the camera is at a particular place, and as the camera moves the subject changes. The writer has to know the point from which the subject is to be viewed — or argued, or analyzed, or discussed, or examined, or explained, or told.

During the planning process writers stalk their subject, moving around it, circling it, looking at it from this point and that point. Point of view, however, is not only a physical matter — the placing of the camera — but also a matter of feeling. Point of view is another way of saying opinion. Effective writers often find the focus of the subject by discovering their own opinions of it. This can be an opinion based on logic, or an opinion based on emotion, or an opinion built of both the intellectual and the emotional.

The Problem

Another way to find the focus of a piece of writing is to discover the problem that will be solved through the writing of the piece. We are problem-solving animals and we need problems to solve. Some studies of creative persons have shown that they see problems to be solved where others do not. We see a pile of beer bottles, and the artist sees the problem of catching the way the light reflects off the brown and green glass. The writer sees, in the same beer bottles, a story in the way Joe kept coming on too strong to the girls at the party and the kindly way that Judy put him down. The social worker looks at the bottles and sees the problem of alcoholism on campus that needs solving.

What Is the Reader's Question?

An effective piece of writing answers a reader's question, and to do that the writer must learn to anticipate the reader's concerns. Sometimes I will sit down and formally write out such questions as:

○ What does the reader need to know?
○ What will interest the reader?
○ What can the reader use?
○ What will help the reader?
○ What will surprise the reader?
○ What will make the reader an authority?
○ What will the reader rush to tell someone else?

Voice

Voice allows the reader to hear an individual human being speak from the page. Good writing always has a strong and appropriate voice. Voice is the quality, more than any other, that allows us to recognize exceptional potential in a beginning writer; voice is the quality, more than any other, that allows us to recognize excellent writing. We respond to voice when we hear it. Voice gives the text individuality, energy, concern.

Voice is, of course, closely allied to style or tone, but I prefer the term "voice" for it seems more accurate and more helpful for the beginner. However we discuss style, it seems to get related to fashion. Style sounds like something you buy off the shelf. It is made by someone else and it changes with the season. The term "style" encourages the misconception that writing is inherently dishonest, that the writer has to say what someone else wants the writer to say in manner appropriate to someone else. But good writing is honest — honest in what is said and honest in how it is said.

When Dr. Donald H. Graves of the University of New Hampshire started his monumental studies of children writing, one of the first things he noticed was that the most effective young writers were always practicing what they would write in their heads before they wrote. He called this process "rehearsal" and identified those children who were in an almost constant state of rehearsal.

As is the case of most good ideas, it seems obvious — after it has been mentioned. Even beginning writers are virtuosos of rehearsal. They have rehearsed speeches asking permission to stay up late to watch TV, to stay overnight with a friend, to use the car, to make a date, to get a job, to marry and unmarry, to get a raise. We all rehearse what we are going to say — and how we are going to say it.

The how is voice. We speak differently at home and on the street corner, in class and in the locker room, at the Saturday night party and the Sunday morning church service. The concept of voice is sophisticated, abstract, and theoretical, but everyone already recognizes voice and makes use of it.

Voice can also tell the writer what the subject is. The way we write about the subject tells us how we think and feel about it, what is important to us and what is less important.

Every beginning writer has a way of speaking that is part genetic, part regional, part social, part native language, part personality. We all begin with the voice that is natural to us, and then try to write as naturally as we speak, getting our voice down on the page.

Once the beginning writer can recognize his or her own voice on the page, the young writer can begin to adapt that voice to a specific purpose or reader.

The voice is most often heard in the line, a unit that is more than a word or a phrase, but less than a sentence. The writer is constantly searching for the instructive line. During the planning process, writers pay attention to those significant fragments that tell us how the writing may be written. These fragments contain the music of the writing, its rhythm, its pace, its beat, its song. Once you hear a fragment of the voice that will be developed in the draft, that voice can be held in the head or on the daybook page until the writer has time to write. I use the term "daybook" to refer to the log or journal in which I play with ideas, drafts, and notes. It is an ideal place to try out possible voices.

Some techniques for rehearsal are:

○ Talk to yourself. Speak silently what you may write and listen to the sounds of language in your head. Go somewhere (in the car, the john, in the woods) where you can speak aloud, hearing the way you may write.

○ Write fragments of language in your daybook that may demonstrate a voice appropriate to what you want to say. Test it by reading it aloud.

○ Read a draft aloud to hear the voice — when it is most effective and when it is not. Have someone read the draft to you so that you can hear its voice. Tape it and play it back to hear its voice.

Design

The writing process is organic. It grows and changes during the act of writing. What is being said changes what was intended to be said. The structure of the piece of writing must be adapted to the evolving message that is being delivered to the writer by the draft and will be delivered to the reader in the finished version.

There is no one way to design a piece of writing. As we study effective writers we find some pieces of writing that were written without the slightest hint of the order that would be imposed by the raw material on itself and other pieces of writing that were constructed from precise blueprints. The type of plan depends, to a large degree, on the personality of the writer. But I think it is dangerous for any writer to feel that he or she can never work from a careful plan or, on the other hand, must always have a careful plan.

The academic article I wrote before starting this draft was written without any formal plan at all. It evolved from the first paragraph as naturally as a river flows to the ocean. It seemed to flow naturally from a plan that was unconscious, if it existed at all. Each part of the writing came to me as if I were following invisible instructions. I accepted that; who wouldn't?

Then I turned to write the final draft of this book, and found myself making the most detailed plan I have ever made. It was necessary, and it was helpful, so I made the plan. But, of course, I haven't followed the plan, not exactly. (And when I revised and edited the book, I had more plans: three that I mailed to the editor in separate envelopes in one day. Each plan — I thought — was the final one. None was.) The outline is only a plan; the writing demands its own direction and development. I have had to leave things out and make room for new pieces of information. I have had to change the order and the pace, the proportions and the dimensions. I have had the excitement of writing a book that is more than the plan, but that does not mean that I didn't have to have a design from which to work. In fact, I had a number of designs, each one more complicated than the last, until I saw a new simplicity. And then that, in turn, became more complex, until it led to a simplification.

The writer needs a plan as an explorer needs a map. It's the guess of how things may go from past experience. But it is only a guess. Yet nothing will happen most of the time if there is no design. The writer will simply wander and have to try to impose a design later on, when it is much more difficult to do. Each sketch of what may be the design of the writing is a predraft, in which problems are identified and solved. And the more experienced the writer is and the more difficult the writing task the more likely the writer will begin to work with sketches of what may need to be written before the first draft is begun.

Genre

Inexperienced writers have the idea that the genre, the traditional form of a piece of writing, is something that is imposed on the writing instead of something that rises from the needs of the writing. Too often that is true, and it accounts for some of the bad writing we read. The teacher assigns a form and the student has to force the subject into that form; the editor assigns the form and the professional has to fill in the blanks even if the information doesn't match them; the writer declares that he or she is a poet or journalist or essayist or novelist and therefore jams information into a specific genre even when it is not appropriate.

Organic Form

Form — or genre — is too important a matter to be imposed from the outside. Form is one of the most significant elements in thinking, and the form we discover in the act of writing is essential to our understanding our subject and helping others to understand it.

When we begin to write we usually have a wonderful mess on our hands. Our raw material is a jumble of information and misinformation: memories, facts, rumors, speculations, guesses, quotations, half thoughts and full thoughts, details, fragments, ideas, theories. It is a glorious collection of stuff.

What we have to do in writing is to try to figure out what it all means, and one way we do that is by arranging and rearranging the mess of information in our minds and in our notebooks until we can see a form that brings the raw material together in a meaningful shape. The form arises from the material. We do not say this is an argument as much as see the pieces of information relating to each other in a way that we call argument. If we study the material and see people interacting with each other in a significant way, then we may have an order we call narrative. The form lies within the material, and it is our task to see what forms are there and which form helps us understand the meaning of the information.

We should always remember that form — or genre — is meaning. When we choose the form in advance of studying the material, or when we have the form imposed upon us by a teacher or an editor, we are told how to think and what to think. Story says there is a beginning and an end, and a series of motivated actions that get us from beginning to end. It tells us we must impose a rational order on what we are observing. When exposition is commanded we must find an explanation. A critical essay commands criticism. Comparison and contrast tell us to make comparisons and contrasts. No form is wrong. There is nothing wrong with a motorcycle or a trailer truck, but it may be difficult to ship the contents of a house from New York to California on a motorcycle.

We have to make sure that we look at the task and then discover the form within the task whenever possible.

Genre as Lens

When beginning writers discover the power of genre to give meaning to material they will begin to understand that genre is a lens they can use to examine life. The more skillful they become with a specific genre, however, the more danger that they will see the world through that single lens. While walking across the same campus the poet finds poems, the journalist sees news stories, and the essayist discovers essays.

There is something necessary and wonderful about this. We need people who see poems where we do not, but we should make sure we try out the great variety of lenses available to us. We should all be sure that we don't fall into the unthinking habit of using a genre because it is customary, because we have had success with it, because we think someone else expects it or because it is what we wrote the last time we wrote. We should use genre — the entire range of genres — to help us explore our subject.

Genre as Vehicle

Genre may be considered a vehicle which carries meaning to the reader. Each genre has been designated for use — to tell a story, to persuade a listener — and has been continually redesigned by use. The writer can consider a genre by deciding which form will carry the writer's particular message to an individual reader.

Structure

Young writers have to discover that a genre will not tell them how to solve the problems of building a piece of writing. It helps in the same way it helps to know if you're building a ranch house, a church or a supermarket. In any case, you have to build a specific structure.

Experienced writers spend time designing the writing structure that will help them develop and communicate their meaning. Plans are never final — the football game plan changes with what happens on the field — but plans still solve many problems in advance of writing.

Title

I'm a title nut. I often write 50, 100, 150 titles before I begin writing. Years ago when I was an editorial writer I would take a turn at working on Sunday because I could be alone in the office. I fell into the habit of writing the title or headline before writing the editorial. It was marvelously efficient, for I could write a headline of one word, or two or three, and capture the direction of the whole piece. It saved me from writing draft after draft of editorials that did not work.

I've held to the habit of writing titles, because it serves me. I can put titles in my daybook in small fragments of time during a commercial on a TV show, while I'm in a parking lot waiting for my wife, during a department meeting. It takes only a minute or less to write a title, five minutes to write five to ten titles. Each time I start I put down the titles without looking back at the others, and then I go back and look at the earlier titles and save the best ones. Sometimes, of course, I write seventy-five titles and find that the third title is the best one. But I didn't know it was the best one until I wrote the other seventy-two.

Note what a title does for the writer:

- It establishes the subject.
- It sets the voice.
- It points the direction.
- It limits the subject.
- It attracts the reader.

An effective title is not a label that simply tells what the piece of writing is — *Strawberry Jam* — it should go beyond that — *Minnie's Wild Strawberry Jam.*

An effective title is:

- *Honest.* The author can deliver on the promise of the title.
- *Short.*
- *Lively.* It has an individual voice.
- *Pointed.* It has an opinion or a point of view towards the subject.
- *Energetic.* It has drive, or energy, often carried in a verb.

There are specific attitudes and techniques that will help the title writer:

Attitudes

- Make title writing a game. Titles are too important to be written with high solemnity. The happiest and most insightful connections are often made when the writer is being a bit silly, loose enough to create the unexpected.
- Welcome the unexpected. Title writing is at the heart of the process of discovering meaning; title writing is thinking.
- Be wasteful. Promiscuity is virtuous in title writers. The more titles you draft, the more interesting combinations you'll have to consider.

Techniques

○ Write titles that are too long, then cut.

○ Try one-word titles. Few will work but they will help you focus on the key words in the piece.

○ Write with nouns and verbs.

○ Make the nouns and verbs as specific as possible.

○ Make the verbs as simple, direct and active as possible.

○ Combine the elements that fit together in the story in the title.

○ Combine the elements that are at war with each other in the title. Many good titles contain the tension or the forces within the piece in the title.

○ Watch out for alliteration; like the third drink, it can lead you astray.

○ When you have a title that seems close to working, change one word, trying a dozen other words. Focus on the verb.

○ If you can't avoid it, use a double title with a colon and a second title that qualifies it. For example, *My Life with an Alligator: Love in a Bathtub.*

○ Listen to the language of your subject and the voice you think you will use in writing about it, to hear words and phrases that might be used in the title.

○ Keep cutting until you have the title as short as possible.

○ Continue to check back to your subject. Make sure your title is honest and helps you — and the reader — understand the subject.

Lead

We know that a reader takes three to five seconds — or less — to decide to read an article. Professionals know how quickly they have to capture the reader, and the journalistic term "lead" comes from the need to lead the reader into the story.

John McPhee says, "Leads, like titles, are flashlights that shine down into the story." In teaching leads, I usually concentrate on the first sentence or the first paragraph, but McPhee goes on to remind me, "Some [leads] are much longer than others. I am not just talking about the first sentence. I am talking about an integral beginning that sets the scene and implies the dimensions of the story. That might be a few hundred words. That might be 2000 words, to set the scene for a composition 50 times as long."

John McPhee, incidentally, is a writer every teacher of writing should know, and there is an interesting and detailed account of his writing methods in the introduction to *The John McPhee Reader* by William Howarth (New York: Random House, 1977).

What we often forget is that the first line, sentence, paragraph, page or even pages is a flashlight to help us see the story we may then point out to our readers. Writers, however, do not forget the importance of the lead.

"What's so hard about that first sentence is that you're stuck with it," says Joan Didion. "Everything else is going to flow out of that sentence. And by the time you've laid down the first two sentences, your options are all gone." Paul Horgan states, "The most important sentence in a good book is the first one: it will contain the organic seed from which all that follows will grow."

Most writers do not proceed with a draft until they have a working lead, because the lead establishes the:

- *Voice* — the writer needs to hear the music that will be played during the writing of the piece. The voice is the element that binds all the other parts of the writing together, and the writer must hear it and feel it before beginning to write. Most writers test the voice by drafting and redrafting leads.
- *Subject* — the content that will be dealt with in the piece of writing.
- *Meaning* — the point of the piece of writing and why it should be read.
- *Perspective* — the point of view from which the subject is seen.
- *Authority* — the authority on which the writing is based, the place on which the weight of the story rests.
- *Spine* — to which everything in the piece is connected.
- *Direction* — in which the piece is headed.
- *Limits* — what is in and what is out.
- *Dimensions* — the size and shape of the piece.
- *Proportions* — the balance between the parts of the piece.
- *Pace* — the speed with which the reader will move through the piece.
- *Genre* — the tradition into which the writing fits or the form that contains its meaning.
- *Structure* — the way in which the reader's questions will be answered.

All of these things in a line or a few lines? Yes, and perhaps more. But the attention paid to leads is not wasted. Each lead is, in a real sense, a draft of the entire piece, an implied draft that can be tested and responded to by the writer, the classmate, the teacher. Writing leads is a shorthand way of testing all sorts of approaches to a piece of writing.

I had mentioned that I might write 150 titles; that was about my average when I was a full-time magazine free-lancer. At that time I averaged about 60 leads per piece. I'm not compulsive about writing leads. If I think the first lead is exactly right I'll go with it, but I don't usually know that the first lead is right until I have tried many more. My first leads are usually drafts of ways I might approach a story, and once the lead has taught me the correct approach I keep polishing it until I have a lead in which the entire piece, in a sense, is packed so that it will grow from that seed.

I must remind myself when writing leads — and remind you — that I will, like all writers, often write badly to write well. It is play in which I am engaged, and I do not expect to be graded. In fact, no one ever sees my leads unless I am writing on writing — or teaching writing — and feel compelled to expose what goes on in the writer's workroom.

Lead writing, like title writing, is best done in the head and on the page in small chunks of time. It must be play, a game in which you try to find what you have to say and how you have to say it. The attitude should be the same as those attitudes encouraged during the process of writing titles: play, welcome the unexpected, and be promiscuous.

Some types of leads:

• *Direct statement.* A good starting point is to say what the piece of writing is about, or what it says, in as few words as possible. Usually this means a subject, verb, object sentence. Once the lead writer knows what the piece of writing will say, then the writer can sharpen that sentence, making the words more specific and the verb more active. If it doesn't work as a lead — if it wouldn't attract a reader and establish a way of writing for the writer — then the lead writer can move on to other alternatives.

• *Anecdote.* An effective way of starting a piece of writing is to use an anecdote — a brief story — that reveals the essence of the piece of writing in a paragraph or so. The or so comes in when there is a dialogue, for we usually start a new paragraph every time a different person speaks. These little stories are extremely effective in involving the reader in the story, but the anecdote must be accurate. The danger is that we will use a good anecdote that isn't quite appropriate to what we want to say, and it will drag the whole story off target.

• *Quotation.* An effective lead is often a quotation from a person within the story. It has the ring of authority, and a good quotation has its own voice. The danger is that the quotation, like the anecdote, will be a bit off target. The writer should be careful not to pick a quotation that is vigorous but inappropriate.

• *News.* The writer tells the reader immediately what is new about the subject. The news lead, in a sense, tells the reader why he or she should read on. It usually includes the five W's: *who, what, when, where, why*.

- *Informing detail.* The writer gives the reader a specific bit of information that will interest and intrigue the reader, who will want to read on to find out more. That bit of information may be a statistic, a fact, a revealing detail, an action, a behavior.

- *Dialogue.* The dialogue lead is rarely used, but it can be effective, for it puts the reader front row center, where the conflict in a piece of writing can be observed immediately. Drama is built on conflict, the interaction of opposing forces, and the reader should see these forces in action as soon as possible.

- *Surprise.* The writer may deliver the unexpected to the reader. This surprise may come from the information in the piece of writing or from the way it is written, but it must be an honest surprise. The writer should not tease or trick the reader.

- *Description.* A specific, detailed description is often a good way to attract the reader. The reader likes to see a place, a process, something that is central to the subject. That description should be packed with visual details, and will be richer if it includes details that attract the senses of hearing, tasting, touching and smelling, as well as seeing.

- *Mood.* Often a reader will be led into a piece by a lead that establishes the atmosphere or climate or a situation. The lead may present the reader with the feeling in the locker room, on the accident ward, in the student government office. This can be a powerful technique if the climate or atmosphere is central to what is being said in the piece. If not, it will just be self-conscious overwriting.

- *Face.* One of the most effective leads is to reveal an individual who is central to the piece of writing. Readers like to meet new and interesting people. It is important for the writer, however, to give that person a strong physical presence. It's usually good for them to be seen in action, doing something significant in the article. And the reader should have a dominant impression of that person by the end of the lead.

- *Scene.* A lead that combines a place, a person or persons, and an action, of course, develops into a scene. In a lead the scene must be short, but it can be very effective in establishing the texture of the piece to be written. It draws the reader in immediately and makes the reader an observer, almost a participant in the article.

- *First person.* The writer is often denied the use of "I" in academic writing and is forced to hide behind false objectivity and such awkward constructions as "one observed one's class doing one's assignment."

The reader, on the other hand, can be attracted to the first person in the lead when the writer speaks honestly and directly of the writer's own ideas from the solid base of the writer's own authority.

● *Third person.* Those who write in the first person may find it productive to stand back and write in the third person — "he" or "she" — to gain distance on their subject.

● *Tension.* A good way to start many stories is to reveal the forces within the piece of writing as they collide with each other, or as they pull in opposite directions. The reader is interested in these forces and in how they will work out.

● *Problem.* Often it is helpful to the reader to set up a problem so that the reader can be involved in its solution during the reading of the piece.

● *Process.* Readers like to see a process unfold, and the lead that can plunge the reader into that process — the winning of the game, the passing of a law, the discovery of a scientific theory — will attract and hold the reader's interest.

● *Voice.* Sometimes the writer can use language to lure the reader into the piece. The danger is that the writer will be cute or overwrite and get between the reader and the subject. But if the voice is true, it can set the tone for the entire piece.

There are other lead-writing techniques that rarely work but that appear logical and are used by the inexperienced writer. There are no absolutes in writing. They may work but they usually don't. Some of these are:

● *Second person.* Inexperienced writers often try to begin a piece by addressing the reader directly, saying "you." It rarely works in a lead. It *can* work as the piece is developed (I use it in this book, in fact); but in many cases the reader identifies much better with the third person — "he" or "she" — or even the first person — "I" — than with the second person. The second person can seem patronizing to the reader and should be used with care.

● *Rhetorical question.* The rhetorical question — "We do want to take our medicine, don't we" — is often used by beginning writers. It doesn't work, for the reader knows that it's not a true question. The writer knows the answer and is not going to listen to the reader. It puts the reader off — and it should.

● *Background.* Inexperienced writers usually start by giving the reader the background, or what led up to the subject that's being written.

The reader, of course, often needs background material, but has to know why it is important to read this material. A lengthy introduction keeps the reader away from the subject. Although it came first in life it can rarely come first in the article. The reader usually likes to get this material in a context paragraph after the lead, or likes to have it woven in when it helps the reader understand a point that is being made.

- *Introduction.* I've kept the formal introduction to the end. One way the writer can begin is by telling the reader what will be said before it is said. The introduction is the beginning demanded in many academic papers, but it is also the least effective beginning, because readers who are not paid to read student papers are impatient and will want the writer to get on with it. The introduction tells the reader slowly, and usually rather generally, what will be said further on. It's much better to say it.

The experienced lead writer will usually follow a few simple principles:

- ○ *Honesty.* The lead is a contract with the reader. The lead must deliver on its promise to the reader. It cannot be a tease and refuse to deliver what it promises.
- ○ *Simplicity.* The lead writer tries to make the meaning clear in as few words as possible.
- ○ *Immediacy.* The lead writer tries to get to the subject right away with as little delay as possible, so that the reader is plunged into the story.
- ○ *Information.* The writer provides the reader with specific information, information that is so interesting the reader will be compelled to read on.
- ○ *Voice.* The lead writer tries to establish the tone of a single writer speaking to a single reader. The reader wants to hear the writer's voice and to have the illusion of a private conversation with the writer.

I have spent so much time talking about leads because the lead, for most writers, is the whole of the writing in miniature. All of the elements of the writing can be attempted and tested in the writing of that first paragraph or so. But the writing of leads must not become a theological absolute. There are writers who plunge in and write leads later. There are pieces of writing that have to be worked at, and can be worked at, without a lead. An obsession with leads can be, for some writers, a blocking device, and writers often have to start without consciously writing the lead, sometimes by starting a letter to a friend or an editor. Usually writers have to write many leads, but some writers can go with the first lead — especially those writers who are constantly rehearsing leads in their head.

Writers know that the time spent on leads is not wasted. It helps the writer focus on what is essential in the story, and it allows the writer to discover and polish the voice. In addition, leads that are not used will pop up as crucial paragraphs during the development of the draft. They will appear at turning points and at the end, and will make the draft more effective.

End

When I was in the paratroops I knew people who had never landed in an airplane, and when I was on a newspaper I knew journalists who had never written an ending, whose stories just trailed off. I am embarrassed to admit that I didn't know the real importance of planning endings until a few years ago, when John McPhee gave a reading at the University of New Hampshire and talked about writing endings first.

To be honest, I didn't really believe McPhee, or other writers who had talked about this. "If I didn't know the ending of a story, I wouldn't begin," said Katherine Anne Porter. "I always write my last line, my last paragraphs, my last page first." William Gibson testifies, "I always know the end. The end of everything I write is somehow implicit from the beginning. What I don't know is the middle. I don't know how I'm going to get there." "I don't know how far away the end is — only *what* it is," says John Irving. "I know the last sentence but I'm very much in the dark how to get there." Eudora Welty ends her discussion of endings with the image of the seed Paul Horgan used to discuss the importance of beginnings or leads. "I think the end is implicit in the beginning," Welty says. "If that isn't there in the beginning, you don't know what you're working toward. You should have a sense of a story's shape and form and its destination, all of which is like a flower inside a seed."

But it wasn't until I was working as a writing coach at the *Boston Globe* and asked the most effective writers early in the planning or drafting stage if they knew where they were going to end, and they did, that I recognized the true importance of the end. Effective writers would, of course, change the ending if it didn't work, but they knew where they were headed.

What is even more embarrassing to confess is that I also know where I expect to end before I begin a draft. If you looked through my daybooks you'd note I often use a capital *K* (for kicker) to mark notes or drafts of endings I might use.

And the ending is important for the reader as well as the writer. Many studies have shown that the reader remembers what is read last more than anything else in the piece. Certainly an effective ending gives the reader a sense of fulfillment or closure. It draws the piece together and reinforces what the writer has said.

Writers rarely use the formal conclusion — the summing up — that is written directly to the reader. More effective endings come when the writer finds a way to conclude by implication, by giving the reader something specific that will make the reader come to the conclusion that the writer wants. To do this, writers usually use the same techniques that are used to produce an effective lead.

The Trail

When young writers have a beginning and an ending, then they can begin to see the trail that will lead them through their material. Writers know they must write from abundance, and they expect problems in selection. Sometimes, of course, the trail will be instinctive, or immediately clear, but many times writers will need a map. But unlike geographic maps, the one they draw themselves is usually more helpful than the one drawn by someone else. Writers have to find their own destinations and their own way to get there.

The Sketch

At the end of the planning process the writer may be able to draw a sketch of the writing to be drafted. Some writers, by their nature, need an extremely detailed sketch; others need only scrawled reminders of key points; and still others, especially fiction writers, say they need no such sketch at all and are, in fact, frightened that a sketch will keep them from the accidental discoveries essential to a good piece of writing.

Of course writers who create fine pieces of finished writing without a sketch should never use one. Even those writers who are most opposed to sketches will run into writing tasks that demand the successful completion of a sketch. And if you talk to effective writers who do not make sketches on paper while they are in the prewriting stage, you will find that they have a very good idea of where they are headed. Their sketch is in their head, not on paper.

I'm talking about outlining, of course, but the term "outline" has a connotation of formal, rigid planning which is contradictory to what the writer does. The sketch is not a blueprint that has to be followed; it is a way of guessing what the piece of writing will look like so that the writer can take a look at the piece of work that may be constructed and make changes before the time-consuming process of completing a draft.

There are also some pieces of writing that are almost impossible to outline or sketch: humor, a mood piece, most poems, much fiction, especially that which depends on character more than plot for its success.

There are a number of different ways to sketch a piece of writing in advance:

- *Frame.* The sketch I most frequently use builds naturally from the planning techniques used in this section of the book. I have a title, a lead, the three to five main points, and an ending. I have built a frame around what I want to say. I know where I will start and how. I know where I expect to end, and how. And I have a strong sense of how I will get from beginning to end. I have the same feeling, I am sure, that a builder has when a house is framed in; there's a lot of work to do, but the entire job can be visualized. This sketch allows me to examine the voice as well as the structure of the piece of writing. In an article or a chapter I usually write a draft very fast at one sitting, or two, and I'm able to do this because the sketch is so complete.

  As I build this frame I may look back and use titles, leads, endings, trails I have sketched earlier. I may look back and use some and use new ones that come to mind, or I may choose not to look back but just to sit down and make a new frame, knowing that all the work I have done is in my head, where it belongs. I can check back later if I feel it will help.

- *Query.* Non-fiction, both magazine articles and books, is often proposed and sold by a query. Many writers use a letter to query an editor, but I find that letters tend to become discursive, and do not allow the writer to show how he or she intends to write the piece and do not help the editor visualize the piece.

  I write my address and phone number, single-spaced, in the upper left-hand corner of a piece of plain paper. Two lines down, in caps and underlined, I put the title, and under it, in upper and lower case, centered, the name I intend to use in writing the piece. Two more lines down, single-spaced, I write the lead as I think it will be written in the final copy. I do not tell the editor about the piece, but reveal it through this lead, which is ordinarily not more than ten lines. Then, indented, single-spaced and bulleted, I make, in five lines or less, the three to five main points. Then back out to the normal margin, and single-spaced, I write a paragraph or two telling the editor about any special qualifications I have, permissions to get the story, research materials, market possibilities, anything the editor needs to know. This takes no more than one page, unless I am proposing a book, in which case the bulleted items become chapters, each one with a title and five lines telling what would be in the chapter. In that case the proposal is two to three pages long.

  The query, of course, is not appropriate for the mood or humor piece. Such pieces have to be written and then submitted because the editor has to see and hear the voice to decide if it should be published.

Here is a query I might write:

Name
Address
Telephone Number

THE GOOD OLD DAYS WEREN'T
by Donald M. Murray

"I don't see no corrections on John's papers. You'd oughten to get with it and teach the way I was taut by Miss Norris in what they call the good old days. Every paper I wrote was marked all over you can be sure of that. In red. We did'nt get by with nothing and I don't see no reason John can't get as good an education as I. My father didn't pay no taxes like I do."

Our teachers receive such notes from parents, are told off on Parents' Night and in the supermarket, receive threatening phone calls, are the subject of complaints to the school board, attacked publicly at school board meetings and budget hearings, ridiculed in letters to the editor and newspaper stories, unintentionally insulted by Presidential candidates.

Even though such notes as the one above should make teachers question how the basics were taught in golden yesteryears, many teachers really believe the good old days were good. Often our best teachers feel guilty and leave the profession because they can't educate their students to the imaginary standards of the good old days.

A realistic look at the "good old days" reveals:

○ Many children didn't attend or finish high school in the years before World War II and few went on to college. In many parts of the country blacks were forced into an inferior system of segregated schools. Many other ethnic groups — Mexicans, Franco-Americans, Irish, Polish, Jews — were kept out of college preparatory courses in every part of the country. In those days, many medical and law schools limited the number of Jews they would accept. Women were simply not accepted at many professional schools. Across the country, women were pushed into secretarial courses and were discouraged from attending college.

○ Teachers were often poorly prepared. Many teachers had not even attended college or were graduated from poorly funded state normal schools which didn't intend to give future teachers a university education.

○ Classes were large — fifty to sixty was normal — when I went to high school and there was little individual attention for the average or below-average students. There were no programs for students who had learning problems, came from a poor educational background, or spoke another language than English at home.

○ The one-room schoolhouse or small local high school offered very few courses, and they were often taught out of ancient textbooks that were out of date. There were few science facilities or courses that required special equipment or special teacher training. Teachers taught many subjects for which they were unprepared, staying a day ahead of the students if they were lucky and had not moonlighted at another job the night before to make ends meet.

○ Teaching methods were primitive, dull and repetitive. Spelling, for example, was usually taught through the spelling bee. Poor spellers — I was one — were eliminated, not taught. All the attention went to the good spellers who survived and competed against each other.

The article will obviously have a strong, personal point of view. I am still angry at the education I did not receive in a school system which was considered one of the best in the nation. I do, however, have access to records — even some student papers — from the good old days between World War I and World War II, and I will document my case with objective evidence. I will lighten up the statistics with quotes from students and teachers about the good old days, and a few anecdotes of my own, such as the day the teacher was removed from class because her engagement had been announced. There was no evidence that she'd done "it" yet, but the engagement announcement showed she intended to do "it." Married women teachers were against the law in most school districts and many teachers had to support their parents and could not afford to get married during the Depression because they would lose their jobs. They were caught in a trap. No wonder Miss Carey broke a ruler slamming the desk every few weeks and jammed bad students, myself included, rump down into a wastebasket.

• *Column*. Writers need a sketch to control the abundance of material they accumulate before beginning a draft. Donald Graves, who studies the writing of children and also writes himself, draws a column down the left side of a page. He puts everything that might possibly be in the article or chapter in that column. Then he draws three additional columns and heads the first one "beginning," the second one "middle," and the third one "end. " He places items in each column. Obviously some things are left out, and new items occur to him that have not been in the left-hand column.

- *Box.* All these sketches are a way of visualizing the finished product, a way of drawing a map of what may be explored. One interesting way to do this is to draw a sketch that is based on the impact the parts of an article will have on the reader. The lead might be represented by a box that takes a quarter of the page. The end might be as large, and one or two turning points almost as large. The sketch would show that the first paragraph has enormous impact on the reader, and that the next six pages, for example, before a major turning point have little impact. The point of the sketch is to make sure the writer knows those points of impact and then discovers how to get the reader to them.

- *Box plus column.* The working writer constantly experiments, adapting techniques he or she learns from colleagues. In outlining the chapters for one book I made Graves' left-hand column half the page. Then, with the other half, I made a sizable box for the title, the lead, and the end. The space in between was for the sequence on the left-hand side and the documentation on the right-hand side. Working through this sketch helped me make a much better book — and a more interesting one — than I could have imagined.

- *Readers' questions.* Anticipating the questions the reader must have answered if the writer is to produce an effective and satisfying piece of writing is a technique I have mentioned earlier in this section on planning and will mention in Chapter 3 in the section on revising. It is also a good way to make a sketch of a book. The easiest way to do this is to draw a line down the center of the page, space the reader's five questions or so in the left column, and sketch in the answers in the right. You may have to number and move the questions around until you are able to anticipate the order in which the reader will ask them.

- *Bracket.* Many people working with computers make a sketch that works from right to left and uses brackets to enclose the extremes within a subject or problem to be solved. For example, I used this technique for a chapter on writer's block that I had difficulty organizing. I put "writer's block" at the left of the page, then at the top of the page I put "good" and at the bottom of the page "bad." Then I worked out the extremes of good and bad in a series of brackets. In the end I wrote a piece that was exactly the opposite of what I intended before I did the sketch. I wrote about the importance of writer's block and the benefits for the writer.

- *Tree.* Another way to see ahead to what may be written is to draw a tree that shows how the subject — the trunk — may branch out and grow in many directions.

- *Shape.* We have all seen shaped poems, in which the typography imitates the subject — a poem about a bird appears in the shape of a bird. Shape is important to a writer, and it's helpful for me, sometimes, to sketch the shape of the piece of writing. It may be a triangle, a fever chart, stairsteps, a sideways cone leading to one point, or its reverse expanding from one point. These sketches may help me see the structure I may attempt in the writing.

- *List.* Lists are a powerful tool, and the simple list may be the best way to sketch what is written. The writer can start by putting down everything that has to be in the piece of writing, and then either numbering or renumbering to achieve a working order. The writer usually also uses arrows and circles and lines to maneuver the parts of the piece into a coherent and logical order. I used a variation of a list in sketching this book by writing increasingly detailed tables of contents. That helped me see where all the small parts of a large topic — how to teach writing might fit so they would be available to a teacher in a logical order.

- *Story board.* Most film writers make a sketch by using three-by-five-inch cards. Each one will have a word or a few lines about a potential scene in the movie. The writer pins those up on a corkboard and moves them around until they are in the best dramatic order. I have found this technique helpful for non-fiction writing. The writer puts each element that may be in the final piece of writing down on a card or slip of paper, and then plays around with them until the writer has a sketch to follow in the writing of the piece. Often certain elements are discarded and new ones added.

- *Folders.* If the writer is doing a complicated research subject it is often helpful to set up a series of file folders. Then notes, tear sheets and copies of articles, even books, can be placed in folders, and those folders can be moved around as the writer works towards an effective sketch of the book. The earliest sketches of this book took place in that way in my file drawer.

- *Outline.* The formal outline can be a helpful way for some writers to sketch the subject. The advantage of a system of Roman numerals, Arabic numbers, capital letters and small letters is that it allows a detailed form of planning. An early version of the table of contents helped me see this book, and I used a whole symphony of typographical marks to divide topics into subtopics, then divide them again and again.

     The danger of a traditional outline is that the writer will take it too seriously. It was helpful for me to make a detailed outline for this book, but it was important for me in drafting the book to loosen up and improvise from that outline, the way a jazz musician uses a melody and a jazz tradition from which to depart in performing.

Remember that the amount of planning for a given piece of writing will depend on the cognitive style and experience of the writer as well as the nature and familiarity of the writing task. Writing is not a military exercise, and students should not be marched through writing by the numbers. Each piece of writing should be searching for its own meaning and its own way of expressing meaning, with the writer following along, helping but not interfering with the natural process of discovery that takes place in all good writing.

3 Drafting, Revising, and Editing

The writer's moment of truth arrives when all the collecting and planning are completed and the writer faces the blank page. Until that moment everything is possible. Then the first word is on the page and the possibilities diminish. The second word follows and the possibilities shrink. The first line is finished and the writer's vision confronts the reality of the text.

Develop

Now writers — amateur and professional, famous and unknown — must find a way of maintaining faith in the vision while creating the reality of the text. All writing is an act of faith, belief in self, belief in the subject, belief in its form, belief in its voice. Teachers — and editors — must recognize how hard it is to maintain faith — and how essential.

This is a significant reason for teachers to write. The toughest critics on every faculty are usually those whose vision of what they would write remains unblemished by the drafts they *might* produce. They demand unrealistic high standards of others because they are not trying to measure up to those standards themselves.

There is a time for criticism and high standards, but at the moment of beginning a draft, every writer needs faith. Avoidance is real. Sit down to write and you need a new pen or pencil, different paper, a new notebook, a new desk or a new arrangement of desk and file cabinet and bookcase. A blank page always inspires a visit to the bathroom, hunger, thirst, caffeine addiction, a demand for more research, consultation with a colleague. Of course writers act this way. They should.

The page will never be as good as the imagined page. The writer always discovers the writer by writing, the real writer who uses the not-quite-right word, who creates the phrase that rings with the resonance of plastic, the sentence that wraps around itself and strangles the meaning, the paragraph of meaning hidden in the underbrush of the paragraph that grows into a tangle on the page.

And the lack of faith may be justified. Many writers fear the first page because they are not ready to write. Writers should have a feeling of fullness and immediacy when they begin to write. Virginia Woolf said, "As for my next book, I am going to hold myself from writing it till I have it impending in me: grown heavy in my mind like a ripe pear; pendant, gravid, asking to be cut or it will fall." The writing should demand to be written. Other times it is impossible to maintain faith in a draft because the draft doesn't deserve it. Again, the writer wasn't ready to write.

Writing Readiness

There are some good indicators of writing readiness, and students who are familiar with planning techniques should have little difficulty answering the questions which indicate the writer is ready to attempt a draft. Not all of them have to be in place every time, but the writer should be able to answer these questions before starting a first draft, most of the time:

• *Do I have enough specific, accurate INFORMATION to build a piece of writing that will satisfy the reader?* Beginning writers constantly try to produce a draft before they have an abundance of information. Then they discover it's like trying to write with a pen that runs dry after a page or a few paragraphs. As Catherine Drinker Bowen said, "One of the marks of a true genius is a quality of abundance. A rich, rollicking abundance, enough to give indigestion to ordinary people." We may not be geniuses, but all writers — poets as much as science writers — need quotations, facts, statistics, concrete details, observations, anecdotes, all the information that may be appropriate to the subject. Writing is not so much written with language as constructed with information. Words that are merely words and do not carry information to the reader will never produce writing that attracts and satisfies a reader.

• *Does the information focus on a single, significant MEANING?* All the planning activities, in a sense, are a search for meaning. The writer should not write to display the baton twirls of style but to discover a possible meaning; to explore, develop and refine that meaning; and to share the explored meaning. In the finished draft everything in the piece should be connected to the meaning and move the reader forward to a clearer understanding of meaning. The dominant meaning of the writing does not need to be clarified before the first draft — in fact it may be a good idea to allow that clarification to come during the drafting — but a possible meaning should be sighted. As Denise Levertov says, "You can smell the poem before you can see it. Like some animal." "It's like being led by a whisper," according to Jayne Anne Phillips. The draft is an experiment, and before starting the draft the writer should have a glimpse of meaning, a hunch, a guess that can be tested in the writing.

• *Do I see an ORDER in the material that will deliver the information to readers when they need it?* Planning will allow the writer to spot a trail in the woods, a way through all the material that the writer has collected, material that both enriches and confuses. If the writer writes from abundance, and all good writers do, then the job of the artist is to impose order on chaos. Planning does not necessarily reveal only one way to write the piece, but several ways that can be tested by a draft.

• *Do I know readers who NEED the information I have to give them?* Effective writers usually have a sense of need. They have a compulsion to share with — inform, persuade, explain, entertain — someone else. That someone else is a reader who needs to hear what the writer has to say. The writer should not change the truth of the message but should shape it to the needs of the receiver. If the message is to be heard and understood it must satisfy a reader's needs and answer a reader's questions.

• *Do I hear a VOICE that is strong enough to speak directly to the reader?* Experienced writers will not move forward to the writing of a draft until they hear the voice that is appropriate to the piece of writing. Voice is the glue that holds it all together. It is what attracts (or repels) the reader. We will be discussing voice in great detail in this book because it is one of the most important elements — if not the most important element — in writing. Planning provides the writer with a hint of the voice. That's all the writer needs to start producing a draft.

The writer does not need to march through this checklist all the time, only when it might help — or when the writer cannot understand why a draft is not starting well or why a draft runs down in a few pages.

There are times when the writer is not ready to write but must. The deadline has arrived — the guests are at the door before the house is picked up and the roast in the oven. The checklist can help here too because it is a way of reminding the writer of the important elements of effective writing and helping to survey what is on hand. It may not be what the writer wants but it is what is available and the writer must go with it.

Writer's Block

Writer's block is real. Anxiety becomes paralysis. A writer has a block when the writer cannot write even if the writing readiness checklist is answered affirmatively.

We need to understand, first of all, that many times writer's block is a natural and appropriate way to respond to a writing task or a new stage in the writing process. What we have to do is to see the block as a rational, normal response and to provide possible solutions. Some common causes of writer's block and solutions are:

● *The writer sets unrealistic standards.* What a writer proudly produces one week suddenly turns rotten in the writer's eyes — and nose — a week later. The writer is unable to produce the work that once came easily. The best writers are most likely to suffer this block, because they learn fast and their standards leap ahead of their writing skills. They learn what good writing is and they read published work — and their own — with an increasingly critical eye — and then cover that eye while creating a first draft.

The poet William Stafford says: "I believe that the so-called 'writing block' is a product of some kind of disproportion between your standards and your performance. . . . One should lower his standards until there is no felt threshold to go over in writing. It's *easy* to write. You just shouldn't have standards that inhibit you from writing."

Does this mean that the writer says "Wow!" in response to every draft? Of course not. It means the writer writes as well as he or she can but does not try to write beyond what is possible this day, on this draft.

● *The writer focuses on a writing skill inappropriate to the stage of the writing process in which the writer is working.* The best example of this, of course, occurs when a writer is free-writing to discover what may be said, but is concentrating on getting spelling, punctuation, mechanics, usage, even handwriting or typing exactly right. If we demand only first-draft writing and correct it only for editing skills, then we force ourselves into this blocking situation. Whenever beginning writers sit down to write they will try to write perfectly the first time. It can't be done. If you look at the first drafts of great pieces of literature, you will see an amazing scribble of intention not yet achieved. Syntax, spelling, penmanship, everything goes in the face of the effort to capture a meaning not yet sighted or defined or made clear.

Writers learn they usually have to write badly to write well. Sentences reach for a meaning that cannot yet be grasped, and fail even to become sentences. The wrong words lead us to the not-so-wrong words, and the almost right words may reveal the right words.

• *The natural writer becomes self-conscious.* Of course. We see this most obviously in young children who write or draw or sing without inhibition. Whatever they do is wonderful. And suddenly they become self-conscious and lose that magic. It is sad, but inevitable and appropriate. And that will happen to the writer during the writer's entire life.

We write with ease, and then through learning develop an appropriate unease. This is not just a matter of high standards, it is a matter of learning, of being able to repeat purposefully what we once did accidentally. The fumblings of the first date change over years of marriage. For most of us that's a vast improvement. We must grow and learn in our writing, and we do that by absorbing the lessons of experience until they become natural. Your students should realize that they will become self-conscious. It's a sign of growth. But at the moment of writing they should try to achieve an ease and naturalness. Good writing can't be forced.

• *The writer tries to be someone else.* One of the problems of youth is that it is a time in life when everyone tries on different roles, wearing the clothes and the gestures and the speech and the behavior of someone else to see what they may wish to become. Some people, in fact, do disappear and become someone else. It is sad to watch it happen.

Writing is self-exposure. The writer cannot be someone else and write effectively. The pose is exposed in the draft — to the writer and to the reader. I would like to write as someone else does, because I would like to be someone else. I would like to write better than I can, but I cannot, I have to be myself. I cannot be younger, or prettier, or stronger, or more graceful than I am. My thumbprint and my voice are my own, and I must make use of what I have, not what I wish I had.

Many writers become blocked because they confront themselves in the mirror of the page. Of course. Seeing yourself in the mirror can be a good reason to go back to bed in the morning, but writers have to understand that being yourself, whoever you are, is a great virtue in writing, and the student writer has to be helped to accept and respect that self that continually reappears on the page.

• *The writer tries to write for someone else.* Writers are blocked when they face a new audience that they imagine will be critical, or an audience that has proved to be critical in the past. It is natural to choke on a first draft before this kind of test. What students need is experience in facing audiences that are appropriately critical, so that they will learn how to deal with a variety of readers.

At least for me, the imagined audience is usually worse than the real one, although the real one can be pretty bad at times. You simply have to know that you can only do your best, nothing beyond that. You will be revealed, you will be exposed — that's the nature of writing.

This may not get any easier, for those teachers and editors and colleagues who write the least will often be the most critical and the least helpful. Your real draft will never measure up to their imagined draft. You have to accept this and learn to be tough enough not to write for others, but for yourself, to make something of which you can be proud, regardless of what others say about it.

I find this very hard. I want the praise of others; I want to be loved and admired. I want, in other words, to impress. But when I sit down to write to impress someone else my page usually remains blank. If it doesn't, my writing is false. It sounds like someone writing to impress someone else.

- *The writer is paralyzed by praise.* That sounds contradictory, but it isn't. Many students, especially those with the greatest potential, are blocked by the praise we give or their peers give.

There can be a number of legitimate reasons for this. One of my colleagues praised my poetry in such a way that I could not write poetry for months. What he saw in my poetry was not what I wanted in my poetry. Criticism would not have blocked me, but his praise bothered me. Was I really doing what he said was so wonderful, and what sounded so wrong for me?

Praise also blocks because it sets standards that are higher than the student wants set. I see more potential in my students than they see in themselves. Many of them are not prepared to make the commitment to writing my praise implies. I will never fail to mention potential when I see it, but I have to be careful to control my praise, for it can inhibit students, who feel they have to do something far beyond what they've been doing to justify this unexpected praise.

Oddly enough, this is most paralyzing for the best students. Behind a whole series of intricate defenses they have felt that they have a special gift. Suddenly a reader has torn down all the fences, and they have to deal with this gift. They have no more excuses. We have to realize as teachers it's important to tear down the fences, but we should not be surprised that this sudden obligation causes writer's block for at least a while.

- *The writer is saying what the writer does not want to say.* Writing is discovery, discovery of the world, discovery of a particular subject, and most of all, self-discovery. As writing teachers we inevitably encourage our students to look critically at their world. We should not be surprised that students become blocked when they see their home, their family, their friends in an unexpectedly bright and critical glare. I'm often worried that I'm wrenching my students away from the illusions and myths and beliefs they've brought to school. I worry that I'm casting them adrift without giving them new beliefs. But that is not my trade. I am not a priest or a minister or a rabbi; I am a writing teacher, and the writer inevitably looks critically at the world. The writer's eye is tough to live with.

But the writer is looking not only at others, but also at himself or herself. The writer in the draft often discovers what the writer does not wish to discover. The talk-show guest says, "I'm trying to find myself." Another guest leans over and says, "You won't like what you'll find." We laugh, because we recognize the truth in this. We may not like what we are thinking or feeling if we write.

- *The writer tries in one draft to make up for the past.* It is natural for the writer to try to make up for the writing that hasn't been done, or the writing that was done and didn't work. But you can't carry the burden of the past to the writing desk. You simply have to write as well as you can write that day.

I try to write every day, and when I miss a day or two, or a week, it becomes harder and harder to write. I want to write for all the days I haven't written; I want to write more than I can write, and better than I can write. And therefore I cannot write at all.

As writers we have to keep reminding ourselves of what Stafford said, and do the writing we can do right now. We cannot make up for the past, but we can have a new beginning.

Tricks for Getting Started Writing

Even without writer's block, most students — and published writers — have difficulty starting a draft. Here are some ways to start writing:

- *Habit. Nulla dies sine linea.* Never a day without a line. That advice is attributed to Horace and Pliny, and allegedly has been hung over many writers' desks through the centuries; it hangs over mine. Writing is like jogging. If you do it every day it becomes a natural activity, and so I try to write every day. Writers who are in the habit of writing find it is far easier to begin than those who do not have the writing habit.

- *Time.* Most writers try to get to their desk at a regular time. Student writers may find the best time is late at night, but most writers evolve into morning writers. I hate to get out of bed; I do not like mornings; I do not bound to my desk clapping my hands in delight because I am so eager to write. Most writers work in the morning before the phone rings, before there is a knock at the door, before the world intrudes.

- *Place.* The experienced writer usually has a place in which the writer is used to writing. That becomes part of the ritual of writing. It may be an office, but it can also be a chair, or an automobile. I do a lot of writing in the car, and in good weather I have a chair on the porch, and in bad weather a chair in the living room, where I can write. There is no ideal place for everyone. Some people like quiet; some like noise. Silence is the most distracting noise for me, but others have to have silence to write. Some writers have desks that point toward the view, as I do; others turn their back on the view. The point is that most writers develop a space in which they can write, and they return to that space regularly to write. One trick I use to make any place a writing place is to take a bean-bag lap desk with me. It's a simple plastic top with a beanbag underneath it that makes a good writing surface for my lap wherever I'm sitting.

- *Tools.* Indulge yourself in tools. You are practicing a craft, and the texture of the paper, the feel of the pen make a difference. Writers are always seeking the magic pen. One reason that word processors are so popular with writers is that they are marvelous tools, grown-up toys with which to write.

- *Traveling office.* I have the many tools of my trade with me wherever I go — paper, clipboard, daybook, folders with working drafts, pens, pencils, ruler, scissors, glue, stapler — all the things I need to work in a car in a parking lot, on a rock at the beach, in a hotel room, on an airplane, at school, between classes or meetings, at home.

- *Write a letter.* Many writers find it helpful to start a difficult piece of writing as a letter is started, saying "Dear Joe" and then writing the piece. I hate to write letters, so it never helps me, but apparently it helps others.

- *Ghostwrite.* Put someone else's name on the piece. I am always amazed at how easy it is to write when I ghostwrite for someone else. Putting someone else's name on the draft may be a helpful trick to get going.

- *Experiment.* Consider the draft merely an experiment in meaning. Experiments usually fail, but they usually show what doesn't work, which is important to know, and what may work, which is also important to know. Attempt a writing experiment.

- *Free-write.* Return to the technique of free writing, and write as fast and uncritically as you can, letting the pen or typewriter or word processor lead you towards meaning. Get into the writing so quickly that you'll have as many accidents of voice and form and meaning as possible.

- *Dictate.* Use a tape recorder to dictate a draft. Most of us speak more easily than we write. We have more experience with oral language, and we can dictate far more words in an hour than we can write. Much of this book, as well as most of all my non-fiction, has a first draft that was dictated to my wife. We started the technique years ago when we had an impossible deadline, and one of the reasons I continue it is that it's easier for me to suspend critical judgment and get something down that I can correct and revise later.

- *Consult.* Talk to a fellow writer about what you think you might write. Many times when we do this we hear ourselves saying a draft, and once we have heard it we can go and write it down.

- *Write a chunk.* Most of the time it's helpful to have a lead. But if the lead doesn't work and it becomes impossible to get started at the beginning, move to any part of the piece that may be ready to be written and write it. A piece of writing does not have to be constructed in logical fashion. It can be written in chunks, in the same way that a prefabricated house is manufactured. Then the writing can be assembled into a coherent whole.

- *Write backwards.* Start at the end, and once you have developed and polished that destination, then you may be able to see more clearly where to begin — and how.

- *Quit.* I can't force writing, and when a draft won't come it hits my stomach, and then my head. I literally get sick. So what do I do? I quit. I walk away from it. I can do this because I establish personal deadlines ahead of publishers' deadlines. But I come back after a break, or the next day, and take another run at it. You can't force writing, but you can keep putting yourself back into the position where writing may come.

Tricks for Keeping Writing

- *Don't look back.* Once a draft is started it's dangerous to look back; the writer should move on through the draft. It's always a mistake for me to go back. I see so many things I want to change. I lose faith in the draft, and it's hard for me to pick up the text and advance it.

- *Stop in the middle of a sentence.* When you're interrupted, or when you have a draft you have to keep going over a number of days, it's always a good idea to stop in the middle of a sentence. Then, when you return to the text, you can finish that sentence and slide right into the writing.

• *Set a quota.* It helps to establish a quota of words or pages, not only because it stimulates productivity, but also because it allows the writer to suspend critical judgment. "How did the work go today?" The writer is not prepared to answer that question asked by someone else, or by the writer. Instead, the writer can answer, "I did five hundred words," or "I wrote two pages." Quantity, for the moment, protects the writer from the question of quality that will have to be answered later. Young writers may be helped by the advice of writers such as Janwillem van de Wetering, who said: "To write you have to set up a routine, and promise yourself that you will write. Just state in a loud voice that you will write so many pages a day, or write for so many hours a day. Keep the number of pages or hours within reason, and don't be upset if a day slips by. Start again; pick up the routine. Don't look for results. Just write, easily, quietly."

• *Keep score.* Count the words or the pages so that you see the progress you have made, hour by hour, day by day.

• *Don't write the whole, just the part.* A few years ago I saw a woman on television who had spent days climbing up one of the tallest cliffs in the country. When she got to the top she told the television interviewer that she kept remembering that you eat an elephant a bite at a time. And that's the way you write, a paragraph or a page at a time. If book writers contemplate three, four, or five hundred pages they find it impossible to begin or keep going. Most of us who write books just try to do it a bite at a time. John Steinbeck wrote: "When I face the desolate impossibility of writing 500 pages, a sick sense of failure falls on me and I know I can never do it. Then gradually I write one page and then another."

• *Don't stop.* As you write you will need to look up a quotation or a statistic, or other details. Don't do it. At *Time* we put the letters *TK* right into the text at such spots; it stood for "to come." We did everything we could to keep the story flowing. Later we would go back and check our notes. You may want to leave spaces for what's to come, or put "check" in parentheses, or put a question mark in the margin. But don't stop. Keep the writing flowing.

Writing the Draft

The writer's task is to get black on white. Writers are people who write. All the writer's — and teacher's — energy must be focused on the production of the draft, that crucial activity that turns what may be into what is.

This is always the central anxiety for the writer. At one moment everything is possible, and a moment later there is the reality of the page. The first draft is always the most important draft. From that moment on the writer has something tangible to work on. It can be tossed out or revised or edited. It is something to be dealt with. Before that all is dream and hope and expectation.

I always hesitate before writing a first draft, fearful I may go up to the plate and strike out. Recently, my wife gave me this note: "The most important thing is to get words down, let them flow, suspend critical judgment. Just write. The surprising accidents happen, and then you have something to work with, something to add to, something to depart from. The writing has to become palpable. Once you have a draft you can sense rhythm — or lack of it — see the holes, the redundancies, the awkward spots, the need for more explanation, etc. Obviously a first draft is the result of conscious and unconscious planning — collecting, connecting — but until words appear there can't be shape or form, rhythm or flow, impact, logic, information with which to build a good piece of writing."

A wise lady who knows me better than I know myself and knows more about the writing process than many who think themselves experts. Writers have to learn a strange intense letting go to produce good writing. Writers have to force themselves by the most compulsive forms of self-discipline to get to the writing desk. But then that intensity has to be relaxed.

Writers, when writing, are listeners. They have to listen to the fragments of language that point towards meaning. They have to relax enough to write with ease. They have to prepare themselves so the writing will come as if it were merely passing through them. The task is, I suppose, at the center of the forces that always pull during the creative process: the force of freedom against the force of discipline. The writer has to attempt to combine what happens in free writing with everything — subject, tradition, order, language — that comes with the formal training and experience of the writer to the moment of the first draft.

The Discovery Draft

The purpose of the first draft is to discover. It is not a final draft; it is more of a late predraft. Peter Drucker calls it a "zero draft." Other names might be a trial draft, a test draft, a dress rehearsal draft, a practice draft, an explanation or an experimental draft. The element that distinguishes it most from the fragments of writing that have gone before is that the writer pushes on to the end, no matter if there are holes and parts of the writing that clearly do not work. By writing the first draft the writer is able, from that point on, to work with a completed whole.

What does the writer discover by writing the first draft?

- ○ What the writer knows.
- ○ What the writer needs to know.
- ○ If the writer has a subject — or needs to find a subject.
- ○ If the subject needs to be limited — or expanded.
- ○ If the genre works — or if a new genre needs to be explored.
- ○ If the structure answers the reader's questions — when they are asked.
- ○ If there is a voice — and if it is the appropriate voice.

Writers have to be prepared for failures of expectation. They remind themselves that they want to be surprised, for the purpose of the draft, above all else, is thinking. The writer produces a draft to think about the subject, and that process of exploration will cause the mind to take sudden leaps backwards and forwards and sideways. When that happens the rhetoric or structure of writing and the structures of language itself will become tangled and break down. That is a condition of surprise, and we must be prepared to accept the draft that staggers and stumbles towards its own meaning as well as the first draft that flows evenly and steadily towards an expected meaning. We write the first draft to discover what we have to say and how we may say it.

The Deadline

I do not know any writers who write without deadlines, or who write at all before there is a self-imposed or external deadline. There must be some, but they are few indeed. Whenever I stop giving myself a deadline — a minimum number of pages by a certain hour on a certain day — then I stop writing. Without deadlines I do not write.

The deadline does not need to be for finished writing, but it needs to be expressed in terms of quantity and time. There must be a moment of truth, of completion, of delivery.

Deadlines are always arbitrary. Few writers, no matter how well they collect and plan, ever feel they are ready to write. There are always more things to research or think about, more planning and warming up to do, more rehearsal before opening night. So the deadline must be imposed, and it must be met.

Write with Information

Specific information. Concrete details. Facts. "I would want to tell my students of a point strongly pressed, if my memory serves, by Shaw," writes John Kenneth Galbraith. "He once said that as he grew older, he became less and less interested in theory, more and more interested in information. The temptation in writing is just the reverse. Nothing is so hard to come by as a new and interesting fact. Nothing is so easy on the feet as a generalization." The writer, while writing the first draft, should feel a sense of building with information, brick by brick, detail by detail.

Information, specifics, details — these are code words that have an almost mystical meaning for most writers. Many well-trained academics cannot understand writers' fascination with detail, the theological significance writers place in an awareness of fragments of information. In school, teachers demand that students seek the theory, the abstraction, the generality first, then find evidence to support it. But writers — and theory makers — usually work from the specific to the general. Academics have been trained to value accurate, specific information as supporting evidence. So do writers, but they also see details as inspiring meaning.

The academy too often limits its instruction to completing assignments that have an expected conclusion or to fulfilling an established thesis statement. Writers do just that at times; and my description of the writing process certainly emphasizes planning. Still, our best writers report, again and again, that they work from the specific to the general. Eudora Welty says, "What discoveries I've made in the course of writing stories all begin with the particular, never the general."

Writers are aware of the power of the specific, the image, the metaphor, the revealing fragment to inspire or illuminate the whole. And writers believe this process is repeated when readers enter their pages. What many writers hope to do is to present information on the page that will create the generalization — the thesis, the argument, the conclusion, the feeling, the thought — *in the reader's mind*. Writers are subversives. They know the best writing often works by implication, not impressing the reader with the thinking the writer has done but — through the crafty implantation of information — forcing the reader to think what the writer wants the reader to think.

Accurate, significant fragments of information also give the writing authority. They convince the reader that the writer knows what he or she is talking about. They satisfy the reader's hunger for information and make it possible for the reader to become a source of information for the people around the reader. Readers, above all, read to be informed. This is true when they read poetry or fiction, history or journalism, textbooks or essays. They want to be given the information they need and want to know.

Information is the raw material of language. Often young writers believe they write with words. They are, as someone once said, word drunk. Their words are disconnected from meaning. They need to learn they really write with information and that words are the symbols for information. Writers must focus on the information itself if they want to write in a vigorous, compelling and effective voice.

Write Fast

Writers, students and professionals alike, have their own writing pace. But there's a great deal to be said for producing the first draft as fast as possible. When they write at a discomforting speed, they force the happy accidents that are essential to good writing.

Speed concentrates the writer's attention on the larger questions of meaning that should be dealt with in the first draft. Fast writing makes it difficult for the writer to pay attention to the details of spelling, syntax and form. The fast writers are forced to let those go as they pursue a voice that is trying to deal with the essentials of the subject.

The energy it takes to write fast seems to provide the energy to make those connections — meanings — we see in good writing. Writing fast causes the leaps forward, the wonderfully half-baked ideas and undeveloped references and not-yet-quite-right analogies, the almost appropriate metaphors, the phrases that do not yet clarify, the words that are moving towards an unexpected meaning but haven't made it — all the productive, instructive failures that are essential to an excellent piece of writing. The chances of these failures are multiplied when the writer is moving fast, not carefully producing a cautious text, but racing almost out of control towards a destination that cannot be seen by the plodding writer.

Write Without Notes

The writer should put aside all notes while writing a first draft. What is remembered is usually what should be remembered, and what is forgotten is usually what should be left out.

The writer has a special kind of memory that is activated only by the writing itself. Students should not think that they are unable to remember quotations and statistics. They may be, and that is no matter, because they can always go back and check such facts after the writing is done. They will, however, be surprised at how much they do remember during the act of writing.

The writer who is constantly referring to notes loses any sense of the flow of the writing. All the material in the notes should be absorbed by the brain of the writer, then released by the process of writing.

Write by Ear

A few years ago I covered up my typewriter so I could not see the text I was producing. I thought that it would bother me that I was building my writing on the text I could see coming up before me. I should have known better because I had been dictating much of my work for years. I think most effective writers dictate, in the sense that they hear the text they are producing. The writer's ear tells the writer how to modulate the language the writer is using.

The ear hears the voice — and hears when that voice fades or is lost. The ear is aware of the rhythm and melody. The ear adjusts the pace to the subject and to the abilities of the audience to hear it. The ear plays up the subject or plays it down.

Beginning writers should read aloud, not just after they have written a draft to test it, but while they are writing or editing to produce writing that the reader can hear.

Reveal the Subject

In teaching fiction we say, "Show, don't tell." In writing non-fiction we vary that. Occasionally we say, "Tell, then show," but we should work towards "Show and tell, show then tell," and in the most effective writing, "Show, don't tell," because if you show well enough you don't need to tell. The reader will come to the conclusion you want.

It takes great skill to get out of the way of the subject, not calling attention to yourself but giving the reader the illusion of experiencing the subject firsthand. George Orwell said, "Good writing is like a window pane." We should do whatever we can to present the information to the reader in such a way that the reader will be forced to absorb and react to that information.

While we are writing we should constantly have in the back of our head the goal of exposing the subject, of pulling the curtain and standing aside so that the reader sees the stage and is not even aware that we have been tugging at the curtain to get it out of the way.

Vary the Documentation

Most writers fall into the habit of using one form of evidence with which they feel comfortable, regardless of whether it is appropriate to the point they are making. Students should be reminded to utilize the whole spectrum of documentation — anecdote, quotation, description, first person account, interview, scholarly citation, narrative, statistic — when they are writing, choosing the form that is most appropriate for the point being made and the reader who needs to understand it.

Whatever you remind yourself before and during the draft, remember to do nothing that stops the flow of writing. The draft is the goal because once you have a draft you can, if necessary, rewrite and rewrite until it works.

Repeat to Revise

Until I started to write the new version of this book I considered revision an integral part of the writing process. In fact, there was a time when others, reading what I had to say about writing, thought I was interested only in revision, and I certainly did explore, and therefore seem to emphasize, revision.

Since I am both a writer and student of the writing process, my academic concerns often mirror my own professional needs. When I moved from first-draft news writing to magazine and book writing, not only did I have to revise, but I also discovered the obsessive joys of revision. I became a virtuoso of revision and, naturally, emphasized revision in my classes and in my speculations about the writing process.

Revision is important, and for most writers, especially inexperienced writers or experienced writers dealing with a new subject, a new audience or a new genre, writing is indeed rewriting. I explored revision to my own satisfaction. That certainly does not mean that I learned everything there is to learn about revision, but I found my eye glancing more and more at what came before, not after, the first draft. In addition I noticed that more and more scholars were doing stimulating research into revision but that relatively little research concerned prewriting. That's one of the delights of an academic life. You can follow your own curiosity, attempting to answer your own questions in your own way — and using your students as laboratory rats.

This new emphasis has been evident in my publications in recent years and was reflected in the early design of this book, but I can remember the moment when it took a radical turn and made it possible for me to see revision in a new way. I was at the Second Miami University Conference on Sentence Combining and the Teaching of Writing at Oxford, Ohio, a stranger in an alien land where material that was familiar to me was looked at in a way that was unfamiliar to me — ideal conditions for creativity — when I took a long walk across that lovely campus not thinking but prepared to accept a thought if it arrived.

Suddenly I realized what was instantly obvious to me, and hadn't been obvious before (and may not be obvious by the time I write about the writing process again). I saw revision as simply that. It is not another step in the process, it is the process repeated as many times as is necessary to produce a text worthy of editing. I no longer see revision as a separate part of the process but merely as a repetition of the process until a draft is ready for editing.

The Craft of Revision

The writer creates a draft:

> COLLECT   PLAN   DEVELOP = Draft

Then the writer passes through that same sequence, again and again, emphasizing one stage of the process, or two, or all three — or even part of a stage — doing what is necessary to produce increasingly effective drafts:

> <u>COLLECT</u>   PLAN   DEVELOP = Second draft
>
> COLLECT   <u>PLAN</u>   DEVELOP = Third draft
>
> COLLECT   PLAN   <u>DEVELOP</u> = Fourth draft

That might be one sequence, an unusually logical one, in which the emphasis moves from collect to plan to develop as indicated by the underlining. The important thing the writer must know is that there is an inventory of writing tools available to perform the task necessary to make each draft work better than the last one.

As the writer moves from early draft to late draft, there is an increasing emphasis on the specific. At first the writer pays attention to the global concerns of subject and truth and point of view and organization, but as the larger problems are solved, the writer moves in close, paying attention to detail, picking every nit so that nothing will get between the reader and the subject. This parallels an increasing attention to audience. In the early drafts, the writer is his or her own reader, but as the draft evolves, the writer stands back to see how it will communicate to a reader.

Students may find it helpful during the revision process to use the following checklist:

○ *Do I have enough information?* If not, then I will have to COLLECT more information.

○ *Do I say one thing? Can I answer the question, "What does this mean?"* If not, then I will have to PLAN a new *focus*.

○ *Do I speak in an appropriate voice? Does the writing sound right?* If not, then I will have to PLAN how to *rehearse* so that I will hear an appropriate voice.

○ *Do I answer the reader's questions as they occur to the reader?* If not, then I will have to PLAN so that I can create a DESIGN that answers the reader's questions.

○ *Do I deliver enough information to satisfy the reader?* If not, then I will have to DEVELOP the piece more fully.

Reading as a Writer

The writer's first reader is the writer. Too often people forget how much reading is involved in the writing course. It is possible to teach a reading or literature course without writing, but it is impossible to teach writing without reading. The writer must be able to read a draft in such a way that the writer is able to make another draft more effective. This reading while writing is a sophisticated form of reading that is essential to the writing process.

The first problem the student writer faces is achieving enough distance to read what the reader will see on the page, not what the writer hopes is on the page. When young children write they think whatever they put down is wonderful. As they begin to grow, they become less egocentric and more aware of readers. This causes anxiety and, often, paralysis. They go from being proud of everything to being proud of nothing. Writers veer between excessive pride and excessive despair all their lives. It is understandable; writing is a private act with a public result.

The writer must be egocentric to write. It is a profession of arrogance. But then the writer must stand back and become the reader, and that requires an objectivity and distance essential to the craft of writing. Ray Bradbury allegedly puts each manuscript away in a file drawer and takes it out a year after it has been drafted. I don't know any other writer who is organized enough to even consider that technique. Most professionals write the way students write: to deadline. The writer has to develop some methods of distancing that will work in a short period of time. Some ways to achieve distancing include:

○ Role-play a specific reader. Become someone you know who is not knowledgeable about the subject you are writing about and read as that person.

○ Read fast, as a reader will read.

○ Read out loud. Tape-record the piece and play it back, or have a friend read it so that you hear it.

○ Have a friend read the piece, asking the friend to tell you what works and what needs work, what is on the page and what needs to be on the page. Be sure to use a friend who makes you want to write when you return to your writing desk.

It's important for the writer to concentrate first on what works. Too often we concentrate only on what is wrong, ignoring what is right. Yet the most successful revision comes when we identify something that works — a strong voice, a pace that moves the reader right along, a structure that clarifies a complicated subject — and build on that strength.

It is too easy to identify all the things that are wrong and to be discouraged and unable to produce a more effective draft. Of course there will come a time to deal with what is wrong or what doesn't work, but the solutions to the problems in the piece come from the points of strength. What can we do to make the piece consistent with the good parts? What can we do to bring all parts of the piece up to the level of the best parts?

Many pieces of writing fail because the writer does not take advantage of what is already working well in a draft. For example, I may read a draft and feel despair. I'm good at despair. Nothing seems to work. But if I remember my craft I scan the disaster draft and see that, indeed, it is badly organized; that it does include too many undeveloped topics and lacks focus; that its proportions are all wrong — too much description and too little documentation; that the language is uneven, clumsy, stumbling at times and then, yes, there are moments when the language works, when I can hear a clear and strong voice. I read the strong parts aloud and work — cutting, adding, reordering, shaping, fitting, polishing — to make the voice consistent and strong. As I work on the draft line by line, I find I am following the clear sound of the voice I heard in fragments of the draft; I make one sentence clear and direct, and then another, and another. The draft begins to become better organized. I cut what doesn't belong and achieve focus; I pare back the description; I build up documentation. I work on what is most effective in the draft, and as I make that even more effective the writing that surrounds it gets attention and begins to improve.

Notice that the writer really looks for what *may* work. As I attacked my disaster draft, the voice was pretty uneven and downright poor most of the time, but I grabbed hold of those few moments of potential success and took advantage of them. They gave me a clue as to how I might improve the draft, and that was enough to get going. It's hard to look through the underbrush of messed up typography, misspellings, tangled syntax, wordiness, and writing that runs off in five directions at once, to see what might work. But that is what the writer has to do. And the writer can best do it by scanning, reading loosely, looking for what meaning lies behind the tangled text.

Writers have to keep reminding themselves that a draft is an experiment in meaning. In the early stages it's important to get beyond the etiquette of writing to see where the draft is pointing the writer. I'm intrigued by the fact that my students often make the most significant breakthroughs towards meaning where syntax breaks down — and I do too. We are obviously reaching for a meaning that is just beyond our ability to express. What I have to do and what my students have to do is to identify that potential meaning. Once we know where we are going we may be able to figure out how to get there.

The reading writer also has to see what doesn't work: to recognize that the beginning simply delays and the piece starts on page four, that the first-person piece would be more effective in the third person, that the essay can't say three things of equal importance but has to have one dominant meaning, that the point of view is built on unfounded assumptions, that the draft is voiceless.

The writer reads, above all, to discover the text beyond the draft, to glimpse the potential text which may appear upon passing through the writing process again, and, perhaps, again and again.

Is Revision Always Necessary?

No. The first draft may work well enough for the writer to edit the piece of writing. Revision is sometimes taught as if it were a federal law. It is not. Some pieces of writing are so well planned and rehearsed that they work the first time. Some writers have enough skill that they do not need to rewrite. Newspaper writers, for example, usually just produce first-draft copy. But as they move to magazine or book writing they usually find that they have to revise to achieve the more subtle meanings or rise to the increased writing standards of the new genre. Many writers feel that writing is rewriting. But the decision has to be made by the reading of each draft.

Students should realize that rewriting is not punishment but opportunity. As Neil Simon says, "In baseball you only get three strikes and you're out. In rewriting, you get almost as many swings as you want and you know, sooner or later, you'll hit the ball." Bernard Malamud states, "I love the flowers of afterthought." Revision allows the writer to resee the text and discover in it what the writer did not expect to find.

The Writer's Need for Readers

After I finish a draft that works pretty well, I have to have a reader. I suspect most writers have a small band of special readers that give support and criticism — in that order.

I'm blessed with many writing friends, and I shamelessly exploit them. They know how to nod or grunt and not say too much, to support without undeserved praise, to make a suggestion or two without taking the piece away from me, to tell me what works best for them and what may need work. They are readers who make me itch to get back to my own writing desk and I value them above gold.

Edit to Publish

Publication completes the act of writing. Until publication the writing has been seen only by the writer, the editor or teacher, and the writer's fellow writers. The writing has been read in process. Drafts have been examined to see how they might be improved. Now the piece is ready to be prepared to be read by strangers, readers who do not care about the writer or who do not even care about the subject, readers who certainly are not interested in helping to make the piece better. These are real readers who simply want to be informed by the piece of writing.

When writers publish they are read by people they rarely see. Their writing detaches itself from them and goes its own way. I'm always touched — and amused — by the effect that first publication has on beginning writers. They don't have to tell me they have been published; I know it from the way they walk, the way they carry themselves. There is a new confidence, a new identity. They have made something that was not here before; they have spoken in their own voice and they have been heard. They are writers.

Many of my teachers made it possible for me to publish in school papers. Mortimer Howell of Tilton Junior College in Tilton, New Hampshire, made the extra step typical of the great teacher. He knew I was going into the Army before the end of the school year and he sent one of my editorials off to the *Christian Science Monitor* and it was published in that distinguished international newspaper. He did it so that I would know I was a writer and that if I came home I could follow that calling.

In editing, it is even more important than it was in the revision stage that the writer achieve a distance from the text. The writer must become his or her own first — and toughest — editor. When someone is considered for sainthood in the Catholic Church an investigator is named to find out everything bad about that person. This investigator is called the Devil's Advocate. Each writer must become a devil's advocate to the writer's own page.

Now the writer must step back and view the work as it will be seen by a reader. The writer may use any or all of the techniques mentioned in the last section to achieve distance.

The writer will also discover surprises in the process of editing, and the writer should delight in them. They should be accepted and utilized; it's those little surprises that will give the reader delight and keep the reader interested. The writer will also be working, while editing, from strength towards weakness whenever possible, but now it is the time to correct any error in the writing, to plug the holes in the argument, to rearrange the order of the text so that it anticipates and responds to the reader's questions, to remove any break with the tradition of language that gets between the reader and the subject.

During the editing of a piece of writing most writers read aloud, muttering and mumbling to themselves as they listen to the sound of the text. We are all more experienced with oral language than written language, and in modern writing we attempt to create the illusion of an individual writer speaking to an individual reader. What is on the page is not speech, but when read aloud it should have the flow and rhythm and pace and music of fine speech. During the editing process we should again and again read aloud any section of the text that is giving us difficulty.

Most writers — and editors and teachers — emphasize the trivial when they read, paying close attention to detail right away. That is a waste of time and it interferes with an efficient job of editing. It saves time — and establishes proper priorities — to read each draft three times:

- *First,* concentrate on content. Is there anything to say? Is there any information with which to say it? This reading can — and should — be fast. The questions are large and can be dealt with quickly. If they have to be answered, there is no sense in wasting time on a more careful reading.

- *Next,* respond to questions of structure. What is the focus? The logical sequence? The proportion between the parts? The pace? Is there adequate documentation? This reading may take more time, but it is still not a line-by-line reading. If these questions require answers, there is no point in the writer — or editor — going on until they are answered.

- *Finally,* the writer — or editor — must deal with all the questions of language that refine and communicate meaning. Now there is a careful reading, with the writer/editor going over and over the word, the phrase, the sentence to make sure that each detail works to develop, support and communicate the writer's main point.

Experienced writers may find they can edit and deal with the larger and the smaller problems of the text simultaneously, since they interact with each other. Each word must relate to the overall meaning of the text, and if a word is changed it will affect the overall meaning of the text. There is no one right way to edit any more than there is one right way to write.

A checklist such as this may help the student:

○ Is the information correct?
○ Is it specific?
○ Is it in context?
○ Does it add up to a single meaning?
○ Does each point move the reader toward that single meaning?

○ Is each point documented?

○ Can the reader hear the voice of the writer?

○ Is that voice consistent and appropriate?

○ Are the traditions of language broken only if it clarifies the meaning?

○ Do the mechanics of language help make the meaning clear?

○ Is each word spelled correctly?

○ Is the manuscript neat?

The Editor's Attitudes

As in writing, the attitude may be as important as the skills involved. Here are some attitudes that may help during the editing process:

○ The editor must try not to bring preconceptions to the draft, deciding on the basis of previous experience what this new text should say and how to say it.

○ The editor should enter into the text, understanding its message, accepting its purpose, listening to its own voice to see how it can be made to work better on its own terms.

○ Editing will produce further surprises. The writer, while editing, will discover connections and tensions and orders and insights that clarify the subject for the writer and, therefore, the reader.

○ It is better to catch and correct a problem in the text yourself than to have a reader catch it when it's too late to be corrected.

○ The text knows what it needs. If you listen attentively to the text, it will tell you what it needs.

○ There is a satisfaction, even a joy, in the physical act of making the text work.

Tricks of the Editor's Trade

The editing writer has to maintain four levels of concern while performing surgery on a text:

○ What does the piece say?

○ How is the text organized to advance that meaning?

○ How does the voice express that meaning?

○ Will the reader understand — and care?

What follows are some tricks I've found to help me edit my own copy — and the copy of others:

● Most editors find that this work is so intense that they can be effective editors only for short periods of time. I find that after fifteen minutes I start being too kind to myself, and I have to stand back and do something else for at least a few minutes so I can return ready to cut.

- I have to keep reminding myself not to cut too much. If it works, leave it alone.

- It's often helpful to put a few key questions or admonitions at the top of the text or on a separate piece of paper that is in sight during the editing. The questions or reminders might be:

> Why should anyone read this?
> Why would anybody believe this?
> What would make the reader turn the page?
> Remember to use examples.
> Document each point.
> Vary the documentation.
> K.I.S.S. — Keep It Simple, Stupid.

- Remember George Orwell's advice that good writing should be like a window pane. Get out of the way, don't call attention to yourself, call attention to the subject. (Yes, you can use the first person, and you certainly can express your opinion, but you should only do those things when that's the best way to get the message to the reader.)

- Aim for simplicity. This doesn't mean to oversimplify; it does mean to write in the simplest manner appropriate to the subject. Some information is complicated and will deserve complicated sentences and paragraphs, but even those should be as simple as possible. The more complicated the subject, the more important it is to find simple — but accurate — words, to use short sentences and short paragraphs at the points of greatest complication.

- Respect the subject-verb-object sentence. When meaning is tangled, consider the solution of a direct sentence.

- If it can be cut, cut it. Everything in the text should develop the meaning of that text.

- Attempt to make use of a natural order in the piece. Let the reader discover the meaning with you. Allow the reader to walk through the school with you or hear the clock ticking, or have the reader see what would be seen first, second, third.

- Make the writing flow so that it is easy to read and the writer is carried along with the flow of the sentences.

- Make the verbs as active and simple as possible.

- Make the nouns as concrete as is appropriate.

- Make sure that the meaning is carried by verbs and nouns, not by adjectives and adverbs.

- Be as specific as possible.

- Reveal what you have to say to the reader. Get out of the way, allow the reader to see, to think, to react.

- Place significant information where the reader will see it. In a paragraph, for example, there are clear points of emphasis.

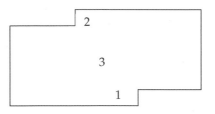

The greatest point of emphasis is at the end; the next greatest at the beginning, and the least point of emphasis in the middle. Remember that 2-3-1 principle. Not every paragraph or section of writing or piece of writing should follow that principle, but it will clarify many a complicated text.

- Get people on the page if possible. The more specific people the better. Reveal them in action that is significant to the story.

- Use quotations to give authority to important points — and to allow the reader to hear a voice different from your own. (Make sure the quotations sound like the person speaking, not you.)

- Make the piece both factually accurate and honest — make sure that the facts are in context.

- Don't try to trick the reader or deceive the reader. Most of the time it won't work, and if it does work, it shouldn't.

- Let the reader dive right into the piece of writing. A long and unnecessary introduction may have to be cut during the editing.

- Limit the subject so that there is room within those new borders to develop the subject properly.

- Make sure that everything in the piece is there on purpose — that it serves the reader.

- Don't tell the reader what the reader needs to know ahead of the time when it is needed — no background, no long introductions. Anticipate where the reader needs a definition, a supporting quotation, a documenting statistic or anecdote and deliver right there.

- Write with abundance. Information — lots of information — may need to be added during the editing process. That abundance should, of course, be under control, and it should not be an abundance of words but an abundance of information. A great deal of writing is superficial; it skates over the top of the subject. Readers want a rich, full meal of information, not a thin gruel.

- Make sure there are no elements in the writing that get between the reader and the subject. Common interferences include misspelled words, inappropriate punctuation, words that are off target, words that are only words, breaks with the traditions of usage that do not clarify the meaning, and just plain messy copy.

Putting the Process to Work

Time to Write

A rule attributed to Horace and Pliny, and followed by such writers as Trollope, Updike, and many other productive writers is: *Nulla dies sine linea*, never a day without a line. The line does not need to be final text. It can be notes, outlines, sketches, fragments, even designs, editing, revision, drafting. But the writing muscles need daily exercise.

As Flannery O'Connor said, "Every morning between 9 and 12 I go to my room and sit before a piece of paper. Many times I just sit for three hours with no ideas coming to me. But I know one thing: If an idea does come between 9 and 12, I am there ready for it." We do not know when we will write well, when the surprises will land on the page, but they will not arrive unless we are writing. Our students must be in the habit of writing so that they will have the possibility of surprise.

Every writer dreams of the uninterrupted morning when there is no knock at the door, no phone call, no letters to be answered, no distraction outside the window; a morning when the writer is rested, prepared; a morning when the world does not intrude with a family, neighborhood, or world crisis; a morning when there is no headache, indigestion, sneeze, no wandering thought. I hear of writers who have those mornings, but I do not know them, and I must confess that the mornings I have that come closest to those insulated periods of time are often wasted. Conditions are perfect, but no writing arrives.

I continue to battle for quiet time, for hours without distraction so that I can be productive. But I am a productive writer, not because I have success in achieving many such hours, but because I have learned to make use of fragmentary time — five minutes here and five minutes there.

I really need an insulated chunk of time only for writing a first draft, and that's a central but small part of the writing process. Most of my time is spent planning, and most of your students' time should be spent planning. Planning can be done when walking, jogging, going to a movie, sitting in a boring class, eating, going to sleep, taking a shower. Recently I identified some of the environments that seemed to stimulate me to get ideas or to solve problems in writing. They include:

○ Driving.
○ Browsing in bookstores, libraries and magazine stores.
○ Listening to a good poetry reading or a boring lecture.
○ Sitting in a car in a parking lot waiting. Sometimes in traffic jams.
○ Sitting in an airplane at thirty thousand feet.
○ Sitting on the john. (I used to read. Now I think.)
○ Eating by myself in a restaurant. (I hate to eat by myself in a restaurant.)
○ Reading. Especially when reading something so good it ought to tell me to quit writing. Instead it's contagious; it makes me want to write and ideas start to flow.
○ Watching sports on television.
○ Taking a nap.
○ Taking a nap watching sports on television.
○ Walking.
○ Sitting doing nothing. Porches are better for sitting and doing nothing than patios.
○ Sitting alone at a boring party. Better: sitting alone in a room while a party is going on in the next room. (All parties are boring, but writers are never bored because they can write when people think they are just staring.)
○ Writing. Writing breeds writing.

Make your own list of the times and places when you write. Five minutes may be all you can get, and need. Ten minutes is fine, fifteen is great, twenty is better, half an hour is marvelous, an hour is luxury. Ninety minutes is about ideal for me. I feel wealthy when I can get two or three hours. Few writers ever write more than four hours a day.

That's more than enough, because they're writing all the time, in their head and on their notebook page.

The Daybook

I am able to make use of fragments of time because my tools, first and foremost my daybook, are with me at all times. My daybook — or writer's log — is what some writers call a journal. When I wrote in a journal, I would swell up like rice in water and fill the space with wordy pronouncements. I tried to be Camus or Gide or someone famous and probably secretly imagined students reading my journal after I was dead. I was unbearable, unreadable — even by me. I'd write for a few days, read it over and laugh. I lost years, whole decades, when I could not keep a journal. I also tried to keep a diary, but the trivial details of my life were so trivial I was embarrassed reading them. The term "daybook," however, somehow freed me. It was a working document, a sort of lab notebook, and since I have called it a daybook, it has become the most valuable resource I have.

I use an eight-by-ten-inch notebook because it fits in the outside pocket of the case I sling over my shoulder. I keep that case with me at school and at home, in the car, when I'm traveling, and by my chair in the living room or in my office, or out on the porch — I may be just sitting, remembering Flannery O'Connor, "But I know one thing: If an idea does come . . . I am . . . ready for it."

The daybook has a page large enough to allow me to get a good chunk of writing done. Smaller notebooks seem to compress me; I don't have the area in which to explore ideas. Larger books become cumbersome, they stop traveling with me. I use a spiral book because it can be bent back easily and made to fit my lap or whatever surface I have in front of me. I also like green-tinted paper because I often write outside perched on a rock or a log and the green page limits the glare.

It takes me about six weeks to fill a daybook, and when I'm finished with one I go back through it and pick out anything that I need to work on in the next book. Usually this means a page or two of notes at the most. I keep the daybooks on a shelf, and since everything is entered by date I can usually remember about when I wrote something and go back to it if I need to. The fact is I don't go back that much, but the process of writing down is vital. I'm talking to myself, and the daybook is a record of my intellectual life, what I'm thinking about and what I'm thinking about writing. I use little code words in the left-hand margin. The initials for this book were *AWTW (A Writer Teaches Writing)* and that was the code I put next to notes about what might be in this book. It's easy for me to review the daybooks to see what I've written on a particular project. Many of my articles and books evolve over a period of years, and the daybook both stimulates and records my thinking.

If you decide to try a daybook or a log, remember that it does not contain finished writing. It can be a place for writing, a draft, but my book, at least, has all sorts of other writing that doesn't even look like writing. Everyone's daybook will change and evolve as the writer changes and evolves, but mine includes:

- Observations of people and places (not as many as I'd expect).
- Questions that need answers (and answers that need questions).
- Lines that may become poems — or stories or articles or books.
- Notes for class or for talks I'm going to give.
- The notes I've used to talk from in class or at meetings.
- Plans for what I may write (and schedules — pages of schedules, all unrealistic — of when I may write them).
- Titles, hundreds of titles, for what I'm writing.
- Leads, dozens of leads, and often ends, for what I'm writing.
- Quotations from writers about writing, pasted in or written down. My daybook is first cousin of the eighteenth-century Commonplace Book, in which people copied down observations, reflections, and pieces of wisdom from what they had read in a lifelong self-education plan.
- Outlines.
- Diagrams that sketch the form of what I'm writing.
- Drafts of poems, articles, chapters, scenes from a novel I'm working on.
- Ideas for pieces of writing or talks that will become pieces of writing.
- Discussion with myself about writing problems I'm trying to solve on my page or teaching problems I'm trying to solve in my class.
- Quotations from my students or my colleagues that I need to think about.
- Postcards or other pictures that stimulate me.
- Paragraphs from newspapers or magazines that I want to keep.
- Chunks of drafts that haven't worked or pieces of writing or planning or notes that I've typed up or done on the word processor. I print them up and paste them in the daybook so they're with me and I can work on them or think about them.
- Titles of books to read.
- Prewriting.
- Notes on lectures.

When Tilly and John Warnock of the University of Wyoming looked through some of my daybooks they were surprised to see no sign of effort, no strain, no angry crossing off, no frustration. Of course not. The daybook is where I play. It is fun. It's where I fool around, noodle, connect and disconnect, doodle. I do not strain, force. I accept, receive.

The spirit of play should never be lost. It is central to the conception of this book. What I am trying to do in this book is to explore for myself, and for you — in that order — the writing process and a way of teaching that will make that process available to my students. This is such a ~~serious business it must~~ not be taken too seriously.

Word Processors and the Process

I do not know of any writer who has used a word processor who is not impressed with this writing tool. It will not make a poor writer a good writer, but it does make the act of writing, revision, and editing much easier.

We need to understand the word processor because some schools are requiring students to buy them, an increasing number of students have access to word processors and often schools are making word processors available to writing students.

No one should be apprehensive about using a word processor. When they first appeared most people who used them outside of a business office were computer addicts. I was put off for years from using a word processor by jargon-babbling computer addicts. They spoke a private language that I could not understand, and it was so filled with offensive jargon that I did not want to understand it.

I had the illusion that there would be a great deal to learn, that I would have to know mathematics (my worst subject in school), that I would have to understand the world of science (my next-worse subject), and that I would have to be familiar with the intricacies of electronics and the whole spectrum of modern technology. That was ridiculous, but I didn't know it. When I had a chance to get a word processor I found I did not have to know any more than I have to know to use the telephone, automobile or television. I do not understand how those devices work, and I cannot repair them, but I can use them.

It took me about twenty minutes to begin producing an article on the word processor. I've now had the word processor for months, and this book was written on the word processor. Of course I have learned new tricks, but there really aren't many to learn. The computer makes it easy.

Mostly what I had to learn was that the computer is immensely dumb. It makes no intuitive leaps; it simply follows orders. When things go wrong I have to find what order I gave it that makes it do what I don't want it to do. Once you learn how to trace back and find those commands it is a snap to use the word processor.

The writer can plunge in and start creating text right away. When the writer needs to edit — to delete, insert, or reorder — then the writer can learn the commands for those functions.

The principal advantages of a word processor include:

• A good typist can type faster on a word processor than on a type-writer, because the typist is typing only one continuous line. The machine does the carriage return automatically, and this speeds up the process immensely. A poor typist can type quickly on the machine and then clean up errors easily later.

• The writer has increased freedom to create a discovery draft without worrying about anything that will have to be corrected later. The writer can feel an enormous freedom to get something down that will be developed and refined later. I have found, for example, that sometimes I write in bursts of one to five paragraphs on the word processor; then cut, add, and reorder, shaping the fragment; then polish it line by line, checking each word, each phrase, each sentence; then write in another burst. That's a very different pattern for me, and it's made possible by the word processor.

• The writer can produce a section of a longer piece of writing when-ever it comes to mind, because it can be moved around easily and in-serted wherever it belongs later on.

• The writer doesn't have to worry about the internal order of para-graphs as much as in normal writing. The writer can get the paragraphs down, then reorder them easily later.

• The three main functions of revising and editing — cutting, adding and reordering — can be done with amazing skill and ease on a word processor. The writer can cut — zap — just like that. The writer can in-sert easily, and since most writing is undeveloped, the word processor makes it easy to do the necessary developing. The writer can reorder words, sentences, paragraphs, sections, and re-reorder.

• The writer can see a clear text immediately after each change instead of the messy, scrawled-over drafts that are normal for a writer.

• The act of writing that always has been a satisfying form of play for most prolific writers is available as play to more people. For many peo-ple, the word processor does seem to make writing a game. They can en-joy the fun of making a text come clear on the tube.

• Many word processors have programs that spell. Educators may worry about this, but the fact is that many writers — present company included — are poor spellers, and the ability of the machine to check this allows spelling to be put in its proper place, at the end of the writing process, so that it is not a matter of primary anxiety on every draft.

• The writing can be stored away easily and recalled whenever the writer has something to do to the draft. These changes may be small or large. No matter, they can be added to the draft, and the draft can be stored away efficiently, ready to be called up again.

• Most writers will confess that in the past they have not made changes that should have been made because of the time and energy it took to produce a new draft. With a word processor you don't have to worry. The draft remains flexible, changeable, until it is printed.

• The writing remains in process for a longer time. There is a wonderful impermanence about the draft on the video tube. It is always writing in process, ready to be changed.

There are also some disadvantages of the word processor. They include:

• Writing is so easy that it becomes too easy. The word processor can encourage hasty writing, wordy writing, unpolished writing.

• It looks too good. Since bad writing looks as good on the word processor as good writing, there is a danger that the writer, or even the editor or teacher, will not see the struggle of crossed-out words, reordered sentences, and syntactical tangles — the hesitations and clumsiness — that signal problems on a normal text. Everything looks neat — too neat — on the word processor.

• It's so easy to reorder sections that the writer can move things around and lose the sense of order.

• The ease of moving things around combined with the ease of insertion leads to a redundancy, a tendency to say the same things twice — or thrice.

• It's easier to see a small chunk of writing, but harder to see the entire piece. If the writer does not print out the text and spread it out the writer is likely to lose sense of the whole. This is increased because the printed text soon becomes irrelevant or old-fashioned. The reality for the writer is on the screen, and the screen displays only a small portion of any text.

Adapting the Process to New Writing Tasks

Remember that there is not one writing process, but many. I have described a process of writing in this book, because that is the only coherent way to introduce and demonstrate the concept of process. It should not ever be seen as gospel. It is only a working model that can be examined, changed, or discarded.

As we have said, the writing process will change according to the cognitive style of the writer. Some of our students will move slowly and steadily, developing their writing by accretion. Others will plunge in, make leaps, skip back and forth. Neither process — or all the range of processes in between — is correct. In writing the end justifies the means; the good draft justifies the way it was made.

Each writer will also have a range of varieties within the writer's own writing process, or will have entirely different processes. Most writers, for example, will go back to a rather formal writing process when they face a new writing task, and they will usually have to revise many times, passing through the writing process again and again. As they become more experienced with the writing task they will be able to plan better. That is understandable; they know the territory; they know the form; they know the problems of clarification and communication involved in that particular writing task. And they can solve more of those problems in the planning stage. The weight of the writing moves from revision to planning, and there are usually fewer drafts.

The very nature of the writing task will cause the writer to make large adjustments in the writing process or to create a new writing process for a particular task. A student, for example, may be in the habit of writing a very rough early draft of an academic paper, then polishing and shaping it over a period of time. When that student takes a bluebook exam the student will have to produce a finished draft the first time. The writing process that works for the student will have to change. The idea of process can help the student see, for example, that it may be wise to divide the twenty minutes allowed for answering a question into five minutes of planning, twelve minutes of developing, and three minutes of editing. The concept of the writing process allows the student to break down the procedures in any writing task to a logical sequence of activity.

Why Teachers Should Write

Teachers should write, first of all, because it is fun. It is a satisfying human activity that extends both the brain and the soul. It stimulates the intellect, deepens the experience of living, and is good therapy. As

Graham Greene says, "Writing is a form of therapy; sometimes I wonder how all those who do not write, compose or paint can manage to escape the madness, the melancholia, the panic fear which is inherent in the human situation."

Teachers should write so they understand the process of writing from within. They should know the territory intellectually and emotionally: how you have to think to write, how you feel when writing. Teachers of writing do not have to be great writers, but they should have frequent and recent experience in writing. The best preparation for the writing class, workshop, or conference is at least a few minutes at the writing desk, saying what you did not expect to say. If you experience the despair, the joy, the failure, the success, the work, the fun, the drudgery, the surprise of writing you will be able to understand the composing experiences of your students and therefore help them understand how they are learning to write.

4 The First Hour of the First Day

Writing teachers and writing students share a similar fear. The instructors fear they have nothing to say. The students fear they have nothing to write.

They are both right. There is little worth saying about writing in advance of writing. And writers never know if they have anything to write until they get words on the page.

Effective instruction in composition comes in response to writing in process. The best way to begin a writing course is by writing.

No instruction is needed. Any assignments, directions, commands, discussion may get in the way of the students' writing the way they write. It is not possible for even the most experienced writing teacher to predict in June what instructions a class may need in September. Each student has to produce a draft before the writing course can start.

When the teacher reads what students write on their own, without excessive instruction, the teacher begins to see individuals. A category — a class of freshmen — becomes a community of individual writers, each with his or her own expertise, interests, problems, skills, styles, potential. As soon as possible — and the first hour of the first day is possible — the students should write and read what they have written aloud so the other students in the class will hear the same diversity and individuality as the teacher. And in hearing each other they will hear themselves.

The class will respond to the diversity of voices within the class: Carl's sense of the ridiculous, Letitia's anger, Bob's eye for details, the way Joanne's language flows, the information packed into Betty's account of a scientific experiment. The stereotypes fall. Roger is the poised preppy, but his prose is hesitant, insecure. Peter is the hulk, a dumb jock, but his writing is sensitive, delicate. Robin appears mousy, dressed in brown, small, tentative looking, but her voice is the strongest in the class.

Of course, none of the writing is finished. They are drafts of fragments, all that can be written in five minutes or so, but there are fragments within those fragments that are just right, that could be written only by the person who wrote them. You begin to know the strengths as well as the weaknesses of the individuals in the class, what they know and what they need to know.

And the class needs to know your own strengths and weaknesses, your own individuality. You should write too, under the same conditions — on the board or in your notebook — and share your writing first. It's a matter of ethics. You are going to be seeing their work; it's only fair that they see yours. More than that, your engagement in the process demonstrates that writing isn't a magic trick to be mastered, but a craft that is continually explored. It is a skill that is alive, ever changing, ever challenging, not the boring old English that so many of your students think it is, not a matter of etiquette but of meaning, of discovering your own meaning with your own voice.

The writing instructor becomes a member of the class. That is a special privilege writing teachers can enjoy: they can enter into the learning. Teaching composition does not need to be — and should not be — a matter of correcting mountains of dull papers. It can, and should be, a matter of helping students discover what they have to say and how they may be able to say it.

There are many ways to start writing the first day. There are only two rules:

1. No topic is suggested.
2. No genre is assigned.

Later, depending on your curriculum and your teaching method, you may have to suggest topics and limit the genre, but not now, not the first hour of the first day. The students must speak their own messages in whatever form that speaking takes. If you tell your students what to say and how to say it, you may never hear them, only the pale echoes of what they imagine you want them to be.

Make up your own format — role-play a beginning student and imagine what would start you writing, ask your colleagues how they initiate writing, or try one of the suggestions below. The goal is always to underteach — just a hair — to give the students room to learn. One of my students complained the other day, "I feel as if I'm teaching myself." Exactly.

If you are still floundering the way I floundered in the weeks before — and after — my first teaching, here is a range of activities you may want to consider using then. They may also be helpful later, but remember that your students should write first. There is no need to talk at them. If they write, you will know who they are and what they need to learn next.

Here are some first-day activities:

- *Free writing.* When Janet Emig started a workshop a few years ago, her students came to the classroom and saw a woman quietly writing. On the board was a simple message. "I'm writing. Please join me." After a while, Janet said, "I'd like to share what I've written," and read her draft. She invited the students to read theirs.

That's all you have to do. Try on Janet's teaching style to see if it fits, or develop your own. The important thing is to get the students writing. Don't allow your students to worry about subject or genre, length or structure, spelling, mechanical correctness, or neatness at this point. just have them write to see what surprises them on the page.

Keep the writing period short, four minutes, five, seven, just enough to produce fragmentary drafts or fragmentary beginnings — something that can be shared within the first class period.

Explain to the students that this is a writing game on which no one is going to be graded. The purpose is to have fun — and to produce writing. And announce that you are going to write yourself — to find out what you have to say.

When there is a text — usually a very rudimentary text, a few lines or a few paragraphs (although you and your students may be surprised at the quality, length or complexity of some drafts) — that text should be shared. Teacher goes first. That is an ethical question. If you are going to see their writing in process, they have a right to witness your own struggles with language and meaning. When you have revealed yourself, most students will be willing to reveal themselves. If they aren't, don't worry about it at this point, just move on.

Later we will talk more about the teacher as writer, but don't worry if you feel that you are not a good writer. just write naturally as well as you can. The more trouble you have, the worse the writing is, the more effective the demonstration may be. The students will be taken backstage. Few students have ever seen anyone write. They have seen people talk, use the telephone, but not write. A child who had never seen anyone talk, or walk, or eat would be at a disadvantage in conversation, in strolling down the street, in bellying up to the dinner table. In the writing course students must see writers writing from the first day. They should see unfinished writing, writing that doesn't work as well as writing that works, most of all, writing that *may* work if the writer rewrites and rewrites.

No formal response to the text is needed. This is not a time for evaluation — that comes later in the writing process — it is a time for enjoying, appreciating, responding with nods, smiles, groans, laughter, silence, whatever is appropriate to the subject and the voice in which it is being read.

• *Autobiography.* Another way to get the class started is to have the students write a brief autobiography, taking only ten minutes or so to introduce themselves. Sometimes it's fun to have them write the autobiography as if it were an obituary of themselves at the age of eighty, a retirement announcement, a story of receiving an award, but I think there is a danger in allowing the class at the beginning to become dependent on the teacher for the topic. And in each of those assignments there is a fundamental dishonesty. That kind of dishonesty in such an assignment is not a capital offense, but it does give to some students a message, or reconfirms a message they had heard earlier, that writing is disconnected from honesty. That's dangerous, for good writing depends on honesty.

If you are going to ask them to write their autobiographies in a matter of minutes, then you should do the same thing, preferably on the board, perhaps commenting, "This is a ridiculous assignment, but I want to get to know you and you to know me so we can work as writers together." Your students need to feel that classroom writing activities are purposeful play.

You should allow enough time for the students to introduce themselves to each other, not necessarily reading, but speaking from their autobiography.

• *Interview.* The interview is a fundamental technique the writer uses to collect information for writing, yet many students have never been taught how to interview. It can be helpful for them — and you — to team up and interview one another. I pair the students from different parts of the classroom, since they often know the person they're sitting next to, and one of the purposes of this activity is to get the class to know one another so they can become an effective writing community.

You should tell the students to find out one interesting thing about the person they are interviewing and then to find out enough to develop that point. It may be a job, a hobby, a place where the student has lived, an experience the interviewee has had, but it is the job of the interviewer to discover something significant about the person being interviewed. In college, loneliness often seems to be a condition of existence, even in some relatively small schools. The writing class provides the opportunity for students to get to know one another, to discover the challenging diversity that should be a part of a liberal education.

It takes time to do this, and the students should have at least fifteen minutes or more to complete this assignment. They may even have the first hour — and the time before the next class to write it up. When the interviews are completed the students can simply go around the room and introduce the persons they have interviewed, telling the most important thing about them.

All the interviews will probably not be presented during the first class period. Fine. You are getting to know your students and their writing and they are laying the foundation of a writing community by getting to know one another.

It can also be fun, and helpful, to have the interviewees read their own interviews and edit them. There can be an interesting and significant discussion in how we see ourselves and how others see us. The point will probably be made that there is no absolute vision. Each writer sees the world differently.

- *Writing case history.* It may be helpful to get your students to reveal their writing history — what writing they have done, what they have been taught and what they have learned — and when these histories are shared they may ignite some profitable class discussions and illuminate important misconceptions about how effective writing is produced.

The students may just free-write or you may have them pick one of the following topics:

How I write.

What is good writing?

How I have been taught to write.

What I know and need to know about writing.

How I would teach writing to this class.

When you write your paper it gives you a marvelous opportunity to reveal your own history. You need to know the conceptions — and misconceptions — your students have about the writing process, and they need to know your own ideas as well.

- *Authority list.* One of my students, Johanna Sweet, described a method for developing a student authority list in the *English Journal* ("Experience Portfolio: An Approach to Student Writing," the *English Journal,* Sept. 1976) that allowed the students to check off things they knew how to do and to add skills and knowledge they had. You may want to develop such a list, or just to have your students list what they know, the things they can do, the jobs they've held, the courses they've taken, their hobbies, their knowledge of places, organizations, events, people.

By doing your own authority list on the board or having the class share theirs in small groups and then go back to add additional skills, the students will begin to see that they have a lot to write about. In most early writing conferences you'll be doing the same thing, trying to discover, with your students, what they know. Good writing is always based on a firm foundation of authority — there is a significant relationship between the word "author" and authority.

• *The writing-process exercise.* This exercise may help introduce students to the concept of the writing process. The basic principles and techniques of conference and workshop teaching may also be introduced if conferences are included.

The exercise is composed of artificially brief writing and conferencing periods to allow the students to experience the writing and teaching process in a short period of time. There are also benefits to this brevity, for it allows students an overview of the entire process yet is so brief no one feels a great sense of failure when the writing doesn't go well. The pace is forgiving, and everyone quickly moves on to the next task.

Realize, before you start, that attitude is more important than skills — at least in the beginning. Writing should be fun. Failure is normal since writing is a series of experiments in finding meaning, and most times meaning isn't found. Laugh at your own failures in your writing and allow them to laugh at theirs. There is no right or wrong, just what works and doesn't work in the context of the evolving draft. The rules of the exercise can be broken. This is play — significant, profound play — but play nonetheless.

If you need a teaching model for this exercise, think how we teach babies to walk, providing experience, encouraging each effort, laughing at each failure, establishing increasingly difficult goals, but making each of them reasonable and not worrying if they aren't met immediately, while always displaying confidence the baby will walk one of these days.

Pass out 5 three-by-five-inch cards to each student (using different-colored cards may dramatize the process) and tell the students to take a card and *COLLECT* specific details by writing them down on the card. They should not worry about sentences, spelling, or punctuation at this point — just get the details down. The specifics may center on one topic or wander all over the countryside. Not to worry, sometimes it works one way, other times the other.

Write on a card or blackboard yourself. Allow about three to four minutes, then share what you have written. Go back over it and circle any detail that surprised you and draw arrows to connect any specifics that relate. These surprises and connections may indicate an area where writing is waiting to be written. Have the students circle anything that surprised them and draw arrows between specifics that relate to one another.

Arrange the students into triads, groups of three. One student becomes the teacher, another the writer, and the third an observer. The writer shares his or her card and makes the first response to the text.

The response may be a question: "Does this interest you?" "Do you need any more information?" "Do you think this flows?" The student who is teacher responds to that response. The observer gains by watching this conference process from a "distance." Remind students it is the responsibility of the writer to speak first, because it is the writer who knows, better than any reader, the text, where it is headed and how it was produced. Time the conference and have the students switch roles after two minutes. After another two minutes have them shift again so that each participant acts as a writer, teacher, and observer.

Have the students return to being writers and look at the material on the first card and *PLAN* by deciding the *focus*, the single most important thing they *may* have to say, on the second card. Remind them, of course, that the focus may change as they write; they may take a different point of view, change their idea of what is most important, or have to start an entirely new piece. Add that if they discovered the focus on the first card and a draft is flowing, that's fine. They can continue that draft on the next card, following their text toward meaning. The process is introduced to help the writer, not to get in the way of writing that is working. Write on a card or the blackboard yourself for two to three minutes, then share your writing with the class. Return the students to their triads and time them in the same way as before.

Students may have as much trouble listening in conference as teachers, but listening is what the writer needs. Most of the time a good listener will encourage the writer to describe and analyze the process — and the problems — discovered in the writing. Solutions are best proposed by the writer, and they will rise from the writer's own testimony. If they don't, the listener may make a suggestion or model the questions the writer should be asking the writer: what works best, what needs work, does it take too long to get to the main point, will the reader believe what's written?

Have the students *PLAN* by *rehearsing* what they may write on the third card. Suggest that they draft a few sentences in different voices to hear which one is appropriate. Voice is simply the way writing sounds. Encourage the students to listen to see if the writing sounds angry or sad, positive or tentative. Share your own search for voice, and have the students confer in triads once more, listening to what the sound of the writing tells them and trying to decide if it leads the writer — and the reader — towards a meaning.

Tell the students to *PLAN* by *designing* the piece they may write on the fourth card. The writer may draft the first sentence, what may be in the last sentence, and then indicate a few landmarks that may help the writer find the way from beginning to end. Share your own design, then have the students return to their triads.

Finally, the students — and the teacher — should *DEVELOP* what they have to say on the fifth and final card. At this point the students do not stop for details but keep the draft moving. They may want to put *TK* for "to come" in the text where there is a fact or a quotation they have to check later. Share your own first draft, and then have them meet in triads for the last time.

If you have time left, it may be helpful to have all the students read their fifth card aloud so the class — and the teacher — can hear each writer's voice before penmanship, misspellings, and mechanical and grammatical problems get between the writer and the reader. Those editorial problems, which will have to be solved eventually, may produce an unfair opinion of the writer by the teacher or the class.

You should point out to your students that they have produced a draft and experienced the essential part of one writing process as it has been described in Chapter 2.

THE WRITING PROCESS

    Collect

      +

    Plan

      +

    Develop

      =

    A draft

This is enough for the first hour of the first day. Your students have written and you have written with them. You have introduced and shared one writing process. In the weeks ahead you will discover other processes and other variations on this process as you write and share your writing.

These activities — and any others that you design yourself or adapt from your colleagues' suggestions to begin the writing course — should be based on the premise that writing must precede talking. The instructor cannot talk effectively about writing in advance of writing, and the student cannot learn from listening to talk about writing in advance of writing. Writing, writing, and more writing create the environment in which this book can be understood. We are taught to write by our own words on the page as they seek their own meaning; we are taught to teach by our own students on their own pages as they tell us what they need to learn.

5 Inviting Writing: Assignments and Demonstrations

You can command writing but you can't command good writing. Good writing — writing that surprises the writer and the reader — comes only by invitation, and many more invitations are mailed than accepted.

To teach composition, teachers have to learn how to create invitations that attract writing. Instructors can't teach effectively until there is writing, drafts rich with potential, individual, quirky, failed drafts ripe with possibility.

Lectures, presentations, handouts, texts, demonstrations, discussions, critical examination of models — all the techniques of the traditional-content course that may have their place in a composition course — will not work until the students are in the act of creating the principal text of the course: their own writing.

Until there is that evolving text, the teacher's materials are abstract, unrelated to the student's knowledge or experience. When there is a text, however, the instructor and the class can begin to discover what each writer knows and needs to know. As the students run into the problems of using language to explore, understand and communicate a subject, they become hungry for solutions — they need and want instruction from the writers around them. The students seek teaching from the instructor, from their classmates and from themselves.

The need for production before instruction frustrates many writing teachers who have had only the experience or the model of the traditional classroom with its lecture/question/test format. It is hard for them to realize that there isn't anything much to say before writing. Many English instructors assigned to teach composition but who have not been trained in composition instruction — and even some who have — attempt to teach composition by ordering writing: "Give me a comparison and contrast on rye. Hold the mustard." They get what they deserve, something slapped together in a hurry and shoved across the counter.

Other instructors are obsessed with motivating writing. When they share their techniques I am reminded of cattle prods that "motivate" the steer up the ramp towards hamburger land. Good writing is rarely "motivated" from the outside but has to be drawn out of the student. That idea infuriates many traditional teachers who feel there is little in their students to be drawn out. They believe it is their mission to inject all knowledge into the student so the teachers may receive the faint echo of their own brilliance.

Successful composition teachers may use some of the techniques of other teachers, but they all share the ability to send out invitations that attract writing.

Inviting Surprise

There are conditions that not only tolerate but also encourage surprise, and the composition teacher should explore ways to adapt these conditions to the teacher's own personality.

Need

Writers need to write. They have an itch they have to scratch, a compulsion that makes it necessary for them to write. Few students, of course, have this need — or know they have this need — but I am amazed at how many people express a secret longing to write.

For many writers this need lies deep in the personality. I think, in my case, the need to write came out of loneliness and confusion. I could not understand the strange home into which I had been born, an only child in the land of giants. I wrote by dreaming, night-dreaming and day-dreaming. I wrote by creating fantasies, stories of a life that I could understand. I became addicted to leading the multiple lives that went on inside my head. When I first could put words on paper I must have realized that I could record and play with those secret lives I was leading.

It is not fair to our students or to ourselves if we attempt to isolate composition from what is called "creating writing." The strongest impulse to write is to make meaning of chaos, to celebrate, to record, to attempt to understand the world in which we are living. We should allow our students the opportunity to use writing to see and explore their worlds.

The need to write is the need to think. We are the animals who can record and re-create the past as well as create the future. We can develop and extend ideas, moving out from ourselves to others by writing.

One student's need is not another's, and the need may not be the same for a single student on other days. We write for power — to persuade and influence others; we write to entertain, for applause; we write to share, to escape our loneliness; and we write to retreat to loneliness and mine it.

We cannot tell our students of their need to write. But if we allow our students the opportunity to write, it is amazing how often their needs come clear. We share our writing, which makes our need apparent, and we have others in the class share their writing, and their own needs come clear. Soon other students find they have their own need to write.

We give our students an opportunity through writing to make use of what they know, so that they can manipulate this information into further knowing. We allow our students the chance to look at the world, capture it, examine it, and develop an opinion on it.

Time

Writers need space in which to write. That not only means time, but a particular kind of time. Effective writing comes when the writer has the room to reach out and research a topic, gathering an abundance of information, far more than will appear in the piece, or when the writer has the room to search within, waiting to hear what writing may come. In many cases the writer needs both room for searching and room for reflecting.

Writers need time to watch themselves thinking, to observe and re-observe what they have learned, time to make connections and disconnections, to experiment with relationships and patterns, to see orders and to hear voices. We should try to create within our writing classes some quiet time, or to encourage our students to find a place and a way that they can be quiet.

But that time does not go on forever. Writers will not produce unless there is a deadline. Writers need the pressure and intensity of writing to deadline.

Every writer feels this conflict: the need for space and the need for limit. It is helpful for writers — and students — to discuss this continual tension, and to share the habits of work that harness these two essential energies, the energy of waiting and the energy of making.

My own habit and the habit of most writers is to write for relatively short, intensive periods in the morning when the mind is clear from sleep and when there is less chance of interruption. My writing periods are an hour, or an hour and a half, or two hours, occasionally three hours. But most of the time an hour and a half is plenty. Of course it may take three hours to create an envelope of time in which I can do an hour and a half of writing. But an hour or two out of twenty-four is all I need to be a productive writer *if* that hour or two is supported by twenty-three or twenty-two hours of waking and sleeping, in which my conscious, subconscious, and unconscious are working in the back room preparing writing. I have to make sure, as much as possible, they are not disturbed, or they cannot work. It is a daily fight to have the quiet time essential if my morning stint is to be productive.

Reader

The act of writing is not complete without a reader, and most writers need one or two or three readers, perhaps five, but rarely more, who they know will appreciate what is being said and how it is being said.

The possibility of surprise is multiplied when the writer knows there is a reader who will delight in surprise; who will laugh at failure, yet applaud the effort; who will understand success and appreciate it.

Teachers should become readers for whom people want to write. This doesn't mean lower standards. In fact, it usually means higher standards; somebody who expects us to be capable of surprise, somebody who expects us to write better than we think we can write, somebody who can share and understand our difficulties and our successes with the writing process, somebody who can be a helpful mentor, counseling us so that we write of our own subjects in our own way with their help: a teacher.

All writing is experimental in the beginning. It is an attempt to solve a problem, to find a meaning, to discover its own way towards understanding. We must, at the very beginning of our courses, emphasize the necessity of failure and the advantage of failure. How do we do that? By showing our own failures on drafts, by making failure a legitimate and interesting part of the process, by showing the evolution of student and professional drafts through failure to accomplishment. Our students are terrified by failure when they need to know how to make use of it. They have been taught, by teachers and parents, the press, and their own instinct, that everything must be done perfectly the first time. They are inhibited, constipated, frightened — in no condition to produce good writing. Writing that is written to avoid failure guarantees mediocrity.

The way we feel often controls the way we think; the affective controls the cognitive. This is not a comfortable thought for many academics, who idealize a world in which the brain dominates the heart. If we are going to teach writing effectively, however, we must see ourselves as creating the attitudes that will allow ourselves and our students to write to discover what we have to say. There are some other significant attitudes that are necessary to encourage the writing process.

Our first task is to attack the imposition of unrealistic and inappropriate standards at the beginning of the writing process. It is a battle I must fight every day when I come to the writing desk and confront this book, this page. I want the chapter to be impressive; I want it to impress my colleagues, my editor, my readers. I sit paralyzed before the page, and then, remembering my own lessons, I put something down, anything down. I turn to William Stafford for counsel. He tells me, in a quotation I keep in the calendar I carry everywhere, "I can imagine a person beginning to feel that he's not able to write up to that standard he imagines the world has set for him. But to me that is surrealistic. The only standard I can rationally have is the standard I'm meeting right now . . . you should be more willing to forgive yourself. It really doesn't make any difference if you are good or bad today. The *assessment* of the product is something that happens *after* you've done it."

We also need to be part of a writing community, a collection of people who are writing, who understand what it means to write. Writers need to be in an environment in which writing is important. We need to work in an atmosphere that values writing and that encourages writing. We need as writers to be able to fail and pick ourselves up and try another draft. We need the security of knowing there are those people around us with whom we can share our early efforts. Through the sharing of writing in draft — our failures and successes — we get to know each other as writers — and as people. The writing class forges a community as students share and help each other write. Such a community makes writing contagious, and as teachers we should work to create a community in which as many people as possible will be infected with the desire to write.

Reading

When writers read something very good they want to write. It is a curious reaction. When we read something that is far better than we could do we should be discouraged. Instead, we're usually inspired. It's not a matter of competition, but it is a matter of getting into the game, participating in the writing process.

We need to provide our students with two kinds of reading. They need to be constantly reading the drafts in process of their teacher and their fellow students so they share the excitement of writing evolving, so they can experience the surprise of what happens on the page. The better the writing around them the better their writing is likely to be.

They also need to hear the voices of the best writers we have in our language. They need to read those who are working in the same territories as they are, and those who are celebrating worlds far different from the students'. They need to see the possibilities of writing, to read the surprises on the pages of master writers, not so that they imitate, but so that they do see the geography of possibility which surrounds them.

Craft

The craft of writing itself can be inspiring. It is intoxicating to play around with language, to hear the music of what we say, to see more clearly as we speak, to follow the unexpected paths where words take us.

Tools are part of our craft. Writers delight in a certain pen, or a particular pencil, in the texture of paper, in the magic mechanism of a typewriter or a word processor. The craftsperson loves the tools of the trade, and they, themselves, somehow inspire. Painters often speak of a brush as if it were a separate person capable of its own explorations. They are right. Our tools seem to lead us towards significance.

All the other elements of craft, the way we make phrases and sentences, the way we shape paragraphs and build with paragraphs, the tricks of the trade that allow us to make a vague idea concrete, to persuade, to explain, to allow a person to speak on the page, to allow a character to rise from the page and walk — all the tools of the writer's craft are aids to inspiration and surprise. The more we learn the craft of writing and the more our students share in our learning the more possibility for surprise occurs.

Craft breeds craft in another way. We like new challenges, new problems to solve, but we also need a history of success. We need to have made a loaf of bread in the past to be inspired to bake another loaf today.

Writers have the satisfaction of problem-solving. While writing we have problems of content, and structure, and audience, and genre, and voice, and as we develop our craft we have more and more ways to attempt to solve those problems. Writers speak of being inspired by the problem that is before them; they are intrigued by the possibility of solving a problem on the page.

When I share this experience of meeting surprise on the page with my students they begin to get excited about writing. We have too often trivialized writing in the schools. We have given exercises in workbooks, topics, and used writing as tests. We have demanded a kind of fill-in-the-blank writing, ordering our students to deliver *our* messages from *their* mouths, and correcting anything that surprises us. Once our students feel the writer's motivation of surprise, once they see and hear their own meanings coming from their own pages, they become motivated to write. And as those meanings become stronger and clearer, they will be motivated to make their writing better structured, better written.

The Syllabus

I have read thousands of student evaluations through the years and been struck by how highly most students value organization. The syllabus is one of the primary ways of establishing the organization of a writing course. It can set the tone of the course, establish ground rules, and let the students know what the course will attempt to do and how it will attempt to do it.

In my last version of this text I at first resisted publishing a lesson plan or syllabus, because I was afraid it would be taken too seriously. I finally relented and published a range of contradictory syllabi. And they were taken too seriously. Readers focused on one syllabus and said *that* is the way writing should be taught.

In this book I show five different syllabi. They in no way represent *the* way to teach writing, and they do not come close to all the ways I have attempted to teach writing. I use a new syllabus every time I teach a section, and one of the great joys I have in teaching is to create experimental designs. When I first taught I would decide what worked best when I last taught the course, and then eliminate that from the syllabus, or do the absolute opposite. For example, when I found that short daily papers worked I taught a freshman section in which I required 25 pages of free writing the first week, 12½ the second week, and 12½ the third. Nothing is sacred to me in my syllabi, and nothing should be sacred to you. But I think it may help to see a series of designs through which writing may be taught. All of these approaches are created to allow the students a chance to do their best work and receive a response from fellow writers during the process.

I urge my students again and again not to allow the syllabus to get in the way of their education. They can attempt anything — and they do — that pushes them beyond the syllabus. A third of the way into one composition class I gave the students the option of following my syllabus or creating one of their own. One student chose to follow my syllabus; nineteen wrote their own, and they were all more demanding than mine.

Sometimes it helps, as part of a syllabus, to share the goals of the course in written form. The teaching techniques of conferences and workshops are discussed in detail in Chapters 8 and 9. Here is an example of such a statement, followed by six variations on that theme.

When you finish this course:

1. You will be able to find your own subject — and know how to make an assignment your own. You will know how to get ideas for significant pieces of writing and to respond to an assignment in a manner appropriate to your own knowledge.

2. You will have a successful experience with at least one writing process that enabled you to take an idea and develop, refine, and share it with others in a final, edited draft.

3. You will have heard your own voice in your writing and learned how to adapt it to a variety of purposes and readers.

4. You will know how to anticipate and answer the questions your readers will ask while they read your text.

5. You will be able to read writing in progress, identifying what works and what needs work. After reading a draft, you will be able to make suggestions that will help its writer, and you will be able to make use of the suggestions of others when they read your draft. Most of all, you will be able to read your own drafts so that they become increasingly effective.

6. You will be able to write at a range of distances — from personal to objective — and in a variety of genre and forms appropriate to your subject, your reader, and your purpose.

7. You will have discovered through the experience of your own drafts that writing is thinking, that you discover what you have to say by saying it.

Freshman English Variation I

PURPOSE   This course will help you discover what you know and what you need to know to make your writing more effective. You'll be able to pick your own subjects, and therefore the course can be adapted to your own academic, career, or personal goals.

WORKSHOPS   We will hold a two-hour workshop each week, where we will share our writing, our methods of writing, our problems, and our solutions. The main purpose of the workshop is to help the writer improve the draft under discussion. The writer will be asked, "How can we help you?" The writer will respond, then we will read the draft and respond to the writer.

Each student will sign up to publish a draft in workshop, once during the first half of the semester and once during the second. The student will provide copies for each member of the class.

CONFERENCES   Each student will sign up for a fifteen-minute conference with the instructor every week. The student will come to the door at the scheduled time to make sure the instructor knows the student has arrived.

The student will make the first evaluation of the paper and the instructor will respond to the student's evaluation. The purpose of the conference is to help the student become an effective reader of drafts in process so that new papers and new drafts will be increasingly effective. In conference, the instructor monitors the student's reading of each draft.

ASSIGNMENTS At the beginning of class, each student will pass in at least five pages of typed, double-spaced copy on a topic of the student's choice. New attempts at the same subject and extensive revisions will count as weekly papers. Students should attempt to write at varying distances and in different forms when they are appropriate to what the student is trying to say.

The student has the responsibility to make sure that the syllabus does not interfere with the student's education. The student can always do more work than the syllabus requires, and should adapt the course to the student's own needs in consultation with the instructor.

RULES There are no late papers. If a paper is not passed in at the beginning of the class, the student will receive a drop card.

Attendance at class and conference is required. Drop cards are available for those who do not attend.

GRADES You will be allowed to do what I do, submit my best work for evaluation. At the beginning of the last class you will pass in three papers of your choice for evaluation. They may be revised, and they should have no errors of usage, mechanics, spelling, or manuscript preparation. You will not be graded on effort or intention but on accomplishment.

Freshman English Variation II

PURPOSE | This course is designed to give you individual attention. You will choose subjects appropriate to your own goals and work with the instructor to develop those subjects in a manner appropriate for your readers and your goals.

WORKSHOPS | There will be no workshops or class meetings, so that there may be more time for individual instruction.

CONFERENCES | (The same as FRESHMAN ENGLISH VARIATION I, except that the conferences will be twenty minutes long.)

ASSIGNMENTS | (The same as FRESHMAN ENGLISH I but substituting "conference" for "class.")

RULES | (The same as FRESHMAN ENGLISH I, except there will be no mention of class.)

GRADES | (The same as FRESHMAN ENGLISH I.)

Freshman English Variation III

PURPOSE | (The same as FRESHMAN ENGLISH I.)

WORKSHOPS | We will hold two three-hour workshops each week in which all the writing of the course will be done. We will write together, share our writing, and respond to it, so that we help each other become more effective writers.

CONFERENCES | Conferences with other members of the workshop, including the instructor, will be held during the workshop periods as they are needed.

ASSIGNMENTS | Each student will complete a draft of a new piece of work, or a major revision, by the end of the second workshop session.

RULES | (The second paragraph in FRESHMAN ENGLISH I.)

GRADES | (The same as FRESHMAN ENGLISH I.)

Freshman English Variation IV

PURPOSE	(The same as FRESHMAN ENGLISH I.)
WORKSHOPS AND CONFERENCES	We will establish groups of three at the first and only class meeting. Students will be encouraged to pick other students with whom they can share drafts during the week. Each group of three will sign up for a scheduled one-hour meeting with the instructor. At those meetings each student will pass out copies of the draft for the other members of the group and the instructor. The writer will comment upon the draft, and the instructor and the other members of the group will respond, so that we can help each other improve our writing.
ASSIGNMENTS	(Same as FRESHMAN ENGLISH I.)
RULES	(Same rules as FRESHMAN ENGLISH I, adapted to the conference/workshop format.)
GRADES	(Same as FRESHMAN ENGLISH I.)

Freshman English Variation V

PURPOSE	The educational experience is too often fragmentary. There is no time to do one job and to do it well. It takes most of us approximately a semester to write one article. I will write an article this semester, and you will write one. You will have time to find your subject, research it, plan it, develop it, revise it, and edit it.
WORKSHOPS	(Same as FRESHMAN ENGLISH I.)
CONFERENCES	(Same as FRESHMAN ENGLISH I, except for the elimination of the term "new papers.")

ASSIGNMENTS Each student will complete one paper approximately twenty pages long by the end of the course. Each week the student will pass in an appropriate amount of research, planning, drafting and revising evidence so that the class and the instructor can help the student make appropriate progress towards concluding that one paper. Students will, of course, explore varying distances and different forms to discover the one appropriate for the final paper.

RULES (Same as FRESHMAN ENGLISH I.)

GRADES The final copy of the paper submitted for evaluation at the last class meeting will have no errors of usage, mechanics, spelling, or manuscript preparation. It will be graded on accomplishment, not on effort or intention.

Writing Assignments

It should be clear that I feel the entire curriculum should *not* be constructed on a system of teacher-designed writing assignments. I feel that students will learn more when they confront the entire writing process and have to find what to say as well as how to say it. I fear that assignments may limit the student because most assignments are based on a prediction of minimum competency. Although teachers who are most proud of their assignments believe they are setting high standards, in fact their students often do far less than they would if they had the higher standard of finding their own subjects and developing them. Still, there is a role for writing assignments in the composition course, especially in advanced and specialized writing courses when a particular form of writing is to be learned.

If we are to use writing assignments, they should be constructed with care and responsibility, so that we are sure we are teaching what we want to teach and not limiting or diminishing the students' intellectual challenge.

The Closed Assignment

The closed assignment is both a matter of pedagogy and ethics. It has a clear educational purpose — the teacher and the students know what the assignment intends to teach. It also has honesty of expectation. There is no hidden agenda kept secret from the students. The teacher lets the students know in advance of the assignment just what is expected of them.

It takes time to build effective closed assignments. They can't be tossed off between the late-show and bedtime or thought up during the morning traffic jam on the way to campus. Effective assignments take time to prepare and time to present. The students need the assignment given to them orally, or in written form, and they need time to ask questions about the assignment in a climate in which they can be asked.

Writing directions is one of the most difficult writing tasks, for we are always building our directions on assumptions that may not be shared by our students. I say, "Type on one side of the paper," meaning that one side should be blank, and I get papers that are typed down the right side of the paper with three-quarters of the page left as a left-hand margin. It is hard for me to know what most students need to know, and harder for them, I discover again and again, to understand what I have in mind. They must be urged to ask questions and discuss the assignment to make sure we are both on the same wavelength.

There is, of course, a whole range of closed assignments. Some assignments, appropriately, are much more closed than others. The degree of closed-ness varies with the pedagogical purpose and the pedagogical philosophy of the instructor. But there are elements that should be considered in creating any closed assignment. They are:

• *Purpose.* Students must know why they are required to do the assignment if the assignment is to be successful. Students appreciate an assignment with a clear educational purpose. It allows them to know what they are intended to learn, and they feel a sense of accomplishment when they believe they have learned it. I tell my students at the beginning of each course — and repeat it during the course — that they should be able to challenge anything I ask them to do, and I should be able to answer those challenges.

The purpose of the assignment should be as specific as possible. Certainly not "to write better" but more likely "to make your position clear, to respond to the arguments against your position that may be proposed by the reader, and to present your own arguments in favor of your position."

• *The assignment.* Students should know precisely what they are expected to do. The assignment should indicate the degree of openness allowed. For example, the assignment might say, "Interview a person in power who makes significant decisions about how they make those decisions," or "Interview a law-enforcement official — a police officer, attorney, or judge — about how he or she interprets the laws while on the job." The assignment must be clear and well-enough developed to anticipate and answer the questions students will have when they are outside the classroom and working on the assignment.

There certainly should be time in class for questions about the assignment, and it may even be helpful to assign a student to be a devil's advocate to the assignment, or to have the class break into small groups for five or ten minutes, and then have the group leaders give you the assignment so you can hear what they think you are requiring.

• *Topic.* The greatest danger in giving an assignment occurs when we give the topic. Often, we fall into that pattern because we give topics when we are subject-matter teachers and use writing to test our students' knowledge of the subject. But in the writing course we are not testing our students on their knowledge of a subject. In fact, something quite different should be taking place. Our students should be teaching us the subject while we are teaching them to write.

When we give the topic to our students we assume a common experience that does not exist. The topics come from our experience or from our preconception of the students' experiences. There is a great danger that we stereotype our students, and that we decide in advance of meeting the class that they would all have an opinion on a topic we give them. This may not be the case. What interests us — abortion, drug laws, international affairs, the environment — may not interest them. And even if it interests them they may have no knowledge on the subject, and to be an effective writer the student has to be an author — an authority.

• *Genre.* The assignment should make clear what form of writing — or forms — are expected and acceptable. If the assignment calls for an argument, then the students should be told, or reminded of, what the instructor expects in an argumentative paper. One instructor, for example, may have a very formal structure for argument; another may even allow the argument to be made with a personal narrative. The students must know the ground rules.

• *Voice.* I have rarely seen voice discussed in giving an assignment, but I think it is something that should be mentioned. The instructor should tell the students what language expectations are held by the teacher for this particular assignment. If the instructor allows the first person, or does not, that should be known; if the faculty member wants (rewards) complex sentences and extensively developed paragraphs, then the students should know that. The students should also know if the teacher allows the colloquial expressions and contractions typical of personal writing or wants the students to follow the more formal conventions appropriate to academic writing.

- *Length.* The students should know the expected length of the paper, or at least the range that is acceptable.

- *Deadline.* The students should know the final date when the paper will be accepted, and there should be no exemptions to deadline except for matters of serious illness or unusual problems which are discussed with the instructor *prior to the deadline.* These rules should be made clear to the students, and should be followed.

I work with the writers and editors at the *Providence Journal-Bulletin* and find that the professional writers do not like, or respect, editors who allow them to write shorter or longer pieces than had been assigned, or to miss deadlines. They want the opportunity to discuss the length of the piece after the research is done or to discuss a change in deadline, but once the deadline and the length are established they respect the editor who holds them to it.

- *Models.* Many students, in fact most freshmen, may have no common idea of what is meant by such simple terms as *essay, argument, narrative, fiction, non-fiction,* or *research paper.* One student may think *essay* means argument, another may think it is creative writing — a short story. They may well have a clear sense of what another teacher has meant by those terms, but the students need a model in a closed assignment, especially if the teacher has a model in mind. These models may be in a reader; they may be dittoed examples from publications or other students, and they may be posted or on reserve in the library as well as distributed to the students. It is usually a good idea to have at least three models that present a range within the genre so that the students do not think that they just have to fill in the blanks of a writing formula.

- *Drafts.* I will often assign queries or proposals for a piece of writing, early drafts and final drafts. The students need to know the deadline and the standards for each of these drafts. It is perfectly understandable to accept early drafts that are marked up and fairly messy. I do not, because I feel it is unfair for my students to present messy drafts. Their classmates and I may see only the messiness. The students need to know what is expected of them.

- *Documentation.* The assignment should make clear if a specific form of documentation is expected — for example, scholarly citations, government reports — and if certain forms of documentation are not accepted — for example, anecdotes, first-person experiences.

If appropriate, the students should know where to get the documentation and how to give the reader attribution. For example, they should know if footnotes are expected and in what form. Of course, students have been taught this before, but in my experience few have learned it, and there is a great deal of variation from instructor to instructor. The students should know what you expect. It is always important with beginning students to show as well as tell what you mean by direct quotation and paraphrase. The majority of students have not learned this essential distinction, and it is important for you to make it clear to them.

• *Style.* Students should know the style of manuscript preparation you expect for the final draft. You cannot expect students to know the various stylistic rules you consider essential for the successful completion of the assignment.

• *Resources.* If there are special resources for source material, models, or style handbooks or guides, the students should know that.

• *Skills.* If there are skills the students need to have to complete the assignment properly, then they need instruction in those skills before the assignment is given or during the time they are working on the assignment. Such instruction may involve class lecture, demonstration, class activity, references to the textbook, or handouts. Too often we expect the students to demonstrate a skill simply because the assignment, in our minds, calls for the skill. For example, we ask our students to describe, but do not instruct them in the skills of awareness or the skills of presenting description to the reader in such a way that the reader will see what the writer intends the reader to see.

• *Response.* A good assignment will usually indicate the response the writer can expect during and after the assignment. Such response may be built into the syllabus. Students, for example, may be expected to respond to their own draft in process, and even fill out a questionnaire such as the one on page 153. They may have the opportunity to have help from their peers in small group or class workshops. They may have conferences with the instructor during or after the assignment. They may also have a written response from the instructor. And they should know, of course, if the paper is to be graded and on what basis.

That sounds intimidating — and it is. A principal cause of poor writing received from students is the assignment. If you are going to use closed assignments, they have to be well prepared so that the students know the purpose of the assignment and how to fulfill it. Far too many teachers blame the students for poor writing when the fault lies with the teacher's instructions — or lack of instructions.

The closed assignment implies a teaching philosophy in which the students are instructed before the act of writing. The teacher initiates and is in control. This is the traditional approach to instruction, and it can get results. It is not my favorite, but it is a mode of instruction that I use, particularly in advanced classes or in courses such as newswriting or magazine article writing that have a specific vocational goal. And certainly there are students who come to me well prepared who have been taught by this method.

The teacher gets into trouble, however, when there is a contradiction between the instructor's philosophy or style and the assignment. For example, some teachers tell the students that they want to be surprised and that the students should be "creative," and then give assignments that predict only one response and limit student initiative and expression.

We should try to avoid labeling one form of assignment bad and another good. What we should do is attempt to be clear and consistent, so that whatever form of assignment we use allows the students the opportunity to learn.

The Open Assignment

I prefer the open assignment to the closed, for it allows the student to be an authority on the subject. Most of us understand and preach the relationship of authorship and authority. We believe our students should know their subjects, have an abundance of information on the subject, think about the subject deeply and clearly, care about the subject and be committed to it. And yet many of us give assignments that preclude all this.

I am, of course, talking primarily about topic, for when I choose the topic I take away from my students an essential part of the writing experience. But I am not talking just about topic, for in every way I want to make sure that my students have as much control over their material and investment in their material as they can. If it is their subject matter they will make their own discoveries — they will think — and they will discover a voice that is appropriate to them, to the subject, and to their own audience.

The open assignment encourages the productive relationship in which the student teaches the instructor the subject while the instructor teaches the student writing. This is, of course, more difficult when there is a content to the course. When writing is taught as an adjunct to literature or when writing is used to test a student's knowledge of a subject, then the open assignment is more difficult.

It is also more difficult to create effective open assignments in courses with a limited, vocational aim, such as journalism, business writing, science writing, and so forth. But I have found that it is possible and advantageous to do this. It is less important for students to perform a specific writing task and more important for them to be engaged significantly in the act of writing. I used, for example, to have all my journalism students cover a specific zoning meeting. Now I ask them to find out something that is important to their readers in class and outside of class. I get better stories with the open assignment than with the closed one, and we cover the same technical problems they must learn to solve.

It is also important for the students to learn how to find a subject. When we give an assignment we cheat the students of experience with much of the writing process. They are not trained in awareness and in limiting and focusing their subject. We, the instructors, do much of the work for the students — and that is why so many students prefer to have specific assignments. They want us to hold up the hoops so they can jump.

Of course a range of openness is possible. The instructor can simply demand writing with no restrictions whatsoever, or the instructor can provide whatever limitations seem essential.

I find deadlines essential. These pages are being written to deadline. When the deadline was not close these pages were not written. I cannot name a single professional who does not need to establish a deadline. Therefore I provide my students with a deadline, a time when writing must be passed in. I find it helpful to have that deadline at the beginning of the class, and to have the passing in of the papers to deadline a matter of some ceremony. At my institution we have a drop card. When a student wants to drop the course the student must get the card from the instructor, have it signed by the instructor and the adviser, and then take it to the registrar's office. For nearly twenty years I have been initiating drop cards without argument so far — students who miss classes and conferences and do not turn in work are given drop cards. Not every institution will allow such a system, but I think that there should be a strict penalty for not producing work during the course and not just at final grade time.

Depending on the course, I may allow a broad range of materials to be passed in: a research report; notes on interviews; brainstorming lists and awareness lists; draft titles, outlines, or endings; test drafts; proposals for pieces; some form of writing appropriate to the writing to be produced.

I also find weekly deadlines important. I work with advanced students, graduate students and professional writers as well as beginning students, and I do not find anyone who can work well with more than a weekly deadline. If I have a two-week deadline all the work is done at the end of the second week. A three-week deadline, at the end of the third week. At times I've taught a course with a daily deadline, and had no complaints, no missing papers. Apparently there's no time for complaints or tardiness. When papers are due four days out of five I get some complaints and a few missing papers; three days out of five even more. I'd like to have daily papers all the time, but, of course, that restricts the subject matter, length and form of the writing.

Often there is a genre limit that is essential to an open assignment. At my institution I am a non-fiction writing teacher, and we do not allow poetry or fiction in Freshman English. As one who writes poetry and fiction I would be happy to allow all genres, but the institution would not tolerate this. Therefore I must tell my students not to write fiction or poetry. It is quite possible to have an open assignment with genre or form limitations. I might, for example, ask my students to write an article about a person, and that might allow an interview or a profile, a hard news story or a feature story.

I often indicate a minimum length in an open assignment, and generally feel that in a basic writing course five pages a week is a minimum. In some cases this can be several pages — two one-pagers and a three, two two-pagers and a one, one three-pager and a two. I also strongly encourage longer papers, for I find that beginning students underwrite, and they need to get a sense of developing story. Often they do not find their story or their voice until the sixth, seventh, eighth, or ninth page. I can never quite get around the fact, however, that any mention of the number of pages, for example, "a minimum of five pages," is interpreted by many students as an absolute edict of five pages, no less and no more.

It's possible to use models with open assignments as long as the instructor makes clear that they are being used to show the range of possibility, not to restrict the writer. Many writers do not understand what can be done in writing. They are not readers, and teachers often have to use models to extend their students' vision of the possibilities of writing.

And, of course, students should know the purpose of the assignment. If the assignment is an open one, then it's vital that they understand why the instructor is doing this. Students may think — an attitude sometimes encouraged by other instructors — that the instructor is lazy or simply "permissive" in some touchy-feely sort of way. The students should understand why they are expected to find their own subjects and develop them in their own way.

Combining Open and Closed Assignments

Too often teachers divide themselves into camps — Joe gives closed assignments, Amy gives open assignments — when it's quite possible, and advisable, to combine open and closed assignments.

This combination can take place within the assignment. Just eliminating the topic is a big step forward, in my opinion. As I've just indicated, the open assignment is created, in a sense, by eliminating any restrictions in the closed assignment that can be eliminated. You'll have to experiment in your own teaching to see how far you can go. The test is in the quality of work that you get from your students.

It's also possible to use a combination of well-designed closed assignments and well-designed open assignments in a course. Each should be used for a specific educational purpose. This will change according to the institutional goals, the program goals, the course goals, the students, and the personality of the instructor. Never underestimate the importance of the personality of the instructor. I prefer open assignments. My colleague in the next office prefers closed assignments. I respect him as a teacher and a colleague, and I admire the results he gets with his students. We each have to teach in our own way, and we have to learn from our own students how we can help them learn. There is no one way to teach, but many ways. We need to become as familiar as possible with all the ways of teaching, and keep experimenting so that we grow as teachers while our students are growing as students.

Presentations

There is a place for the class meeting in the composition curriculum, although I do not think it is at the heart of the curriculum. First comes the conference, then the workshop, and then the class meeting, a place where the community of writers can work on those matters that concern them all.

Presentations by the Instructor

There is little that can be said about writing in advance of writing, but once the students in the class are writing and the instructor is responding in conference and the students are responding in workshop, each class will develop its own need to meet. One class may need a presentation on leads that shows the class effective leads and how to write them. Another class may need a presentation on brainstorming to find a good subject. Still another may need a session on outlining or time to develop a class checklist for editing.

I find it impossible to tell what any class needs until they begin writing, and I also can't tell when they need it. It is important to time class presentations so they respond to the needs of the class. My rule of thumb is that when a quarter to a third of the class has a problem in writing and is aware that they have that problem in writing, then the class is ready for a presentation. If for example, I find that five students — or six or seven — out of twenty are frozen into one kind of lead or introduction, then it's time for me to expand their horizons.

It doesn't take me long to prepare a class presentation. I know where they are, and I know what they need, and so I make whatever notes are necessary to speak on that topic for ten or fifteen minutes at the most. I encourage discussion, and whenever possible I back up what I have to say with a handout. My handouts are best when they are prepared for a particular class, and I try to lose them afterwards, so I have to keep preparing new handouts. They obviously can have a life beyond one class. I don't think the notes for a presentation can, and I put all of my notes in the wastebasket at the end of each class. After years and years of classes I think this habit of tossing away my notes makes my teaching fresh and interesting to me more than anything else I do.

These class presentations should be informal and conversational, with the tone of a writer speaking to a writer. Here is a chance for an experienced writer to share that experience and to make suggestions which may or may not help the students. If you have this tone you have the opportunity to bring the students into the discussion and to get them to share their own solutions to the problem under discussion. You should not lecture, but invite the students to share your experience with the craft of writing.

Presentations by Students

Tim Linehan said at the end of one of my composition classes, "That's the best class we had all semester." I knew it was. I'd kept track. I hadn't spoken for the last fifty minutes. In some ways I feel that my challenge as a teacher is to eliminate myself as a teacher, to make it possible for my students to teach each other and to teach themselves.

I am a successful teacher whenever I can get my students to do my teaching for me. Therefore, I encourage presentations by the students. When a student has an opportunity in workshop or class discussion to make an informal or formal presentation on a success they have just achieved, that presentation has an authority for the students that I can never have. It also reinforces the lesson learned by the student making the presentation.

One of the best ways for students to make presentations is to have students tell, after they have written a story that has impressed the class, how they wrote the story. This is a technique first cousin to the valuable protocol work done by Dr. Linda Flower and others that allows us to see how writers write, and to learn the techniques of writing from each other. This is one of the basic techniques of my work with professionals. In working as a writing coach for the *Providence Journal-Bulletin* I encouraged reporters to produce accounts of good stories as a way of reinforcing what they are doing and educating their colleagues. Many of these accounts have been collected in *How I Wrote the Story — A Book for Writers by Writers About Writing,* edited by Christopher Scanlan (The Providence Journal Co., 75 Fountain Street, Providence, Rhode Island 02902, 1983).

I find it's helpful to have students do the same thing. Sometimes I have accounts only from the best students, other times I have every student — halfway or three-quarters of the way through the course — write a detailed account of how they have written a specific piece. These accounts instruct me and instruct the class. They are the inspiration for good discussion and they reinforce the lessons the student writers are learning and encourage them to look at their own writing processes in a critical yet constructive manner.

Discussion

I like to allow time for open discussion about writing, so that students have an opportunity to air their concerns and to share their responses to those concerns. Discussion is another fine way of inviting students to become writers, especially when it eliminates misconceptions about what writing is and how it is done.

If the discussion flags — or never starts — in the beginning of the semester I'll sometimes end the class and walk out. That usually startles the students, and the next time there is an opportunity for discussion they're more likely to participate and take advantage of the time to talk about writing.

Each semester I practice a trick taught me by a colleague, Dr. Hugh Potter, that I've adapted to my own use. I distribute three-by-five-inch cards and give the students a few minutes to ask questions about writing. I have them passed in, and I answer them briefly and quickly. I can handle about three questions from each student, usually fifty or sixty questions, in an hour.

This is another significant way to respond to the concerns of a writing class. The written questions I receive are greatly different from the oral questions. They include the "stupid" questions that are often profound and that the members of the class want to ask but wouldn't dare. They also include questions from those people who rarely volunteer in the class. It is interesting and significant how different the questions are in each class. I received over 60 questions from one section last semester and more than 60 questions from another section in the same course. I had more than 120 questions, but only 3 questions were asked by both classes — and it was the same course and the same level of students. That documents the diversity that the teacher must recognize — and to which the teacher must respond.

I find that this is helpful about midway through the course. It gives a chance for students to receive a response to concerns they have, and it gives me a reading on where they are in the course. It is also a good way to inspire discussion. Questions that have come up in this exercise return during future discussions and in conference.

Demonstrations

Most students have never seen writing being made. They believe that teachers and writers know a magic rite that places words on the page in an order that is full of grace and meaning the first time, that each word arrives correctly spelled, each piece of punctuation appears at the moment it is needed, and that all rules of rhetoric, grammar, and mechanics fall into place on their own.

It is illuminating for students to see the way words may flow when somebody writes and the way that they may struggle to find a meaning. I envy my colleagues in studio courses whose students can see them paint, and my colleagues in the music department who can hear them toot and retoot and retoot trying to get the right rhythm and the tone. We need to make writing accessible to reveal the writer's struggle on the page, so that our students do not think that those words went down line after line as neatly as they are printed.

I believe that teachers should occasionally write in public, and whenever possible have their students write in public. I have been surprised when working with professionals to discover their fascination with a public demonstration of writing. Even those who work in a city room or a book or magazine publishing office have not often had the opportunity to observe an evolving draft of a colleague with all the false starts and problems of organization, development and voice exposed.

Teachers should not be fearful of writing in public. The worse the writing goes the better the demonstration, although I will never write down to a class. If I were to suffer writer's block, then it would be an ideal situation, for I could turn to the class and ask for their help with the writer's block.

There are many ways to make writing public. You can share the reproduced manuscript pages of great writers. You can invite professional writers to come to class and share their drafts. You can bring in writing of your own and show the history of a piece of writing as it grew through many drafts. You can invite a student to display and discuss the notes, outlines, and drafts that led to a good piece of writing.

It is possible to actually write in public by writing on the blackboard, on a huge pad of newsprint, or on an overhead projector as your students write, and then go back over your writing with them. It's possible to just write a draft and have them observe you working, to write a draft and explain what you're doing as you do it, making verbal the sort of talk that goes on between the writer and the text. You can invite the class to participate in the writing act with you, suggesting what you might say and what you might have to change in the text if you say it.

Towards the end of the composition course you may be able to have other students of writing share their writing process so that the class sees how different people work. I do not think that the process of writing, although it is essentially private, should be secret. Teachers should demonstrate that writing is not magic, but the craft of trying to make meaning clear with language.

This chapter — and the next — offers an extensive inventory of writing teacher strategies and tactics to which you will add techniques stolen from your teachers, your colleagues, your students and dreamt up yourself, often in desperation, "Well, I might as well try that, nothing else seems to . . ."

Never forget that teaching is similar to writing, a craft and art that cannot be contained by absolutes. There is no one way to teach effectively. You have to change as you learn more about your subject, gain experience, face new students. Eudora Welty says of writing, "The writer himself studies intensely how to do it while he is in the thick of doing it; then when the particular novel or story is done, he is likely to forget how; he does well to. Each work is new. Mercifully, the question of *how* abides less in the abstract, and less in the past, than in the specific, in the work at hand . . ."

Teaching is like that. The teacher needs an inventory of techniques as the writer does, but each class is new, each student a fresh challenge. The effective teacher is always learning how to teach better by trying new things, failing and learning from the failure. The teacher learns how to do it while in the thick of doing it.

6 Inviting Writing: Activities and Environments

We do not know what we will write until we write; therefore, we must as teachers continually invite writing, keep the game of writing going in front of our students, make it so interesting they will want to join in and, by repeatedly waving them over, make sure they know they are welcome.

Fortunately writing *is* fun. Hard fun, but fun because it is hard, because it is significant play. We do not know what we will say until we say it and so we discover, by writing, what we have seen, what we have learned, what we have lived and what it means. Each draft is new, filled with surprise.

The writing class should surprise the teacher — and the student. All teaching plans, discussion notes, activities and exercises should be abandoned in the face of a good question or comment from a student. Welcome surprise in your class as you welcome it in a draft. You will find you have more responses to surprise in your mental inventory than you realize. If you don't, make up a presentation, demonstration or activity to respond to the concern. Teaching should be as experimental as writing. In every class you will fail to teach some students. That's the price of teaching others well.

If you don't have a response in your inventory and if you can't make one up, you are especially lucky. Experienced teachers are often prisoners of their past successes. Invite the class to respond. It's their problem and they should learn how to solve problems. A student may, for example, challenge a principle of good writing and the class can be invited to discuss, qualify and resolve the issue. Mark Ramsdell (now a Washington consultant) described how he used a clothesline across his dorm room to solve an organizational problem. That actually happened.

He told my class how he used clothespins to hang his research material in proper order, then rode across the room — his typewriter and chair were on wheels — writing away.

Activities

As you meet with your students in conference and class you will realize they share common problems and that solutions might be introduced by a class activity.

As I read the papers in conference I may see a repetitive pattern of beginnings and realize the class will benefit from being forced to draft many alternative leads. Organization problems may crop up in workshop or conference, and the class may be ready to play with a dozen ways of organizing writing. It may be apparent to the students and to myself that a class needs to revise a paragraph ten or twenty times to learn revision techniques.

I try to keep these activities short, and generally think of my composition classes in a way that has been taught me by two of my colleagues — Ruth Clogston and Dr. David Watters. I think of the class period as consisting of twenty-minute modules, and I try to give my students a variety of experiences within the class period: an activity, a workshop, and a class discussion, for example. I'm not rigid about this, and obviously can spend a whole two-hour class period on a workshop, for example, but I try to keep my presentations and activities short. We also think of activities or exercises in whole-class situations, but they may be more effective as small group activities.

You should, of course, not use just my activities but develop your own and, even better, have your students design activities to solve writing problems they are facing in their writing.

In designing effective activities, there are a number of elements to consider:

○ Keep it fun. Writing is hard enough, and students need to get a feeling for the importance of play in writing. Activities or exercises are *not* graded.

○ Failure is O.K. In fact, failure may be more instructive than success. There shouldn't be any competitive pressure to achieve. The purpose of the activity is to introduce a writing tool. How well that tool is used will be revealed when the students write.

○ Do not expect the students to use the activity on the next draft and certainly do not make the activity a part of an assignment. If you do that, you'll have students using a sledgehammer to repair a watch.

○ Keep the subject matter on which the tool is being used as open as possible, so that each student will be working a vein where he or she might find ore.

○ Do the activity yourself, on the board or overhead projector if appropriate, so that you can participate, share your problems, and establish the attitudes appropriate to the activity.

○ It's always a good idea to supplement the activity with a handout students can keep and use when they try the activity to solve a problem in their writing.

Design your own exercises, share them with your colleagues, steal and adapt theirs. Invite your students to make up their own. Choose problems that need to be isolated and explored or techniques that need to be introduced and practiced. Here are some activities you may find helpful.

Recall

• Have your students think back to one of the most emotional experiences of their lives — an automobile accident, their first funeral — a time loaded with emotion, because those are times when our awareness receptors are stimulated. Have them list as fast as possible in just a word or two as many specific details as possible. Do the same thing yourself, then share some of the lists, and discuss them. They should have written down all sorts of details they were not consciously aware of remembering.

• Do the same exercise, but break it down according to the senses, with a column for each sense. Time them, three minutes each for visual details, for sound, for smell, for touch, for taste. Have them go back and add any that occur to them.

• Have your students remember a place that was emotionally important to them — where they hid when they were young, a room that frightened them or made them feel safe — and have them write for ten minutes, getting down as many details as they can about that place. Do the same thing yourself, then share and discuss how writing draws from what we know that we didn't know we knew. As Robert Frost said, "For me the initial delight is in the surprise of remembering something I didn't know I knew."

• Have your students remember an important event in their lives — the scoring of a touchdown, the first overnight in the woods, the first trip they took on the subway by themselves — and have them write directions for a photographer who is going to re-create and film the event. Make sure they give the photographer plenty of specific details to look for. Have them share their directions with the partner playing photographer, and indicating what additional information they need to know.

• Have your students brainstorm, map, or write a quick, in-class exploration draft to see what they dredge up. It may be fun to divide the class into thirds and give a different technique to each group. Then in the next class they can meet in triads, with one person from each of the three groups, sharing what they found. Later the class can discuss the advantages and disadvantages of each technique. It also may be fun to have each person in the class use the three techniques on the same subject to see what different information is recalled with each method.

• Have your students remember a written text that made an impression on them. Have them describe the text with as many concrete details as possible. Let them have ten minutes, and then share and discuss their memory — and yours — of this text that was important to them.

Observation

• Have your students go to a specific place — a dormitory floor, a campus hangout, a supermarket — and record as many details as possible in a limited period of time. You may want to set an outrageous quota — 150 details in half an hour — to stimulate the speed they must use to record something of what they are observing. The students do not need to write up the description; they should just share it with each other and with you, perhaps underlining the details that most surprised or interested them.

• Have your students take a square foot of the floor or the wall or a piece of earth — make it an inch, or a yard — and have them describe it in as much detail as possible. They may find in the bark of a tree many colors, shapes, and textures. A piece of brick or a rock may reveal a universe of information. Share and discuss what you and they have seen.

• Have two members of your class stage a sudden interruption with an argument. Or arrange an incident in which a student interrupts the class and has to be ejected. Have the students describe what happened, what the people looked like, what they said and did, how the class reacted. Have them share the different accounts that will come about naturally. This may be an interesting introduction to how we observe, and not always a comfortable introduction. I had a black colleague interrupt one of my classes, and that led to a significant discussion, not only of description, but also of racial prejudice and stereotypes.

- Have your students study a text, and then have them list what they see in it. They should look for revealing quotations, repeated words or structures, key phrases, forms of development and documentation, evidence of style or voice, indications of point of view or opinion — all the dozens of details that a careful student can discover in a few pages of significant prose. You may want them to go on and write up their description in a critical essay that has a point, but there's no need to do that. It is enough at this stage that they realize what they can observe in a few pages of printed text.

Empathy

- Have your students pick a person who is as different from them as they can imagine, then tell them to put that person's skin on and describe the world as they now see it. The football player, for example, might describe a play from the point of view of someone who hates violence, and the student who hates violence might describe a football game from a fan's point of view.

    After the students write their descriptions of the world they should share them and share what they have learned. Obviously one cannot become a jock or non-jock, black or white, healthy or handicapped, well-to-do or poor, male or female in a matter of minutes, perhaps not in a lifetime; but one can begin to look at the world differently through the medium of writing.

- Have the students take an issue — pollution, nuclear war, prejudice — and state their position in ten lines, taking the point of view precisely opposite from the position they would usually take. Make clear that good writing, of course, depends on good thinking, solid research, and strong feeling. They can't be dishonest and write well, but they can use a writing exercise such as this to extend their world. Share and discuss what they've discovered.

- Have your students write a short dialogue between advocates on both sides of a significant issue. Keep the dialogues to a page or two. Have students pick someone in the class to read one part of the dialogue while the writer reads the other so the class can hear both sides develop. Encourage them to share what they experienced writing and reading from a point of view other than their own.

- Have your students become ghostwriters and prepare a statement for a President, a senator, a governor, a university administrator. Have them try to become that person in the way they think and the way they speak. Restrict the length of the statement to ten lines, so that there is a chance for students to share what they have written and what they learned from writing it.

- Have the students become an author with whom they're familiar, and then have them write from that person's point of view in that person's style. Encourage them to pick a writer who would take a position different from their own.

Interviewing

- Tell your students they are going to write a brief article about another person in the class. Have them pair up with someone they do *not* know, have them interview the other person for ten minutes, then have them switch with interviewer becoming interviewee for another ten minutes. If you have more time, extend the periods of interviewing. Then have the students write their article during the rest of the class period. In the next period they can share their stories with the rest of the class. This is a good early semester, or even first-class, technique that helps the members of the writing community get to know one another.

- If you do a second in-class interview, have the students meet in groups of three. One person is an interviewer, one an interviewee, and the third an observer. The observer takes notes, and after the interviews are done there can be an interesting discussion of effective and ineffective interview technique.

- Have the class interview you in press conference format, and allow them a chance to write it up. In this way they can get to know you and can see which questions yield information and which don't.

- Suggest that your students interview somebody in their family, a grandparent or a parent, an uncle or an aunt, to find out something about a crucial part of family history or a national event, such as a war, in which the person took part. This assignment almost always brings wonderful by-products with it. Most families need an excuse to talk about the things most important to them, and the students become excited about discovering the stories that are part of their own heritage.

- Have each student interview a person, or persons, who is an authority on a subject the student is interested in or who has an interesting job: the nurse who makes first contact with a patient on the accident floor, a security officer in charge of protection against shoplifting at the mall, a researcher who is doing work that may contribute to a cure for cancer.

Research

- Have students who are writing on similar topics form teams to comb the library for information that may be helpful to all of them.

• Have your students take a piece of personal writing and develop a bibliography of sources that might extend or support that topic.

• Have your students find more than half a dozen different kinds of information for a single topic of their choice. Information on basketball star Larry Bird might be in a basketball magazine, a coach's text, a physical education film, the *New York Times* microfilm file, and so on.

Plan

• Surprise your students and have them take part of the class period to answer one or several of the following planning questions about a piece of writing they expect to write. Then have them discuss what other questions they should ask early in the writing process.
    Some questions might be:

What organizing specific will help me control material?
What is the most revealing detail I have discovered or can remember?
What image sticks in my mind's eye and seems to symbolize the entire subject?
What person, or face, do I remember from doing the research?
What idea kept coming back to me during the time I was collecting material?
What code words have special meaning to me now?
What is the most important single fact I have learned?
What is the most significant quotation I heard or read?
What surprised me the most?
What is the one thing my reader needs to know most of all?
What do I remember in greatest detail?
What event is central to what happened?
What statistic sticks in my head?
What did I think when I was doing the research?
What did I feel when I was doing the research?
What person impressed me the most?
What story or anecdote do I remember?
What pattern or order did I begin to see?

• Suggest the students go through their notes for a story they are about to write and put an X beside anything that can be left out.

• Tell the students to take a piece of paper and make two columns, one labeled *In* and one labeled *Out*, and then go through their notes and use code words to describe the material that must be in — "Martin's" — or can be left out — "statistic on thin versus thick pizza."

• Tell the students to draw a three-inch square in the center of a piece of paper and put everything outside the fence that can be and put inside the fence what has to be.

• Take the actual pieces of research — notes, photocopies, papers, books, journal entries, fragments, brainstorming lists, whatever is appropriate — and put them in piles, one labeled *In* and one labeled *Out*.

Distance

• Have your students list the important elements in a piece of writing, then use a zoom lens to see which ones would be left out and left in as the writer moved close to the subject. Students should realize that the closer they move in, the larger the writing space. If I write about childhood diseases before World War II in a fifteen-page paper, I'll just skip over the surface. If I write fifteen pages about the ten minutes during which I found I had to have an operation, I'll have a chance to go into some depth.

• Have the students make a frame with their hands, and then move closer and closer to a subject, observing what they see when they look at a person as part of a group from across the room and what they see when they stand three inches away, making sure they realize the almost infinite possibilities as they move forward and back.

• Have the students take an experience that was important to them, and then write a series of sentences describing it, moving from a detached to an involved tone.

Point of View

• Have the student circle the subject and write down the different points from which the subject can be viewed.

• Have the students circle the subject and write down the different opinions that the writer could have of the same subject.

• Have the students draw a sketch or map of the subject, and then put the camera at different points around the subject, seeing with their mind's eye how the subject would be viewed from each camera angle.

• Have the students take a limited subject with which they are familiar a single play in a basketball game — and write quick, short paragraphs describing it from the point of view of an offensive player with the ball, the defensive player on that person, an offensive player without the ball, a defensive player a few steps away, the referee, the coach, a player on the bench, a young observer in the stands, a former player in the stands, a parent, a fan, a reporter, a scout.

Problem

• Students usually find it helpful when they are invited to answer questions that help them discover a problem they may solve through the writing of the piece.

> What keeps me from the information I need?
> Why is my draft unfocused?
> What makes the draft disorganized?
> What keeps my reader from understanding me?
> What keeps my reader from believing me?
> What makes my voice unclear?

Voice

• Have your students free-write for five minutes while you free-write on the board. Then have everyone read his or her piece aloud. Afterwards you can point out the variety of voices that exist in the classroom.

• Have your students free-write on a common subject familiar to them all. For example, their first impression of the campus. When I do this I do get some good examples of variety in voice, and the voice is a bit clearer as an element of writing. But the writing itself is nowhere near as good as when I allow everyone to write without giving the topic.

• Have the students pick a piece of writing from their folder or daybook and read a paragraph aloud which shows them using their voice effectively.

• Have the students take a subject they are interested in and write a lead sentence for five different audiences. Have them meet in small groups and pick the student paper that shows the greatest diversity of voice. Have that writer from each group read the paper aloud to the class.

• Have the students pick a paragraph from the reader that demonstrates a writer's effective use of voice. Have them read that aloud and say a few words describing the voice or the technique that reveals voice. This is a good supplemental activity to their own writing, but it should not take the place of their recognizing the quality of voice in their own writing and in their classmates' writing.

- Have your students think for four minutes about what they may write, encouraging them to try to hear the voice in which they may write — the way the sentences will sound when they write. Then let them write for a minute or two to capture one of those sentences. Let them read those sentences aloud and discuss what they could hear before they wrote and hear when they wrote.

- Have your students pick the topic they are working on, and then describe in a word or so a range of voices they might use when writing: angry, humorous, nostalgic, coldly logical, very personal, detached. Let them make up their own list, and then have them write a sentence that might appear in the piece in each of the voices. It should be the same sentence, and might well be the lead sentence, for the lead establishes the voice.

- Have your students write five lead sentences for five different audiences they might attempt to reach. They might, for example, write about a new alcohol policy on campus in an announcement to be sent to parents, a brochure for students, a memo for residential assistants, a letter to students who have been warned in the past, a warning to the owners of bars in the area.

- Have the students take something that they are working on and write a lead sentence for different genres: an academic essay, a short story, a news story, a government report, a familiar letter, an administrative memo.

- Have your students take a sentence or paragraph of their own and have them write it in the voice of the instructor, of specific classmates, of writers they know and admire — or know and dislike.

- Have your students take a published text and rewrite a key sentence or paragraph in as many different voices as they can.

Genre

- Have your students read through the material they have gathered, or simply think back about it and describe, in a few words or in an outline sketch, the different forms or genres that are in the material. They may see stories, poems, essays or analyses of opinion — any number of forms. It's generally helpful if you don't give them the names of forms, but let them try to describe the forms themselves. They can dictate their names to you on the board. If you want to teach them the formal names afterwards that may be helpful. But if the names come before they look at the material they may only see what you think they will see, not what they should see.

- Have the class meet in small groups — pairs, triads, or larger — and work together to see the number of different forms that may come from the material as it is described orally by the writer. Have the class share the forms or genres that have been discovered in each group.

- Have the class take a piece of writing from the class or from a published writer. Let the class, without formal rhetorical language, discuss the form or genre the author used, and then discuss the other forms the author could have used.

- Create a jumble of specific information — a device we use in teaching news writing — that fills a single-spaced page. Give copies to the class and let them see what forms lie within the material. Have the class decide which form or genre contains the real meaning that is within the jumble.

- Take a poem, essay, or short story by a well-known writer and mix up the lines or paragraphs. Have the students rearrange the parts to discover the arrangement that reveals the meaning of the piece. Then give the class the author's version and let them compare theirs with the published one.

- Have your students make a list of genres — poem, corporate memo, essay, TV play, news story — and look at the material they have and decide which genre might help them discover the meaning in the material.

- If they have decided that one or several genres might work, have them list the internal forms that might be helpful to develop the piece. For example, if they decide the external genre is travel, then they may need the internal genres of description, anecdote, quotation, and narrative.

- Have them go back and look at a jumble, this time picking a series of genres and looking at the material through those genres to see if they help the writer understand it — and might help the reader understand it.

- Have them look at a piece of finished writing through the eyes of several other genres. The essay might be examined to see if it could be a poem, a newspaper story, a government report, a speech, a TV documentary.

- Have students research the genres required in their majors or in courses they are taking. They can do this by:

    Examining the guidelines for writing a paper given out by a professor.
    Asking a professor for guidelines for writing a paper in the professor's discipline and course.
    Asking a professor for a model paper in that course.

Asking a professor, the library, or a professional organization, such as the Modern Language Association, for a style sheet and guidelines for writing in that discipline.

Checking the library and the bookstore for a book on how to write in a particular academic discipline. You may want to request that the library keep such books on reserve or that the bookstore have them available.

Asking a professor for papers the professor has written, or looking up such articles and books by the professor in the library.

Titles

• Pick a subject common to the class — a town or gown institution or person — and have the class help you brainstorm on the board as many titles as possible for an article about that subject. This can even run over from one class to another, with students bringing in new titles, but when the titles are complete the class should vote on the best ones and discuss why they are effective — and how they would help a writer draft the article.

• Have your students bring in twenty-five or fifty titles for a piece they may write. Have them meet in small groups and have members of the group check off the best title on each person's list. Have the group share the best title with the class and then have the class discuss why those titles work.

• Have the class collect titles from popular magazines. Have them share the best titles and discuss how they must have helped the writer in establishing the voice, limiting the subject, and targeting the reader.

• Have the students write a title for each of five different approaches to a story they might write, and then have them write five or ten variations on each approach. Have them meet in small groups to pick the titles that attract the readers.

• Have your students take an essay and write a dozen or more other titles it might have been given. Discuss how other titles might have caused a different essay.

Leads

• Have your students write twenty-four leads for an article before the next class. Tell them to write these leads — just the first sentence of the first paragraph — as fast as possible. They should be able to write faster than a lead every five minutes. In other words, it should take them less than an hour to write twelve leads, less than two hours to write twenty-four leads. At the next class have them pass their leads around the room. Everyone, yourself included, should check the three leads he or she likes the best. You should read fast, scanning the way a reader would, and you should keep the papers moving around the room. It doesn't matter if everyone reads every paper. What does matter is that the class get a chance to read leads and see what attracts them, and the writer gets a chance to see what interests readers.

• Have the students write a dozen leads that demonstrate twelve different ways to approach the same subject. Have these leads passed around the room, or used in small groups, with the readers checking the approach they would be most interested in reading. This should be followed with a discussion of what approaches attract readers, and the point should be made that the writer does not have to follow the most popular approach, but the writer should know which approach is most popular and should make sure that the approach he or she uses can be written so it will attract readers.

• Have the students take one approach to a story and write twelve different variations within that approach. Again, these approaches should receive a response from other writers in the group, for those writers need to see writing in process as well as receive a reaction to their own attempts.

• Have the students bring in ten good leads from newspapers, magazines, or books. The best lead should be chosen in each small group and shared with the class. The class should discuss what these leads did for the writer as well as do for the reader.

• The class should brainstorm its own list of lead-writing techniques and principles. If the class develops its own list and rules after writing and reading leads it can have a dittoed resource to which it can add during the semester. Obviously the discussion of what should be included and what should not be included will be extremely helpful to the class.

Ends

• Have your students imagine five different directions a piece of their writing may go. Then have them write five different endings. They should share and pick the ending that sounds best to the reader, realizing that the reader is very much in the dark. If students have worked on leads they should be allowed to use leads they have written previously that might work as endings.

• Have your students pick five leads that they have done and revise them so they would become effective endings. Have them share these in small groups, picking the best one and sharing it with the class, and discussing why it is best.

• Have your students pick an ending for a piece of writing they are going to work on and revise it a half dozen times, so that the same thing is said in six different ways. Again, they should share and evaluate each other's work.

• Have students pick a half dozen endings from newspaper stories, magazine articles, and books. Have the small groups pick the best one, and lead a discussion which helps the students see how those endings gave the writer a sense of destination and the reader a sense of closure or completion.

• Have the students develop a list of ending techniques, or have them mark those leads they have on their lead-writing resource list that might also make good endings.

The Trail

• Have your students put a few words at the bottom of a page that will remind them of the ending they plan to use. Then have the students do the same thing with the lead at the top of the page. Next, have them mark down the two or three or four or five points they have to make for the reader to get there.

• Have your students write the five (or four or six) questions the reader has to have answered if the reader is going to make it from the beginning to the end. Put those questions down in the order they occur to the writer, then number them in the order the reader wants them answered. This technique is helpful in researching a piece, in planning it, and also in attempting to revise a complicated piece of writing that confuses the reader.

• Have the students take a published piece of writing and identify the key points or landmarks in the trail that lead the reader from beginning to end. It may also be helpful to take a published piece of writing and write out the questions for which each section of the article provides answers. The beginning writer should see the invisible dialogue that takes place between writer and reader. In some brochures the questions are left in, but in most writing the questions are taken out, and only the answers that respond to the anticipated questions of the reader remain.

• Have the students take a published piece of writing and show other trails that might have been written to take the reader to the same conclusion from the same starting point.

• Have the students read an essay, a short story, a poem, an argument on the same subject, and have them identify the trail the writer used to lead the writer through the subject in each genre.

The Sketch

• Have your students choose a topic they are working on and use five different ways of sketching the subject, so they will see how a sketch or outline can reveal the different ways one topic may be developed. Have them report to the class on what they have learned from this activity, or have them share their sketches with each other in small groups, with the other members of the group checking the one they like best.

• Have each member of the class write a one-page description of a sketch or outline that has helped them in writing or in another discipline. Encourage them to find out from the teachers in their discipline what forms of outlines or sketches are most used by professionals. Allow them to develop a new form of sketching or outlining. Have them report to the class and keep their pages in a notebook or folder that is available as a resource for the class.

• Have the students bring in and report on a sketch that is used in an activity in which they are interested. These might include a football game plan, a legal brief, a research proposal, a sales or marketing plan, a military battle strategy or tactic, a menu, a rehabilitation or exercise program. Have the class discuss how the techniques that produced these plans might be adapted to writing.

• Have a few students interview writers, asking them how they plan their writing. Make sure the students choose writers in as many fields as possible — children's book writers, technical writers, journalists, poets, business writers — whoever is available — to provide details on how they plan their writing. Have the students write up their reports and discuss them with the class. They should be allowed to interview good student writers in the class and outside, and on occasion to conduct self-interviews.

• Have the students use three different sketches to analyze a published piece of writing and show how it may have been constructed or how it might have been constructed differently.

Revision

- Have your students share their papers with a reader or readers who scan the paper and indicate to the writer what part of the writing process the writer should emphasize in going through the draft again — collect, plan, develop.

- Have class readers look at a draft quickly and say how further collecting or planning or developing could make the piece better.

- Have a student reader revise a text or part of a text from a classmate, writing a new lead or a new ending, attempting a new voice, suggesting a new structure or genre, and demonstrating it.

- Reprint a piece by a published writer and have the class revise it, making sure they understand the difference between revision — reseeing the piece — and line-by-line editing.

- Have students interview publishing writers to see how they revise their work. Or have a guest writer come to the class with revisions of a piece of published work and talk about how he or she revises. Have the students go to the library and find published revisions of famous authors and report on how those authors have revised their manuscripts. Photocopy for the class revisions of a piece of writing — Robert Lowell, for example, revised many of his poems and published those revisions — and have the class discuss what the writer was doing while revising, why the writer did it, and how well the writer succeeded.

Editing

- Organize the class into small groups in which each group has a person who is a good grammarian and speller, another person who is good at seeing sham and fraud, another person who is good at the larger questions of structure and voice, and have them edit each person's piece.

Do students break down into these neat categories? Of course not, but you should know your class well enough to bring together teams that have a constructive assortment of strengths. And don't forget the importance of the reader who simply does not understand. Writers have to learn to reach such readers.

- Have students edit a few paragraphs in one another's copy. Usually it is helpful to have the writer point out the area where he or she needs special help. The editor should be instructed to be as tough and specific as possible. The writer should be reminded that the point is to learn from what is being done, not to accept it arbitrarily.

• Publish the best piece of writing in the class on ditto or overhead projector, and edit it with the class, showing how an excellent piece of writing can be made better, but also showing that it is just as important to leave things alone that work as it is to suggest changes.

• Work with the class to develop an editing checklist which can be dittoed for the whole class, but leave space for individual writers to add their own items — things they have learned they need to watch out for in their own writing. You may want to leave a space where you or someone else in the class who is familiar with the writers' work can add a few items that particular writers should watch out for. One writer, for example, may have a tendency to be choppy; another to combine sentences into an enormous incoherent train wreck. One writer may need to remember to be more specific; another to make the meaning of the specifics clear. And every writer has special quirks to watch out for — I tended to use "quite"' at least once a page on the first draft of the first edition of this book. I think I've cured that, but you will see other quirks in my writing I should have been aware of and changed.

• Ditto some pages from published writers, and edit them with the class, showing all the different ways that one piece of writing can be edited. This can be a game that will remind the class that anyone can be edited and that there is no one correct way to edit. The purpose is always to make the writer's meaning clear.

• Interview editors to find out how they work and what they think are most writers' problems — and how they can be solved. Invite an editor to class to show how he or she edits, with examples of some edited pages, or perhaps by having them do some editing on an overhead projector, on the board, or on some dittoed pages with the class following along.

The Research Paper

An activity required in many departments is the research paper. I, personally, am not enthusiastic about the research paper in Freshman English. When I was Freshman English director I did a survey and found that every high school in the state had taught the research paper. It was also true that few students learned to produce an effective research paper until they used research themselves and knew the reasons for scholarly conventions. (Students who are especially interested in this subject should be referred to *The Modern Researcher,* by Jacques Barzun and Henry F. Graff, Harcourt Brace Jovanovich, New York, 1957, 1970, 1977, which has been in print for twenty-five years and is available in paperback.)

Students who are assigned research papers should:

○ Keep a consistent record of everything that they have read, whether it has been valuable or not, so they do not circle back through the same material and so they know where they have gotten the information they are using.

○ Clearly mark each note as a direct quote or a paraphrase so they will not plagiarize the information. The best way to do this is to write the note as the writer thinks it will appear in the final article. In either case there should be specific reference to where the material was found.

○ Photocopy significant pages, making sure they note the place the page comes from, so they will have the text in front of them at the time of writing.

○ Scan the material, and then read carefully if it bears on their subject. Many students read too carefully when they are doing research.

○ Practice the art of serendipity, discovering one thing while looking for another. They should be encouraged to glance at the books on the shelf below the one they're looking for, at the article on the page following the one they have found in the directory.

○ Write early so they discover what they know — and what they need to know.

Expanding and Adapting the Process

The writing process the student uses in your course should be seen as a beginning point. The process is not meant to be a set of laws but a dynamic activity which can be changed to meet the students' needs in the years after school. One way to reinforce this idea is to have your students try some of the following activities:

○ Have your students interview individuals in such fields as the laboratory sciences, art, law, and music to see how they work. Have the students report on the results of these interviews and show how they relate to writing.

○ Invite a guest to class — another writer, an artist, a scientist — and have the guest tell how he or she works. Allow time for the class to question the guest.

○ Have your students bring in stories or interviews they have read that show how other writers or other people practice their craft.

○ Have your students write an account of what they do in a craft they practice. Encourage them to draw comparisons to the process of writing, and have them report their findings to the class.

Never forget that the best way to invite your students to write is simply to make writing possible. You write, your students write, you all share what you have written. It sounds simple because it is. Never let your teaching get in the way of your students' learning.

Making a Writing Text Inviting

The principal text of any writing course is the students' drafts. They learn most from seeing their own drafts and the drafts of their teacher and classmates evolve towards meaning. No text should attempt to take the place of the students' own writing.

Additional texts can be helpful if they are designed in such a way that the students can use them to respond to the problems they are having in writing while they are having them. The text becomes a fellow writer, a resource that is available during the writing process. Such a text will allow the students to discover not one way but many alternative ways to experiment with solutions to a writing problem. They will give the students a sense of writing in the making, allowing the beginning writer to enter into the workshop of experienced writers.

Students may also need a text that is a handbook. But again such a resource must be comprehensible to students. Many handbooks are so technical that the only people who can use them are those who don't need to use them. The handbook must put the traditions of writing into the hands of the student in such a way that they can be drawn upon during the writing as an auto repair manual can be used during the process of repairing a car.

It may be helpful to have the students read a writing text in a great burst near the beginning of the course, not so that they will learn everything in the book but so that they will learn what is there and can refer to it as they need it. I find that I need, unfortunately, to have some sort of police action if I use a text. Students rarely read a text unless they are held accountable through a paper or a quiz. My favorite police action is to require a paper in which students relate the lessons of the text to their own writing and ask them to document points of agreement and points of disagreement. Such an assignment can lead to a good discussion.

The handbook cannot be taught in the same way. The students can be asked to learn the precepts, principles, and suggestions in the handbook, and can be tested on what they have "learned." But what they learn this way may not be practiced as they write. The kind of information that is in a handbook is best learned when it solves a problem of meaning for the student, when the engine won't go. I am uninterested in how fuel gets into my van engine, but when the car stops on a remote road in a snowstorm I turn to the handbook with immense interest.

The teacher must find opportunities in conference, workshop, and discussion to make connections between the published texts, the students' texts, and the students' experiences with the writing process. The students must be led to discover that these texts can be responsive to their needs.

Making an Anthology Inviting

The primary form of reading in the composition course must be the reading of the students' own drafts and the teacher's and classmates' drafts. This is how the students learn to spot potential in their own work and cultivate it.

The reading of writing in process can be aided by an anthology or a reader that provides examples of good writing. The advantage of a reader is that it collects the published works of excellent writers. These models establish standards that put the students' writing in a larger context. There are dangers, however. The anthology may establish standards that are out of reach, and therefore diminish the students' writing and discourage rather than inspire the students. Most readers also show nothing but finished writing. What is published is the edited final draft of the best writers in our language. What they do and how they do it is often inaccessible to the student.

If a teacher uses a reader every effort should be made to connect each student with the selections in the anthology. This can be done in class discussion, workshop, or conference when a subject a student is dealing with or a strategy a student is using is in the text. Then the student can be urged to read the example from the point of view of the student's own writing.

The teacher should try to look at the models from the writer's point of view. Many anthologies, with their teaching apparatus and questions, look at writing from the reader's point of view. That is a valid approach in a literature class, but it is of little help to the writer. The student writer needs to get behind the scenes to see the messy drafts, if possible, of great writers, to see writing being made, to witness productive failures, to share the excitement of meaning being made.

Teachers should try to get their students over the worship of print, to rewrite and edit the models in the book, to take apart the work of the best writers and attempt to reassemble it, to speculate on the choices the writer had and the reasons those choices were made.

In every way students should see the models in the text as resources that they can use, drafts that can teach them while they are in the act of producing their own drafts.

Creating an Inviting Environment

The longer I teach the more important I think it is to have a supportive classroom and office environment. I teach not only in my own institution, but also in workshops in schools across the country, and the geography of the classroom has a powerful influence on what happens in the classroom.

This is just as true of the office or room in which I hold conferences. As a professional I pride myself on functioning under the most adverse conditions, but I am amazed at the energy that is drained off in the battle with the environment. And I'm also surprised how few people in our profession realize the importance of that environment. I request specific conditions for a workshop, and fellow professionals who are making the arrangement pay little or no attention to those conditions, and do not seem to realize that the effectiveness of the program is decreased.

Here are some of the elements to be considered in designing an effective environment for the teaching of composition:

- *Class size.* It's possible for composition classes to be too small. I like at least a dozen students. I find that when I have less than a dozen I do not have the critical mass necessary for good discussion and workshop. Fifteen is an ideal number, and twenty quite possible. After twenty the effectiveness falls off dramatically with each five students that are added. I have taught with thirty and even forty-five students in a single composition section, but I taught far less effectively every time the student load went up.

In establishing class size, however, a significant factor must be the total number of composition students who are going to be seen in conference. That's the real teaching load for the composition teacher. I have taught — but I can't remember how — 120 students by weekly conferences. I was young, and I know that I taught badly. Forty conferences a week is fine for me in my experience; sixty is quite possible, especially if I have no administrative responsibilities. Ideally, when teaching three courses, I would like to teach two conference courses with forty conferences a week, and a non-conference course in something other than composition. Eighty conferences can be handled, but this begins to get to the outer limits of effectiveness.

- *The classroom.* The circle of chairs or desks in a classroom has become an educational cliché, offensive to the traditionalists in most departments, essential to the majority of effective writing teachers. The desk, and certainly the desk with a lectern on it, forces the teacher into the role of a priest delivering sermons. The authority is dispensing the law, and the students, seated row upon row, are the congregation, organized to worship the giver of truth.

It is hard for the students and the teacher not to fall into the role established by the furniture of the classroom. There should be encouragement for many teaching styles, but most composition teachers teach sitting down, demonstrating by the manner in which they teach that both teacher and student are writers. There is a difference in experience, but an equality of challenge as they face the craft of writing.

The ideal situation is to meet around the outer edge of a square of tables. If the tables are in a long, thin rectangle, eye contact is lost, the students are at great distance from one another, and the effectiveness of class discussion and workshop diminishes. A square allows everyone to be in contact with everyone else. They can make eye contact and ear contact. The quality of discussion and workshop goes up.

I have even noticed that my dress in the classroom has changed. Before I was a workshop and conference teacher I wore jacket and tie. As I began to learn how to teach in a workshop and conference environment, my dress unconsciously became the costume of the workshop — woolen shirt, sweater, or short-sleeve shirt. The degree of informality or formality in teacher dress will have to depend on the teacher and the institution. A three-piece-suit person in a sport shirt is as ridiculous as a woolen-shirt person in a three-piece suit. But everything should be done to create a class geography in which the students are able to share their writing openly and effectively.

- *The office.* The ideal situation is to have a private office, but few composition teachers can achieve that. The teacher should, however, be able to establish a small area in which the teacher feels comfortable. It's better for student and teacher not to confront each other across the desk but to work at a corner of the desk side by side. If the teacher is comfortable the student will be comfortable, and that's important. Writing induces anxiety, and presenting a piece of writing to a reader increases that anxiety. I notice how many effective writing teachers use posters to create an informal environment, and some even bring in old or battered furniture to make the tutorial situation more relaxed, put a rug on the floor or bring in a bridge lamp so the conference doesn't take place under the glare of ceiling fixtures.

The Teacher Who Invites Writing

The responsive style describes the instructor who learns to teach less so the student can learn more.

This seems a contradiction because so much traditional teaching is conducted on a power model: the teacher knows a great deal and the student knows very little. It is the responsibility of the instructor to force the teacher's knowledge into the reluctant mind of the student. Teaching becomes a kind of intellectual rape.

But as much as the teacher — the experienced writer — knows about writing, the composition teacher does *not* — and should not — know the subject of the student's draft as well as the student writer. The teacher does *not* — and cannot — know what the student writer is discovering that the student has to say about the subject. The teacher does *not* — and cannot — know how the writing is being made as well as the student writer.

The teacher's primary role is to draw out of the student the knowledge and skills of which the student is unaware. By giving the student that experience of self-exploration and self-discovery, the teacher makes it possible for the student to learn a pattern of self-education and self-expression that will last a lifetime.

This is powerful and important teaching, and in developing a responsive style teachers will call upon many of the resources of traditional teaching to support their teaching and assist their students, but whenever possible these resources should be used in response to individual student needs, for that is when they will be meaningful and effective.

7 Responding to Surprise: The Response Theory of Teaching

Walk into a composition classroom in most of our institutions the first day of classes and you will meet a bewildering diversity of students. There are women so young and unformed they seem not yet women sitting beside women who have survived childbirth, marriage, divorce, job discrimination and have come to college with fearful insecurities yet a touching faith in a second — or third or fourth or fifth — chance. Eighteen-year-old males, clumsy as colts, lounge in their chairs with carefully constructed masks of disinterest and sit next to veterans and factory workers with notebooks and pens at the ready because they are determined to catch up and get a better job. In some classes there are senior citizens, retired and hoping to experience the college years they missed.

These students come from a glorious diversity of backgrounds. They arrive in our classrooms from city streets, suburban homes, remote farms. Their parents live on inherited money, work two jobs, are unemployed; they go to Wednesday night prayer meeting, hang out in bars, entertain a different uncle or aunt every weekend, disappear. Our students have attended good schools and bad, private and public, alternative or Christian, learned little or a great deal, are writers and non-writers, readers and non-readers, want culture or vocational training with a practical payoff for each lesson, are academically confident or almost pathologically insecure, don't want to be in school or are working two jobs to get there, come from all those societies within our society — black, white, Oriental, Hispanic, native Indian and Indian Indian, gay and straight, Lithuanian, Turk and Franco-American, Mexican and Canadian, jock and hate jock, Arabic, Jewish, Republican and Democrat, Polish, pure WASP, Greek, management and labor, Italian, Scandinavian, Russian,

Iranian, pro-nuke and anti-nuke, Pakistani, South American and Central American, Yugoslavian and Japanese, East Coast, West Coast and Middle American, North and South.

Those incredible differences among the individual students who come to a writing class provide the composition teacher's greatest problem — and greatest opportunity. The tired old pros of the faculty lounge grumble about such diversity, remembering the days that never were when their students were pretaught by someone else, came from always happy two-parent homes cast by Walt Disney, and produced student essays that never failed to please the ancient gods of rhetoric. But even the loudest complainers — earnestly projecting their teaching failures on other instructors, parents, genetics, the system, acid rain, or chemicals in the drinking water — underestimate the enormous differences between the students who come to our beginning composition classes.

The composition class, however, should be a place where that diversity becomes an advantage, where individuality is nurtured, developed and given expression. We should be grateful that our students are not delivered to us as McDonald's products but are like fingerprints and voiceprints, each different from the other.

The Challenge of Diversity

At the University of New Hampshire everyone takes Freshman English, and we make no effort to separate those students with high scores from those with low ones because we have no faith in the tests that attempt to rank writing ability. We accept diversity of background and writing experience as a natural condition of the composition class. But even those schools that test, exempt and segregate their Freshman English students still have classes in which there are enormous differences between individual students.

Those differences take so many forms significant to composition instruction that we should review them:

• *Cultural diversity.* Every time I go to Europe I am struck by the obvious cultural similarities within each country. There are Germans in Germany, Italians in Italy, Swedes in Sweden, and I appreciate anew the enormous cultural diversity within the United States, and the longer I stay in Europe the more I crave the stimulating diversity of our cultural mix. Our students come from the many cultures that exist on each continent.

At one time it was understood in the best schools that every student would be familiar with the King James version of the Bible. No one makes that assumption today in the United States. Our students come from many religious backgrounds. There are significant differences between students who have grown up in New Hampshire or Wyoming, Georgia or Arizona. There may be as many differences between those students who are streetwise and those who are countrywise, and neither may have much in common with the suburban student whose village is the shopping mall.

The most common cultural background shared by students is music or television. But musical generations seem measured in months more than years, and the television taste changes each season, so that teachers only a few years older than their students may be members of alien musical and television cultures.

- *Economic diversity.* Our students do not come from economic backgrounds as diverse as they should. Family money and family education are still dominant factors in determining who can go on to college. But the United States still offers greater opportunity to a broader spectrum of students than most countries. The differences in family income within a composition class can be enormous. In the same class last semester I had welfare mothers sitting beside children of the corporate rich. They brought stimulating — but significant — backgrounds to each workshop.

- *Diversity of experience.* The average age of college freshmen keeps going up. Our students come to us after they are married, have children, are divorced, have served in the military, traveled, worked for a living. These students do not have common intellectual and emotional experiences but a marvelous diversity of experience to explore and share in the composition class.

- *Educational diversity.* We do not have a federal system that controls the curriculum as many countries do. We have local schools, and even within a state or region there are amazing differences among the educational backgrounds of our students. We also have students who are not college bound and do not have the same courses as the aspiring college student within an individual high school. Our students have electives and many diverse educational opportunities. We see their weaknesses first, but we should see their strengths as well. The condition, however, is not one of strength or weakness, but one of difference.

- *Sexual diversity.* At one time — and not so long ago — our schools of higher education were male dominated. My wife was valedictorian of her high school class in Kentucky, yet it never occurred to her, to her teachers, to her family, or even to her brother who had already gone to college that she could go on with her education. And those women who did go on either came from well-to-do homes or were tracked into polite subjects. We are now beginning to educate our female population, and that creates another creative form of diversity in our classroom.

- *Racial diversity.* Within my lifetime high school students from Irish families or Franco-American families were less likely to go on to college than those from white Anglo-Saxon Protestant families. Now we are beginning to educate people from an even greater diversity of backgrounds: blacks, Hispanics, and recent Asian immigrants. The racial diversity in our schools is not as great as it should be, but it is beginning to get there, and it provides an increasing diversity in our classrooms.

- *Diversity of goals.* At one time a college education meant a liberal arts education. College students went away to school to become ministers or priests, doctors or lawyers. Now we educate people to go into marketing, computer science, physical education, police work, labor management (a wonderful contradiction in terms). People want to have a college education to become airline pilots, social workers, sales engineers, wildlife managers — thousands of jobs that increase the diversity of goals held by our students.

- *Diversity of writing tasks.* When I took Freshman English we wrote papers of literary analysis, and when I returned to teach Freshman English more than two decades later we taught the same papers of literary analysis. Today we realize, in most schools, that our students face a great diversity of writing tasks in school and beyond school. We must prepare our students for the diversity of writing tasks within our own institutions and for the writing tasks they will face after they graduate.

- *Diversity of standards.* It would be nice to believe that there are common standards of writing held by the faculty within our institutions, even within our own departments. But that is not true. Some faculty want students to write long; others want them to write short. Some faculty want an abundance of specifics; others reward abstractions. Some want one form of documentation; some prefer another. We must prepare our students to write to the standards held by their teachers in the diversity of courses they take.

- *Diversity of cognitive styles.* My students have a diversity of thinking styles. Some work best when they plan, others when they just plunge in; some see the design of the writing and tire before they begin, and others sniff their way through the piece a tree at a time. Some work fast, and some work slowly. Some work from external sources of information, while others seem to internalize everything and work from the inside out.

Our students think differently and write differently, and it becomes even more complicated the further we go in a composition class, because the cognitive style of the student may change with experience. I tend to plunge in when I face a new genre or writing task. I get a draft, and then revise it into shape. But when I am familiar with the writing task, I am able to see the problems I will face in the abstract and solve most of them before the first draft, so I revise less and less. My cognitive style seems to change with my experience.

• *Diversity of personality.* Some teachers attempt to avoid the question of personality in the composition class. I cannot. Some of my students are optimists, and others are pessimists. Some need encouragement, and others respond to discouragement; some need support, and others need criticism. Some need privacy during the writing process, and others need sharing. I find each composition class composed of a great variety of student personalities.

• *Diversity of voices.* The students in the writing class bring their own language and their own ways of using that language with them. After a paper or two or three it's possible to recognize each student without reading the name on the paper. The effective composition teacher tries to get each student to use the student's individual voice more effectively. The students do not write the same — or speak the same — and should not. The composition class is a wonderfully cacophonous Babel of voices.

Diversity is the basic condition of our business. We can choose to deplore it, imagine a time or place when there was less diversity, hope for a time when there may be less, but we can't make it go away. In the composition curriculum we must accept the differences between individual students and take advantage of those differences. We must design a curriculum that responds to diversity.

Taking Advantage of Diversity

Many experienced composition teachers do not complain about diversity, but glory in it. Donald Graves, in his extensive researches into young children writing, started looking for the similarities between children and ended up finding that the differences between children and between teachers and between the performance of individual children from day to day was where the significance of his studies lay. It was the differences that revealed the most.

We must teach to those differences, glorying in the variety of backgrounds and voices our students bring to the composition class. We must learn to respond to their diverse needs, their diverse learning styles, the diversity of what they have to say and how they can say it. The solution to the problem of diversity is diversity — diversity of teaching and learning experiences.

A curriculum designed for diversity has a natural evolution from individual to increasingly larger communities in which diversity is respected and enjoyed. The curriculum begins with the individual teacher, moves on to the individual student, and eventually expands to include smaller and larger, closer and more distant, writing communities. But it is always rooted in the individual, the writer confronting the draft in the loneliness of the writer's desk and the writer sharing what was written with an individual reader, teacher, or classmate. The writing curriculum spirals through the following sequence again and again:

○ The teacher responds to the teacher's own drafts.

○ The individual teacher responds in conference to the individual student.

○ The student responds to the student's own drafts.

○ Individual students respond to one another's drafts in conference.

○ Individual students respond to one another's drafts in small group workshops.

○ Individual students and the teacher respond to each other's drafts in class workshops.

○ Individual editors and readers outside the classroom respond to the student's writing.

Accepting Your Own Diversity

To accept your students' diversity, you must discover and accept your own individuality as a writer and a teacher. The best way to do that is to write. This text will be best understood by those who read it while they are writing themselves. The writing experience allows us to make use of the contradictions and differences we see from page to page; it allows us to hear our own individual voices. And those teachers who have a strong sense of their own voice — their own individuality — are most likely to tolerate and encourage the diversity of their students.

Write in your own way. Write of your own subjects in your own voice for the readers you want to reach. And then teach in your own way, responding to your individual students in the way that is right for you, not modeling yourself on your colleagues, your former teachers, or an idealized concept of what a teacher should be, but responding to the writers who are working with you as a writer whose task is to help them write more effectively.

Accepting Your Students' Diversity

Once you have accepted yourself, then you may be ready to accept your students. It is difficult for those teachers who have not heard their own voices to hear the voices of their students; who have not seen language run out of control on the page and surprise the writer with a new meaning to encourage — or even allow — students to write towards surprise; it is hard for those teachers who have not seen their own syntax fall apart just before language leads them to a meaning to understand what is happening on the students' drafts and to encourage the kind of bad writing that is necessary for good writing; it is impossible for teachers who have not passed through failure to success in writing to communicate to students that writing is experimental and failure both essential and productive. It is difficult for teachers who have not felt the roller-coaster ride of hopelessness and pride, despair and joy, to understand where their students are and how to talk to them, writer to writer, so the students will learn to become writers.

Teachers should know where students are in the writing process through their own frequent adventures in trying to make meaning with language.

The teacher must accept the student where the student is. Too many teachers want their students pre-educated, or prepared for their classes in a way different from the way they are prepared. We are educators, and our job is not to educate the educated but to educate those who need education. If our students came to us knowing what we teach, then we would be out of a job. We should be grateful, not angry, that they need to learn. These feelings are natural, but a waste of time. We must accept our students where they are, and we are best able to know where they are if we ourselves are experiencing the process of writing.

There is no way to predict with any accuracy what a class, or a student, knows or needs to know. Each individual writing student has a pattern of strength and weaknesses, and we must find out what they are so that we can respond to them. A group of such individuals — a class — will have its own needs, its own strengths and weaknesses, and we will respond to them.

We start our teaching by finding out what our students know and what they need to know. We do this by getting them to write as early as possible and responding to that writing, from our own experience, with as little prejudice as possible. We look for strengths, and then weaknesses: what they do well and what they need to do better.

You don't learn a skill by learning *about* it; you learn a skill by *doing*. This is forgotten by literature teachers or teachers from other content disciplines who are retooled as composition teachers and who, too often, look down on the teaching of a skill as a low-order intellectual act. Skill teaching, in fact, demands a much more sophisticated, complex form of teaching than the normal I-lecture-you-listen university pattern. To be fair, more and more literature teachers are departing from that pattern. They are learning what composition teachers should learn, that teachers can enter into the learning act with their students. Teaching the skill of writing, listening to students discover and use their own voices, is a most satisfying kind of teaching.

In the writing class, the student writes and evaluates the writing. The teacher reads the writing and listens to the student's evaluation of the writing, then responds. This pattern of instruction I call responsive teaching.

The Response Theory of Teaching

Response theory builds on the observation of learning from the time an infant starts to crawl. We learn best when we see our own problem to be solved and attempt to solve it in our own way. We are usually pleased but puzzled when it works; frustrated and puzzled when it doesn't. If we have succeeded, we want to know what we have done, if there is a better way to do it, and how we can use this new trick to solve other problems. If we have failed, we want to know why, how we can solve the problem and how we can apply that learning to other problems in the future. We need an experienced colleague who watches us, encourages us and stays out of the way until we are ready to learn. Then that colleague, often called a teacher, responds to our experience and our questions. When the writing has gone well, our colleague helps us see how it worked so we will know how to use our successful solution to writing problems in different, but similar, situations in the future. When the writing has not gone well, the colleague helps us think of other solutions to the writing problems we have failed to solve. Response theory takes advantage of the inevitable but potentially productive student failures that frustrate teachers who attempt to teach before learning.

The Importance of Failure

In writing, failure is normal, as in most experimental subjects. Student and teacher both have to realize this. Both the famous writer and the beginning writer experience failure in early drafts. A few times I've worked on stories with well-known photographers, and I was struck with the fact that where I would shoot a roll of film they would shoot dozens, and where I would choose a picture to print they would choose that picture to crop and shade and redevelop. What they were doing was finding from abundance something that worked, and then making it work better. In response teaching we are engaging the writer, the writer's peers, and the instructor in a long process of training to the unexpected and still only potential success amid the clutter of instructive failures.

To do this the best response is a response to a response. In other words, we need to have the writer select what works or what may work and then have other readers respond to that choice. The classmate or the teacher who just jumps in and says something works may be perceptive, and there may be times to do this, but the writer learns far less than when the writer is given the opportunity to make that discovery first, and then to have it verified, qualified, or not accepted by fellow students or teacher.

The student must make the initial response, not because of some vague philosophy about democracy in the classroom, or the importance of "affective teaching," but because the student needs to learn how to produce a text and then how to evaluate that text. The writing course is a writing and reading course. The student needs to learn how to write and, just as important, how to read a draft so its revision will improve.

Responding to Student Papers

Composition teachers often spend a great deal of time discussing the stance of the teacher-reader. How distant should the reader be? Should the reader be a colleague, helping with the draft? Should the reader be a stranger, even an enemy who does not understand or agree with what the writer is saying? Should the reader-teacher be a judge, a literary critic, a cop, a grammarian, a pal? Should the reader-teacher "appropriate" the text, as composition theorist Nancy Sommers revealed that many writing teachers do, or should the reader-teacher remain silent about the text he or she sees within the student's draft?

These questions of stance and many more are valid. The effective composition teacher usually works at a variety of distances from the student's text, moving in close in the early drafts, role-playing a distant reader later on. There are many roles teachers can take that are appropriate to their personality, training, and the needs of the students and the curriculum. There is always the danger of appropriating the text and making it your own, forcing or manipulating the student into writing your vision in your language.

All of these concerns are resolved in part by responsive teaching. The instructor is *not* the primary reader of the text and neither is the fellow workshop participant. The writer is the writer's own first reader. It is the writer who takes the stance of sympathetic reader or stranger, copy editor or literary critic. The writer evaluates the draft and the reader-instructor monitors the text *and the writer's response to the text.*

The teacher should not appropriate the text or the response. It is the responsibility of the writer to respond first and the responsibility of the teacher to respond to that response, helping the student writer make both text and response more effective.

Reacting to the student's opinion of a draft also helps us avoid the danger of being patronizing. If we keep patting the student on the head for good work that we see, the student becomes dependent on our stroking. It's a nice way of manipulating, dominating, and ultimately destroying the student.

It's quite different when we respond to the student's response. If the work is good and the student knows it's good, we can get the student to tell us why it is good. There is opportunity for professional discussion and sharing. If the work is poor and the student knows it is poor, we can get the student to tell us why it is poor and how it might become better. There is opportunity for professional discussion and sharing. If the student thinks the work is superb (I'm surprised at how rarely *that* happens) and we don't; if the student thinks the work is hopeless (I'm surprised at how often *that* happens [watch out for appropriation, warns Nancy]), then there is opportunity for professional discussion and sharing.

In every case the teacher responds by asking for further responses from the writer who, after all, knows the subject and the history of the draft better than the teacher and who has to learn to become a more effective reader to become a more effective writer.

Through positive reinforcement and response theory we work towards a point at which we give neither praise nor criticism. Both responses tend to be general; they blanket the whole piece and summarize. Praise may, indeed, be more destructive than criticism. We are more likely to have a defense against criticism than a defense against praise. What we try to achieve is a professional discussion between writers about what works and what needs work.

What Is Good Writing?

Teachers often express an insistent insecurity about the standards of good writing that inhibits their acceptance of their own writing and their students' writing. Most instructors trained in literature have a standard of aesthetic excellence which does not work for student writing, especially beginning student writing that is hesitant, faltering, fumbling, unfinished, almost unbegun in its search for a meaning and a way to express it.

If you study the early drafts of the most famous writers in the great libraries or in such books as those listed in the Appendix, you will see that even the great faltered and fumbled at first. Often we find that early drafts of the finished writing we are familiar with in our study of literature bears a striking similarity to the early drafts of our students. Sometimes it is helpful to show them the early, scrawled over drafts of the masters. It is our job as writers and teachers, as it was the challenge of the masters, to recognize the potential in the hesitant first pages of copy.

It may be worthwhile to develop a checklist with your students, who may feel that neatness, grammatical correctness, spelling, a particular distant voice, a specific genre, or even one way of thinking is the mark of good writing. Such a checklist, after discussion about what writing the students like and respect, might include:

• *Information.* Readers appreciate a satisfying abundance of specific information. They like to be given information that makes them think and that makes them an authority on the subject so they can deliver that information to other people. Writing that works usually has a rich abundance, a density of information in it. It is not thin or superficial, but has a satisfying depth.

• *Honesty.* Readers are so afflicted with what is false and what is plastic that they appreciate honesty. One false note and the writing is lost; readers no longer believe it. But when we are honest, readers are drawn to us, and they believe in our authority and listen to our message.

• *Focus.* Readers appreciate focused writing, writing that says one dominant thing and then develops it, writing in which each piece of information is connected or related to each other piece of writing.

• *Form.* Readers need a sense of structure. It is, after all, the artist's job to make meaning of chaos. The shape of the writing is satisfying and important to the readers, for shape or form is in a very real sense meaning.

• *Development.* Readers need fullness and movement, ongoingness, the feeling they are being led towards a meaning.

• *Documentation.* Readers need evidence to believe what the writer is saying. The writer has to learn how to get out of the way and present evidence, not just opinion, to persuade the reader.

• *Closure.* Readers need a sense of completeness in an effective piece of writing, a feeling that a destination has been arrived at.

• *Voice.* Most of all, readers listen to a voice, an individual writer speaking to an individual reader in an individual way. The voice needs to be vigorous and appropriate, appropriate to the writer, to the subject, and to the reader.

How are you — and your students — expected to turn from a checklist of standards for effective writing to your own miserable draft, that puny confusion of incomplete intentions and feeble possibilities, tracks run dry, small cries and pitiful groans?

That's exactly the point. You are a composition teacher, and you need the experience of confronting your own writing that isn't yet made, that is unfinished, incomplete. You need to be an expert at reading what is not is, of what may become. This is where we prepare best for the writing course at our own writing desk, trying to make sense of what we have to say before we know what it is that we have to say. It is a humbling and essential experience. We need to participate in the struggle and the satisfaction, the despair and the joy of writing if we are to listen to our students' comments about their writing and read their early drafts with understanding, so that we are able to respond with increasing effectiveness.

The Terminal Response: The Grade

When I first began to teach I was a tough grader right from the first day. I was a professional writer, and I applied professional standards to my students' papers. My students didn't realize I was terrified that they would rise up and attack me. I put them in their place with grades. I was surprised they accepted, and even seemed to appreciate, my F's and D's and C minuses. They seemed to feel that Freshman English was boot camp and if they survived it would be something to brag about.

And the grades could be justified. Since they didn't know how to write and I didn't know how to teach writing, their work was awful.

When our students come to us and we grade their first papers, we are grading what they have been taught — or not been taught — in other courses. Our purpose should be to grade our students on what they have learned in the course they are taking.

I would have gone on cracking the whip if I hadn't had a couple of young colleagues camped at the outer edges of the department who wore beards when I was cleanshaven and who made me rather uncomfortable. I worried they might start wearing sandals. They challenged me to stop grading individual papers. I was shocked and scornful. But they kept after me, and I finally decided to stop grading a set of papers, sure that my students' work would self-destruct and that I would be able to document the importance of grades and shut up the academic crazies.

When the next batch of papers came in my B students — there were no A's — wrote better papers than I could have ever imagined they could write. They suddenly did not know they were B students, and they started to work. I hadn't realized how comfortable they were, lolling around on their B's.

After a few weeks the C students, not realizing they were C students and seeing what the B students could do in workshop, began to surpass their own expectations and mine. After a few more weeks the D and F

students, who I had thought were working but had sensibly given up —
they had a string of D's and F's in the first weeks of the course that could
never be overcome — began to write papers that caught up with the C
students, and sometimes zoomed right past. I was beginning to learn
how to teach.

I did not eliminate grades or standards. I could not and would not
want to. Grades and standards are important. I was delaying standards
and allowing my students time to practice and to learn. I do not send
off my early drafts, my necessary failures, to editors, and yet I had
been grading each draft as if it were final. I realized that my students
had to rehearse and practice the same way that artists, performers, actors, athletes, soldiers, and cooks all have to have an opportunity to
learn a craft through a series of failures and successes before they face
evaluation.

I announce at the beginning of the course that students will be
graded on pieces of their choice — usually three — that are chosen by
them at the end of the course. I have not found that students lie back
and wait. They work harder, in fact, at the beginning of the course,
knowing that they are learning how to write.

I have discovered that I'm a demanding teacher because I expect
more of my students than they expect of themselves. They must show
their work to me every week, and show their work to their peers most
weeks. They know what they are doing, and we know what they are
doing. The result at the end of the course is a certain amount of grade
inflation, because those who do not write drop the course, and those
who do write learn. They are not graded on what they knew or did not
know before they came into the course. They have an equal opportunity to improve.

I do not, however, grade on potential, talent, improvement, effort,
motivation, intention, behavior, personality, weight, height, sex, race, ac-
cent, appearance. I grade on accomplishment, subjectively, I admit, but
to the standards I feel are appropriate to the course. A's represent exceptional work, far above average. B's represent good work, above average.
C's represent average work. D's below-average work. And F's exceptional work in the wrong direction.

It is the work I am grading, not the student. It is work that can be
shown to the student, to colleagues, to administrators; it is work that relates directly to the quality of the reference that would be given for the
student when that student applies to more advanced courses or for a job.
It is a grade that represents my evaluation of what the student has accomplished and demonstrated at the end of the course after the student
has had the benefit of extensive writing and extensive reaction to that
writing.

Responsive Teaching in Practice

Responsive teaching is a difficult, sophisticated kind of teaching. You cannot just prepare yourself and walk in and command the classroom. You must be able to stimulate text and responses to those texts which provide you an opportunity for your own response. You must be able to listen to what is being said in the writing and about the writing. You must be prepared in the greatest sense, prepared by everything you have done, all your own writing and reading and teaching, to bring the information your students need to them at the moment they need it. And you must be quick on your feet, able to make use of the insights and accidents and perceptions that are occurring in the arena of the classroom. And, hardest of all, you must learn how to shut up, to wait, to listen, to let your students teach themselves, for through that teaching they will learn the most.

Later chapters will present strategies and tactics that make response theory workable, but you can also get help on responsive teaching from the best art and music teachers, from those who teach theater, from those who coach, from the great laboratory teachers. But ultimately your students will teach you most how to do this teaching if you can be quiet enough to listen and observe how they teach each other.

Many composition teachers have the advantage, in the beginning, of being graduate students who are being taught as they teach. It is important to steal from your best teachers, to observe with a critical eye how they teach. You may even want to go and visit the classrooms — with the permission of the instructor — of other teachers who are considered successful teachers, and to make appointments to talk to your most effective teachers about how they teach. Don't forget how much you can learn from bad teaching. Observe your teachers who are not stimulating or tolerating learning in their courses. Pay attention to what they are doing, for it will tell you what *not* to do yourself.

I hope that you will consider the philosophy of responsive teaching and study the detailed techniques described in this book, but I hope you will never attempt to teach like Don Murray, or anyone else. You must teach like yourself. A life of teaching should be a life of learning about your subject and yourself. You should continually find ways that are natural for you, the classroom and conference atmospheres in which you can best function, extending the range of techniques and methods that you can apply when you see the need for them.

You learn to write by writing and learn to teach by teaching. You learn from books, articles, lectures, and from experience — most of all from experience — because all that you learn from outside your experience has to be filtered through your experience. Pay close attention to what is happening as you write and as you teach. The classroom is a lonely place for the teacher. Those who have never taught do not realize how exposed we feel before our students. But do not try to hide, for you cannot hide. Instead, revel in the loneliness. Each classroom is self-contained; it is your class, and it allows you to bring all you know and all you feel to bear on allowing your students to learn, each in his or her own diverse and individual way. If you are able to accept your loneliness, your individuality, then you are on the way to accepting theirs and helping them to accept it too.

8 Conference Teaching: The Individual Response

Conference teaching is the most effective — and the most practical — method of teaching composition.

The tutorial — one-on-one — situation allows the instructor to take advantage of the individual differences between students and their texts that are an enormous problem in group teaching.

Conferences allow the student to learn how to read and improve their own texts and allow the instructor to encourage and monitor that essential form of learning.

Most people agree that conference teaching is ideal, but believe it is impractical under normal college and university conditions. It certainly is a methodological challenge, but it is practical and efficient. In fact, the worse conditions are, the more remedial or diverse the students, the greater their number, the more important it may be to develop a conference based curriculum.

In the past fifteen years many schools have developed such programs, and many experienced teachers have published reports on the subject. At the University of New Hampshire, students in Freshman English and Introduction to Prose Writing (advanced composition) meet with their instructors individually every week outside of class. We have more than 64,000 writing conferences a year. This method is not a matter of theology. We do not command this curriculum, although we do strongly recommend it; it has become standard because it is efficient, because teachers who experiment with this method find it satisfying and successful.

There are many variations in conference teaching. I have learned from and with my colleagues. My views of conference teaching are quite different in some ways from my colleagues', and they should not be held accountable for my views. The biggest difference is in the pattern of response. Many conference teachers are deductive. The student comes to conferences to receive the evaluation of the draft and suggestions for future writing behavior from the instructor. Students have an opportunity to respond to the instructor, but they are told what is right and wrong with the paper and what they should do about it.

I fear that such conference teaching does not allow the student to develop as a reader of the student's own drafts and that the student may become dependent on the teacher for identifying problems and developing solutions. I believe it is vital for the writer to learn how to read a draft and evaluate it. My conference pattern incorporates response theory: the instructor responds to the student's response and to the student's suggestions for improvement.

The Conference Pattern

The variations on the writing conference are almost infinite, but the basic pattern is simple. Donald Graves discovered during his research in the schools that it is important for both student and teacher to have a predictable pattern within which they can work and from which they can depart and return when necessary. The pattern is:

○ The student COMMENTS on the draft.
○ The teacher READS or reviews the draft.
○ The teacher RESPONDS to the student's comments.
○ The student RESPONDS to the teacher's response.

The Purpose of the Basic Pattern

The purpose of this pattern is to help students learn to read their own drafts with increasing effectiveness. It is the responsibility of the student to write and to make the first evaluation of his or her experiment in meaning. It is the responsibility of the teacher to listen to the student's response, then to listen to the text, and finally to respond to the writer's reading of the text. Then it is the responsibility of the student to respond to the teacher's response.

These conferences should have the tone of conversations. They are not mini-lectures but the working talk of fellow writers sharing their experience with the writing process. At times, of course, they will be teacher and student, master and apprentice, if you want, but most of the time they will be remarkably close to peers, because each writer, no matter how experienced, begins again with each draft.

The conferences will vary from teacher to teacher, and the conferences of each teacher will vary from student to student. Some students will need more encouragement, and others will need more prodding. Some can be kidded, and some have to be taken seriously. There is a whole range of human interaction in the conference. But it all builds on this basic pattern of student initiation and teacher response.

As writer and reader meet during the development of a series of drafts the relationship may change. At first there is no draft; the student doesn't know what to write about, is unsure that the student can write, and the teacher moves close to the student trying to draw the student out, to fan a faint ember into flame. As a series of drafts evolves, the teacher draws back, becoming first a sympathetic and understanding audience and later a distant audience, a test reader who does not know the subject, the writer, or the writer's intentions. Then, when the final draft is edited and the student faces a new project, the teacher may have to move in close again and follow the same sequence of withdrawal. But this pattern, too, is built on the structure of student initiation and teacher response.

Teaching by conference helps us develop both sides of the student nature: creator and critic. When the creative side of the student is overdeveloped we get writing without discipline, without meaning, a self-indulgent spatter of words. When the critic is overdeveloped we get nothing at all, or an uptight, cautious, anonymous piece of work, a dog with its tail between its legs, its ears pinned back.

The discipline of writing is developed by a productive tension between freedom and limitation. It is the task of the writing teacher to monitor this tug of war, to encourage the creator or the critic at the appropriate time, to make it possible for the writer within the writer's own self to learn how to deal with these dual forces. The only way we can estimate the state of the struggle is by hearing what the writer has to say about the evolving text.

Teaching Reading to Teach Writing

Every writer is a reader. When you write one word — or phrase or sentence or paragraph — you have to read what you have written and read ahead to what you have not quite yet written. For each word written there are many words read and reread, scanned, considered, chosen, rejected, selected, fitted to other words, and reconsidered. Most of us are unaware of this continual, sophisticated reading that is embedded in everything we do as we write and rewrite.

To teach writing, we must teach reading. The writer's first reader is always the writer. The writer reads within the act of writing, and therefore we have to teach the student to be a more effective reader.

Reading during writing is immensely different than the kind of reading we do when we confront a published text. When the writer reads the writer's own text there is the constant possibility of change. The writer faces alternatives, in many cases a drowning ocean of alternatives. The writer must read what is, gaining enough distance to recognize what is for the reader, and the writer must also read what might have been and what might be.

The workshop's primary justification may be that students can see writing in process — writing still seeking its meaning — and learn to read it more effectively. Whole-class activities and class meetings will often introduce or develop this writing skill of reading during the act of making. The most effective place for such instruction, however, is the conference.

The writer knows the history of the draft, knows the unseen decisions that do not appear on the page, and is the person best able to comment on the draft, stating what works and what needs work. If the teacher does the reading for the student, the student is cheated of the opportunity to learn. The teacher should listen to the student — as a fellow writer — and examine the draft in the light of the student's vision, then respond, teaching the student in each conference how to read with increasing skill.

The Trialogue: Student, Teacher, and Text

The writing conference will not be fully understood if it is seen just as a dialogue between teacher and student or writer and writer. The text itself plays an important role, usually an equal role, sometimes a dominant role in the conference. What occurs is really a trialogue between student, teacher, and text.

The evolving text is itself learning during the conference. In a very real sense, it is discovering its own meaning. During the entire writing process there are things that the writer — or the teacher-editor — may want done to the text that become impossible. The text will simply not allow it. As the text grows, it increasingly limits what can be said in that text and limits the options in how it can be said. There is a continual narrowing down as the writing moves forward towards publication. This narrowing down may be described as the text teaching the writer what may be said and the manner in which it may be said.

The primary conference activity might be described as a co-reading. The writer and the teacher-editor-colleague-helper read the text together to see what it is saying, what it cannot say, what it may be able to say. The text is the focal point of the conference. The student speaks first, but the student speaks of the text. The teacher listens to what the writer says *of* the text and checks it *with* the text.

This process of co-reading demystifies one of the most mysterious feelings that the writer has: that the text talks to the writer and tells the writer what to do and not to do. Non-writers confront a writing problem and look away from the text to rules and principles and textbooks and handbooks and models. Writers look at the text, knowing that the text itself will reveal what needs to be done and what should not yet be done or may never be done. The writer reads and rereads and rereads, standing far back and reading quickly from a distance, moving in close and reading slowly line by line, reading again and again, knowing that the answers to all writing problems lie within the evolving text.

The student discovers this in conference as the teacher keeps inviting — even commanding — the student to look at the text, read it, and comment on it and as the significance of the student's comments is confirmed by the teacher's validation and, even more important, by the increasing effectiveness of the drafts that follow. Reading in conference with a co-reader or in workshop with co-readers produces an intensified reading, often more revealing than when reading alone. Soon the student begins to realize that secrets lie within the text and that they can be discovered best by the reading of the writer who has helped that text evolve, who knows its conception, purpose, history and developing meaning.

The Teacher's Self-Conference

The most effective training for a conference teacher is experience in reading and responding to the teacher's own text. I best prepare for a day of conferences when I spend at least a short time, perhaps only fifteen minutes, writing and reading my own text. It tunes me up for responding to my students' reading of their own texts. It gets me in shape to respond individually to the surprises on the page that my students confront.

We need to be familiar with the process of reading and influencing a live text, with words that carry their own meaning to the page. We need to remember how hard it is to predict the effect those words will have on each other. We need to know failure and success firsthand, hear the music of the writing, feel its structure under our hands and sense its changing shape. As teachers-writers we know where our students are in the writing process because of our own recent travels through the process.

Composition teachers should also experience conferences with other writing teachers. I have learned what to do in conference — and especially what not to do — by continuing to be taught in conference by colleagues and editors. I didn't learn much about writing from the *Time* editor who made a glider of one of my stories and tossed it out the twenty-eighth-story window. One poet told me, after reading a sheaf of my poems, that I should write big poems because I'm a big guy. The poet was not reading my texts or my purpose but measuring me against a standard of his own. Yes, he wrote big poetry and was a big guy. I have, on the other hand, learned a great deal from colleagues and editors who listen to what I have to say about my texts, then read them and help me confirm or adapt my reading of the draft so the next draft improves. I am dependent on them for help and I write and rewrite. And the experience of good and bad conferences helps me remember what to do — and *not* to do — in my own conferences.

The Teacher-Student Conference

Students should be prepared for conference teaching by class discussion that makes the following points:

○ Student writers are individuals. They have their own subjects, their own reasons to write, their own way of writing and their own language. They have things they are good at and things that need work. Conferences allow the teacher and the student to work together on what each individual student needs.

○ Not all students need to learn the same thing. In the conference, the learning is tailored to the student's need. And the student participates in the decision about what has to be learned.

○ Not all students learn the same way. The conference allows the teacher to fit the way of learning to the student's learning style.

○ Students know the history of the draft being read better than the teacher. The writer knows the choices that were made and the reasons for those choices. In the conference, the student can tell the teacher what needs to be known to put the text or a problem in the text in context.

○ Students need to learn to read their own drafts so they can improve them. In the conference, the teacher can listen to the students' evaluation of their own texts and help make them more effective.

Students need to know the dynamics of the conference: the student is expected to say something about the draft; the teacher is expected to listen, read the draft, and respond to what the student said; the student is expected to listen to the teacher and respond.

Most students will, of course, be uncomfortable in taking the initiative in their own education. Why not? Most teachers have taken total control of what goes on in the classroom. Now the student is supposed to speak and the teacher to listen. It may be a bit hard on both of them.

The best way to encourage student response in the conference is to allow it. Shut up. Be quiet. Wait. When the student makes a comment, then you can pick up on that. At first the student's responses may be noncommittal. "I dunno about this. I mean, like what do you think?" You have to throw it back into the student's court, urging the student to make some evaluation.

Students may be suspicious — with good reason. They fear a form of teacher entrapment. Many teachers use a false openness in their teaching. They ask questions that are not questions, and they do not listen to an answer that is not the teacher's expected answer. It will take time for the teacher to earn the student's trust. But there is no shortcut. It takes the time it takes with each student.

Most of the time, silence is the only motivator you need. Students can't stand silence. Allow them to sit quietly for a few seconds and they will think it hours. If you don't speak, the students will.

If you want to intervene, you may have students come to conference with a written evaluation — a sentence or a paragraph on a three-by-five-inch card or at the end of the piece — that tells what the student thinks works and what needs work.

I've also used a questionnaire to help evaluate a draft. Janet Emig included a very wise question on a form she used: "Who would you like to have read this piece?" The student had the choice of inviting a conference with a classmate instead of a teacher.

I used the following form last semester and found it helped the student during the writing as well as afterwards.

  I. What does the story say — in one sentence?

 II. Why will the lead capture the reader?

III. What are the reader's five questions?

    1.

    2.

    3.

    4.

    5.

 IV. Are they answered?

  V. What different forms of documentation have you used?

 VI. What does the voice communicate to the reader?

VII. How does the end give the reader a sense of completion?

No forms or questionnaires are necessary however. Just silence and listening and then response to what the writer says about the text and the writing of the text.

How Teachers Respond

If teachers allow students to speak first they will discover that they have a response. Many times even before the teacher has seen the text, the student will express an insight about the making of the draft, and the teacher will feel a shock of recognition and be able to share a similar experience at the writing desk. The teacher will soon realize that the best class preparation is often the teacher's own writing.

Responsive teaching can't be predicted. Even if the teacher has read the student's paper before the conference the instructor still needs to know the student's opinion of that paper in order to speak intelligently about it. The responsive teacher has to learn a waiting game, calm but alert, waiting to take advantage of what the student says.

It is important to create a personal environment in which the teacher can be relaxed, calm, and receptive, concentrating on the student. The student's opinion is vital, and in every way the teacher must deliver that message by careful attention to the student and what the student has to say about the evolving text.

The teacher must keep in mind that there is no single, correct response to a student's response. The teacher is often appropriately noncommittal. The point is not to get in the way of the student, to give the student the maximum amount of room so that the student can instruct himself or herself.

In most conferences only one thing can happen, only one issue can be dealt with. You must be alert to help the student find a significant issue or problem to confront. On an early draft the syntax may break down because the writer is searching for a meaning, and the writer may need to be reassured that technically correct writing is not necessary at this stage. But later, when the writer has a message that an audience needs to hear, it may be important for the writer to pay close attention to the traditions of language, and the student may be encouraged, even commanded, to pay attention to those traditions so that the reader will get the message.

Responsive teaching is often confused with a stereotypical therapeutic role in which the teacher always nods, always encourages, always supports, and never intervenes. That is ridiculous. The teacher is, after all, the teacher, and has the whole range of responses to a text available. It is insulting and patronizing to encourage work that is not good, but what the teacher has to do is to help the student see the potential in the work, to draw that potential out and develop it.

Most conference teachers find the oral response most effective because it can truly respond, not to what the teacher expects to be said, but to what is being said. The tradition that every student paper deserves a written response from the instructor is so deeply ingrained in our system that most of us feel guilty when we do not mark up a paper. In some institutions instructors are even required to mark on each paper, and I've heard of schools where the papers are collected by senior faculty or administrators, and the instructor is evaluated on the *quantity* of squiggles.

It is easy enough to mark up student papers, even professional papers, for that matter. As literature teachers we can carve up Shakespeare and Toni Morrison. In general, we mark according to an inverse order of significance. That which is most trivial can be marked more easily, and so we mark typography, neatness, spelling, usage, mechanics, but we are less likely to mark failures of logic, structure, documentation, style, or subject matter. In fact, it's quite possible to mark up a paper that isn't yet a paper, that doesn't have anything to say worth saying.

I keep trying to find a way to make written comments on papers, and I have experimented with this in my own teaching and in team-teaching. And my failure to find effective ways to comment on papers in writing may simply be my own problem. But I have difficulty in knowing where the student is, and when I write on a paper, therefore, I'm more likely to be overpraising or overcritical. I tend, and I think most of us do, to the general phrase, to the judgmental summary statements that shut off reconsideration and revision.

Even my best, most precise pieces of counsel are often given to students who are not yet able to understand them, or to students who already understand them and feel patronized by my comments. When I edit line by line — a compliment I usually reserve for my best students on their best papers — I run the danger of taking the writing away from the student and making it mine.

When I read papers before conference I try to put no marks on them; I want to be ready to respond to the students' concern. I want to teach them what they are ready to learn. Sometimes I'll put a code at the top of the paper: *p.v.* for point of view, a tiny *e* to signal that it may be time for us to edit a few paragraphs together, for organization.

But I am tempted, oh how I'm tempted, to mark up my students' papers, because my colleagues would be impressed, my students would be impressed, and I would have the opportunity to learn to write by editing their copy and making it mine.

As much as possible — in responding orally or in writing — the teacher should not praise or criticize. We need to discuss with the student how the piece is going, what is working, what needs to be done, avoiding as much as possible evaluative generalizations and focusing on a writer-to-writer discussion of what is working and what needs work.

Some responses to avoid and to use include:

No

○ "This is no good."
○ "Wow. You can write."
○ "Didn't you learn anything about writing?"
○ "This is great, just great."
○ "This is a mess, just a mess."
○ "I've never seen such a good paper."
○ "I've never seen such a bad paper."
○ "I don't know what I can teach someone who writes like you." (Interchangeable: can be used to overpraise or overcriticize.)

We can all add our own favorites. I've never met a writing teacher who didn't have a list of monster responses to drafts. The problem is that these comments all terminate discussion and the growth of the piece of writing. We loll around on our backs with our paws in the air, wagging our tail, when we get praise; and we growl, bark and press our ears back when we are criticized. Both ends of the spectrum close the door on improvement. There's not much the writer can do with — or learn from — such comments.

There are comments, however, that may stimulate and encourage work.

Yes

○ "What do you plan to work on next?"
○ "Obviously some of this works, but what do you plan to attack next?"
○ "Where do you think you get off the track?"
○ "Well you certainly solved last week's problem, what's next on the menu?"
○ "You followed my advice and really screwed it up, didn't you? What do you think you can do to screw it up on your own?"
○ "I like the way you wove the quotes into the text. Are there other things that could be woven in the same way?"
○ "This looks like what happened to my draft this morning. Where do you intend to go from here? I need to find out."
○ "And you said you had no voice. Tell me how you made this draft so different."

These comments — in your own voice and appropriate to your own situation — can be more demanding than blunt, destructive criticism. The writing teacher should not duck critical problems, but face them in such a way that the student is involved in their solution.

The responsive teacher is an encourager, and there are two important reasons for that. One is that the student doesn't know what is good, what has potential, what is working any more than the inexperienced student doesn't know what doesn't work. We learn to write primarily by building on our strengths, and it is important for the teacher to encourage the student to see what has potential, what has strength, what can be developed.

The other reason that we encourage responsive teaching is that we all learn best by positive reinforcement. This isn't Pollyannaism, it is realistic common sense. Observe parents and grandparents with a child beginning to walk. They invite the child to walk, holding out their hands to indicate an achievable goal, and cheer at success and laugh at the inevitable failure. That's all you have to know to be a good teacher of writing. Keep inviting, encouraging, supporting, establishing increasingly difficult goals — and sharing laughter at failure.

The responsive teacher soon finds out, of course, that there are a few things all students need to know. When a sizable minority of the class needs to know something about organization, for example, we can teach a class in organization. But most of the time we find out that our students have their own individual patterns of strengths and weaknesses. Robert has good subjects, but doesn't know what to do about them. Evelyn is too organized, and needs to loosen up. Phil needs to tighten up and get organized. Each student has strengths to build on and weaknesses to overcome. And like the child learning to walk, students have to build on what they have done and attempt what they have not yet done a step at a time.

How Students Respond to the Teacher's Response
Not too seriously, I hope. I always urge my students not to pay too much attention to what I say. It's their work and their responsibility to make it work. My job is to confirm, from my experience, what they are doing or to make suggestions, from my experience, about what they might consider or do, but they are only suggestions. When the writer gets into the act of writing the conditions change, and what might be expected to work doesn't work, and what might not be expected to work may work.

I want my students to leave the conference thinking about what they may do next, and I may even ask them, "What are you going to do next?" I want to get that process going, but I don't want to hold them to it. Many times my students tell me they are not going to rewrite the draft, and I nod in agreement, knowing that many of them will be drawn back to a subject that obsesses them or a draft in which they have such an investment that they must pursue it. It is not important whether they rewrite or not most of the time; it is important they leave the conference planning to write.

The student's normal response to the teacher's response is conversational and continuing. They are people working together to produce increasingly better text. The scheduling of the conversations is artificial, but the tone is natural — two workers at the bench pursuing their craft. And the conversation in the office is similar to the conversation about writing that I will have with students when I run into them across campus, in the supermarket, or at the hockey game. We share our victories and defeats, our moods, our problems, our solutions, for we are learning to write together.

The Student-Student Conference

The student-teacher conference should evolve into student-to-student conferences. This is the second step in developing a community of writers who are not only willing, but prepared, to help each other. Your own conferences have modeled a teaching style that is learned by each student, because they participate in it. You are training teachers within the class, and they should be encouraged to teach each other.

To train them to teach each other you may need a few formal sessions in which the students work in threes with a teacher, a student, and an observer, and then switch roles so that everyone will have a chance to be a student, a teacher, and an observer. I find it helpful to keep the conferences short in these sessions to force concentration on one issue and to limit the teacher's tendency to say too much.

Although the students have been experiencing conferences with you, they should be reminded:

○ The writer speaks first.
○ The writer concentrates on what works and what needs work.
○ The teacher listens to what the writer has to say.
○ The teacher scans the draft to confirm or adapt what the writer has to say.
○ The teacher responds to what the writer said about the draft.
○ The writer responds to the teacher's response.

After the students have had several such experiences you may find ways to allow informal workshop time within your class periods. I also urge my students to confer outside of class, and I have, on occasion, had students who are conferring outside of class come to conference together so that, in effect, I am conferring with each in the presence of the other and also monitoring their conferences by my response.

One of my primary goals as a teacher is to make everyone else in the class a teacher, so that ultimately my students will be able to be both writers and teachers of writing with themselves as their student.

Conference Variations

Writing conferences, of course, do not need to take place in a classroom with a formal structure. A writing conference occurs whenever writers discuss their writing. This can take place anywhere, and there are other variations that can work for both student and teacher.

I often use telephone conferences. I give my students my home number on my syllabus, and urge them to call me at reasonable hours if they are writing and have a question or concern. I'd rather teach at the moment they are ready to be taught than wait days for a scheduled conference. I don't have enough calls to make it a problem, and I hardly ever have a frivolous call. The questions are serious, and we can discuss the issue quickly.

Sometimes I have students whose schedules and mine do not mesh, and we can have our regular conferences by telephone. It is a poor substitute for a face-to-face meeting, but if the student has a copy of the text and I have a copy of the text we can have an effective writing conference.

I've also had conferences by mail when students have had special problems. These are very difficult for me, because there is such a time lag between responses, and because I cannot listen to the voice of the person speaking or see those signals that illuminate what he or she is saying. If you have to do a conference by mail it is essential that the student make the first comments on the text. The same thing will be true when my word processor is connected to my students' word processors.

It is possible to tape-record the teacher's reaction to a text and have the students listen to those tapes, and even respond. This has been a practice in some schools, but I am not comfortable with it because it substitutes a machine for a person and, more important, does not allow the give-and-take that I see as essential to an effective writing conference. If for some reason — sickness, for example — it seems appropriate to use tape, then I believe the student should tape his or her reaction to the text first and the teacher respond to that.

In teaching teachers the writing conference, I started doing demonstration writing conferences in class. I went around the class, listened to what the students had to say about what they had just written, listened to or read the text, and began a conversation with the writer. Many of the teachers started holding public conferences in their classes, and I have tried the technique myself. It may be a helpful alternative once or twice in the beginning of the writing course to model effective writing conferences and to set the stage for workshops. Most public conferences stimulate the rest of the class, and the class members seem to feel a compulsion to help the writer and the writing conference becomes the writing workshop.

The conference teacher must always remember that many conferences won't work — and the teacher will probably never know which ones do work. I haven't found any way to grade individual conferences. I am confident the conference method works, because the papers written by my students and written for my fellow conference teachers improve, and because our vast alumni testify to what they learned. But that does not mean that every conference goes well.

There is a big advantage to conference teaching in that the instructor and the student can participate in making adjustments when conferences don't seem to be working. The teacher reads student response and behavior so that the instructor can repeat, go back, or try another tack immediately. The student can initiate a change in the conference by asking the teacher for clarification, or even a different conference style. When student and teacher feel that conferences aren't working, they can discuss it and try to devise solutions to the problems they can identify. It is a flexible, correctible teaching method.

The Student's Self-Conference

The student-teacher conference, student-student conference, and all the other variations of the writing conference are preparation for the most important conferences. Those are the conferences students have with themselves during the writing process.

We must remember that we are teaching students to teach themselves because they — like us — will continue to learn to write all their lives, facing new writing tasks that require new strategies and tactics. Students have to know how to talk to themselves about what is going on in the writing — what is working and what needs work — while the student is within the process of making meaning. The conferences the student has with others should become the model for the constructive dialogue during the internal conferences at the writing desk.

Conference Techniques

When I first started conference teaching I usually opened the conference with some such pleasantry as "What's new?" or "How are things going?"

expecting to hear some campus gossip or chitchat. Most of my students responded in terms of their writing. This wasn't a social call; they had written a paper and they were going to discuss it with me. Since I had told them they would be expected to speak first, they quickly learned to rehearse an opening statement. The conference opens best when I am pleasant, friendly, and silent.

Pleasant and friendly is fairly easy for me; silent isn't so easy. My students are tolerant of my remarks about the hockey game, the weather, politics, but quickly get me down to the business at hand by initiating the discussion of their paper. I urge you to be as quiet as possible, making yourself receptive, and they will start speaking of what they have written. After all, that's what you have in common.

It's important to keep the conference moving along, to avoid lecturing the student, and not to encourage the student to create an oral draft, telling the entire story. The writing should be done on the page most of the time. Occasionally it helps for a student to tell the story orally, and it allows you to say, "Why don't you write that?" But most of the time you're talking about one thing on one paper, and you want to open doors to the students' thinking about that problem.

Occasionally you may want to give the student a handout, refer the student to a text, remind the student of another student's paper, share another student's paper or one of your own, suggest that the student confer with a classmate or another instructor. But most of the time you want to listen, letting the student talk. The student, in conference, is first of all confronting the student's own work, and the instructor needs to have what William Stafford calls a good "unh-uh" and a good "mmm." The teacher has to nod and grunt and do all those silly significant things we do to show someone that we are listening and understanding without interrupting.

The instructor should remember that the purpose of the conference is not to evaluate or conclude anything, it is a conference about writing in process. It should be inconclusive, somewhat vague, supportive, stimulating. It should encourage the student to reconsider what has been accomplished and to consider what will be attempted next.

There are two important strategies for the difficult conference. One is to keep tossing the ball back into the student's court. It is the student's primary responsibility to evaluate the piece of writing, to decide what works and why, what needs work, and how. It is the teacher's role to discuss those evaluations by the writer, and therefore the student must be given these responsibilities again and again. The reason for them — that the student must learn to read the student's own draft effectively so the student can write it more effectively — needs to be repeated in class and in conference. But the student can't be let off the hook.

When the student and the instructor are both checkmated, and they do not know what to say about a specific draft, then the instructor can suggest that he or she would like to give the draft more thought, and suggest the student do the same. They can make a date for a conference later in the week, or for a telephone conference. But at that second conference the student should again have the opportunity and the responsibility to speak first.

If the instructor does not talk too much the conference will come to a natural end. It is amazing how students pick up the rhythm of a conference. If I am doing ten-minute conferences, students will conclude within ten minutes; fifteen-minute conferences, and it will take them fifteen minutes; twenty, and it will take them twenty. I, of course, have built in my own discipline in having other students come to the door to announce that their time has arrived. But what if there are no other students? I didn't know what I did until one of my students told me. I stand up and start walking to the office door. Sometimes I walk the student down the corridor and to the front of the building, always amused at observing myself doing what I didn't know I'd been doing before.

Conference Skills

Responsive teaching skills are natural to most of the personalities drawn to the discipline of English. It is difficult for many shy writers and readers to learn to lecture and dominate the classroom. But these quiet personalities are often ideally suited to responsive teaching. In my experience most beginning instructors take naturally to conference teaching.

Listening to What Is Said

Listening begins with respect. To be good listeners we have to believe that the person speaking may say something worth hearing.

Unfortunately it can be difficult for some instructors to believe students have anything worth saying. The answer, of course, is to hear what the students have to say, but if instructors do not expect to hear something worthwhile it may not be said, and therefore it will not be heard.

I remember sitting in the back row of a New York theater completely involved with the twisted, disfigured human being in *The Elephant Man.* When Merrick spoke about how he felt when he was listened to for the first time in his life, I felt the hair stand up on the back of my neck. Merrick described what takes place in many effective writing conferences, *"Before I spoke with people, I did not think of all those things, because there was no one to think them for. Now things come out of my mouth which are true."*

Reread that speech again and again, think about it, practice it. If you expect your students to be able to say things that are true about their writing they will. They will be astonished, and in the beginning you will be too. But soon your astonishment will turn to perpetual delight. They will see what you see in their text, and more. And you will be able to share with them their surprise and satisfaction in being able to talk about their writing with such perception and intelligence.

Of course, their comments will not flow out in neat little nineteenth-century essays of literary criticism. They will speak in shorthand, in colloquial English, as we speak to each other. But what they have to say will illuminate the text and help you to understand, with them, what they are doing when they write and why they are doing it.

Listening to What Isn't Said

The experienced conference teacher soon realizes that what isn't being said is as important — is often more important — than what is being said. The writing teacher has to train himself or herself to hear what is being said by inflection, pause, gesture. The way the student walks into the conference, the way in which the student handles the paper — as if it were a golden gift on a platter or a stinking three-day-old fish — can be revealing. The student who writes with hesitation and anxiety often speaks the same way, and the students whose sentences often pile up in a train crash when they speak often rush their words when they write. The volume and timbre of the student's speech can reveal what the student thinks of the writing.

Yes, we have to pay attention to what collects under that jargony term "body language." Hate it or not, I see my students with their physical guard up, protecting themselves against the blow they expect, demonstrating their openness by the way they hold their hands, showing pride or despair by the way they sit in the chair.

We have to pay attention to all the clues that tell us what the student thinks of the writing being done, what attitudes the student will take to the next writing task, and what response the student is having to our conference remarks.

As I talk to a student in conference I'm constantly looking carefully at the student, trying to estimate if I've been understood, if I've gone too far, if I've gone far enough. I'm reading the student to see if my message has been understood.

Responding to the Unwritten Text

The effective composition teacher has to learn how to read what isn't yet written. These texts range from the ones that exist before there is a word on paper through notes and outlines, exercises and journal entries, through early, primitive drafts.

If we try to teach by treating a first draft as a final text our students will not learn to write. We have to deal with students who have not yet written. Our students come to us saying they have nothing to say. We know they do, but they do not know it. Many times they have had no adult listening to them. Their own experience has not been valued at home or in school. We have to draw the draft out of them that they do not know they are capable of writing.

This is usually best done by an easy questioning of the student — what's the student's home town? Major? What courses is he or she taking? What jobs does the student have? Hobbies? Skills or interests? When the student starts talking and we can respond with a legitimate interest, then the student begins to have both an audience and a subject, and we can suggest, "You might want to write about that."

What the writing teacher is looking for is potential, some specific information that's interesting, a strong feeling about that information, an opinion, an area of authority, something the student knows or needs to know, or may want to know. The student's answers to our questions are all early drafts, oral writing to which we can listen and respond.

As the writer moves on to notes and fragments, we have to be able to read these for their potential with the help of the student. It is important to listen to the student, for writers who do not yet know they are writing use code words that have private significance. A writer says "skiing" or "Betsy" or "loneliness," and these are effective code words that bring up very specific memories. We have to ask what they mean, and we may learn that skiing, for example, is the way one student wants to live his life. He is a ski instructor and plans to manage the family ski lodge. He knows a great deal about skiing. Betsy may be the name of a girlfriend who died in a skiing accident. Loneliness may be the hours he sat with her body waiting to be rescued. We have to draw out of our students the meanings behind their code words. And if they want to explore those subjects we have to help them make that meaning come clear to others.

The less the students are skilled or experienced at writing the more we have to help the students learn to read their own unwritten drafts, scanning through memories, reaching out with research, observing life, doing scholarship, so that we can help them see the potential in what they are collecting. Both writing student and writing teacher must develop the skill of reading what isn't yet written.

Reading Students' Drafts During the Conference

Most of our instructors read students' papers *during* the conference. That sounds irresponsible to many traditional teachers, but it has many advantages. Some of them are:

○ The student gets an immediate response from a reader. There is a quick turnaround time. The paper doesn't stay on the teacher's desk but is with the student, ready to be revised or to influence another draft.

○ The teacher is forced to read fast and therefore is more likely to spot the big problems with the paper and not bog down in a swamp of petty problems.

○ The teacher can listen to the student's evaluation of the draft and then read it with the student's eyes, monitoring the student's learning.

○ It encourages a co-reading — and sometimes a co-editing — allowing the student writer and teacher writer to focus on an evolving text.

○ The student is a resource, ready to explain the reasons for the decisions made during the process of producing the paper.

○ The teacher is a resource, available to respond to questions from the student.

○ It allows the teacher to respond when the student has identified a problem and is ready to learn.

○ The student sees a reader responding to the paper and can read the reader's response, discovering how to hold and lose the reader's attention.

○ The teacher is forced to be efficient, responding to the student when the student is waiting for a response. It makes the conference period productive and frees the teacher from guilt of unread papers.

○ It makes the conferences purposeful and brings intensity and energy to the writing conference as student and teacher work together to improve the paper.

Remember that the conference can be short because the instructor is responding primarily to the student's principal reaction to the draft. The teacher probably is seeing a revision and so is familiar with the text. The teacher is also familiar with the student's strengths and weaknesses, which have been discussed in other conferences.

Sometimes the quick reading in conference doesn't work and the teacher and student take an evening or a day to reconsider the draft and then meet again in person or on the phone to discuss it. Not every conference has to work. If one doesn't, then there's time to schedule another.

Responding to the Text in Process

The best way to think about responding to a text in process is through two key questions:

- What works?
- What needs work?

That doesn't mean those questions are constantly asked; it does, however, establish the agenda for most conferences.

The writer needs to make a judgment of what is going well, what has succeeded, and then to decide where to proceed next. These conferences are ongoing. There is a constant picking up of what has been done and a looking ahead to what needs to be done.

It is a natural process. The conference creates a sense of craft, a feeling of workers at a common task. The most difficult thing for the traditional teacher is not to make final evaluative statements, not to play the judge, for such statements halt the growth of the piece of writing. We should not say "bad" or "good" but attempt to speak in a way that responds to what is going on and what can continue to go on.

Conference Questions

In the beginning the inexperienced teacher may need to formulate questions, such as:

- What works best in this draft?
- What needs work in the next draft?
- What did you learn in writing this draft?
- What surprised you?
- What do you expect to do next?
- How have you done that in the past?
- How do you think you may do it differently?
- How is your way of writing changing?
- What are these drafts teaching you about the subject?
- What are these drafts teaching you about writing?
- Is there anything that's happened in conference that may help you with the next draft? In workshop? In class? In the text?
- How is the text different from what you expected?
- What do you think you ought to be working on in your writing?
- What do you enjoy most in writing?
- What do you hate the most?
- What would you tell someone else to do to make this piece better?

○ How would you respond to the piece as an editor? A teacher? A reader?

The questions reel onward, and they are fun, and they may be helpful, but remember that they are helpful primarily to the teacher. They are not necessary to the student. I needed to develop such questions so I had them in my repertoire, and I needed them to reinforce the responsive teaching attitude I was developing. But I found that once I had internalized the questions I did not need to ask them. They got in the way. Students are capable of asking those questions of themselves on their own.

You might invite the class to develop a list of such questions and distribute it to them so they can refer to it during their conferences with themselves at their writing desks, but I would want to make sure the students know that the questions should never get in the way of a productive discussion of the evolving text.

There is a teacherly danger in developing a list of questions, and then a hierarchy of questions that imply, even though the developers may not believe it, that the same questions can be asked of each text and of each writer. I don't think that is true; writers are individuals who are changing through the act of writing, and their texts are changing. The questions must come from that combined process of discovery and learning, not from outside it, if they are to be the best questions.

As a text appears and develops, the student begins to know the text and the writing process. The result is increasingly sophisticated comments on the text and the writing process, sharper questions, more complex proposals for strategies on the next draft. The teacher follows the student if possible, leads the student if necessary — but as little as possible.

The Editing Conference

When a text has developed a meaning and a form, the teacher may want to respond to the text with an editing conference. This works best when the student indicates he or she is having problems with language — "I don't know, it doesn't seem to, well, flow, you know." "Kinda choppy isn't it?" "I keep working at it but it's flat kind of. One tone like. All the way through." "Okay, I've got something to say. At least *I* think it's important, but I still don't know no grammer." "It seems finished to me. It's O.K." Any of those student responses may allow the teacher to intervene and suggest an editing conference.

In beginning an editing conference I ask the student's permission to mess around with the text and ask the student to suggest a place where the student would like to have me edit. The student does have the right to reject my suggestion, and many do. There is no point in doing this unless the student is interested and comfortable. Then I have the student move over beside me and I go to work on the text in front of the student, talking out loud about what I'm doing: "I wonder what would happen if I cut up these sentences here. Hmn. Doesn't seem to do it. Maybe I've just got to make those clauses parallel. Let's see, that might carry the reader along. It's flat. No energy. Verbs, let's try some stronger verbs. No, that's too much. Ridiculous. This is a pretty good one. Oops. You just used that in the sentence above. Well, if we use it here, you may have to change that one."

In this way I work through a paragraph or two or three of text, talking to myself out loud as I talk to myself while editing my copy. It's a process of trial and error, seeing what works, not a matter of absolute rule, and I want the students to understand the game of editing. I don't work too long because the student won't be able to absorb it all and because I do not want to take the text away from the student. Students often tell me, during the editing conference, that my editing is changing their meaning. Of course. I pounce, agreeing with the students, pointing out that they know the subject much better than I do and they'd better edit it themselves, right now. I always try to show the students options, suggesting a range of verbs — "she tip-toed, danced, marched, glided, galumphed into the room" — or connecting sentences into several different orders. I want the students to see there's not one way but many ways to work on a line. Sometimes I urge them to go into another room and continue the editing, coming back and checking it with me later, or I have them bring a marked-up, edited draft to class or conference so I can second-guess their editing. And, above all, I try to make editing fun, a continuing process of finding and developing meaning.

The student writer must leave the writing conference eager to write again, with enough support to face the task with confidence, with some idea of what can be done, but with the realization that the act of writing will probably change what the student and the teacher thought might be needed in the next draft.

Providing a Process Context

During the conferences on evolving writing it is important that the instructor continue to put the draft in a process context. The student needs to know where the draft is in the writing process so the student can apply the skills appropriate to that stage of the process. If the student is collecting material hoping to find a subject, then the niceties of language may be ignored; if the student is editing a final draft for workshop presentation, then no sloppiness should be allowed to get between the meaning and the reader.

The instructor can put the draft in a process context in an easy way that reinforces the process concept. It doesn't need to be a heavy-handed lecture, but simply remarks that are dropped into the conversation, such as, "You're doing a good job of revising, but don't forget you've got to move to editing pretty soon." Or, "In these early drafts you've been trying to figure out the meaning for yourself, it's been private writing, but you're going to have to go public next week. You'd better make sure the readers know what these terms mean."

The student will have a process concept that has been presented in a text, developed in a syllabus, and all the instructor has to do in class and in workshop discussions is remind the student of the process, so that the student will continue to develop a sense of the process that will help the student in the future.

Providing a Student Context

The student also needs to realize that he or she is developing as a writer. A writing history is being written through the drafts, and the teacher should remind the student of this individual history. The student may be told, "This is organized pretty well. I can remember when you couldn't organize a paragraph." Or, "You look like you're becoming the class expert on finding subjects. Remember when you told me you didn't have anything to say?"

In the same conversational way the teacher can remind students of things that haven't yet been dealt with. "I like the way you've got this organized, but doesn't it seem a bit stiff to you? Is it time to start thinking about the flow?" Or, "Now that you've got this organized it may be time to go back and figure how to plug in some evidence that will document what you're going to say."

Of course, this is always better done inductively, and every effort should be made to draw the writing history out of the student, to encourage the student in a sentence or two when you have the chance to say what has been learned and what needs to be learned, to reinforce the lessons of the past and establish the priorities for the future.

Teaching writing is a matter of learning to move ahead one step at a time. It's the task of the writing student to put that sequence of steps, at first tentative and later assured, into an evolving personal curriculum.

Responding to the Finished Text with a Grade

The student has had time, opportunity, encouragement, support, help from colleagues, help from the teacher, help from the text. Now the student should meet the standards of good writing appropriate to the course.

The process approach to writing is often seen as an argument for lowered standards, or for non-existent standards. It is nothing of the sort. The standard should and can be higher and more demanding than in the traditional course.

In the traditional composition course, papers are graded immediately. When that is done the teacher is grading what the student knows before taking the course and before the student has had an opportunity to draft and redraft, to try different subjects, find an appropriate genre or form, clarify the meaning through an increasing attention to the discipline of language. The student needs education and needs time to demonstrate that education in finished drafts that deserve high standards. The student should not be patronized with high grades for poor work. The student deserves the teacher's respect, and deserves a grade that indicates how that work measures up.

The student is not rewarded for potential, for effort, for commitment; the student is rewarded for accomplishment, for producing writing that stands up to a reader's critical eye.

Conference Problems and Solutions

Any teaching theory can run aground on the day-to-day problems of making it work. Conference teaching must be practical and respond to the natural concerns of composition instructors. If you have problems, define them and be open, share them with your colleagues who are teaching the same way and with your students. It is, after all, your students' problem as well as yours.

How Can I Read All Those Papers?

Quickly. We make a serious mistake in thinking that each student draft needs careful correction by the instructor. A million English teachers — perhaps millions — have nailed themselves to the cross as martyrs to their students, correcting each dangling modifier, branding each misspelled word *sp.*, unsplitting infinitives, making colons semi, working night after night to do the learning for their students. Such dreadful responsibility is irresponsible. It takes the opportunity for learning away from the student, and it simply doesn't work. In most cases the student cannot understand the reason for the corrections.

Do not assume your student hasn't been taught all these things. That's too easy. Well-qualified teachers have taught grammar and rhetoric and style and usage and mechanics and spelling year after year.

I work with teachers from kindergarten to graduate school. It's all taught — and mostly, taught well. But it isn't learned, most of the time because it is out of context. The rules and principles are abstract, nothing that will help the student clarify the student's own meaning. There is no need to do again what other teachers, as well trained or better, as hardworking or more, have failed to do in the years before yours. You don't have to correct every single mistake on every single draft.

If you do, you may be wrong. There is no way a teacher can tell the student what is the right word unless the teacher knows what the student wants to say and how to say it. All the traditions of language should be engaged to develop and clarify the meaning of the writing, and that is the job of the student, not the teacher. Instructors can serve as coaches and make suggestions, but the least effective teaching is done when teachers arbitrarily correct a piece of writing, making that writing say what *they* want to say in the way *they* want to say it.

In conference teaching it is often best to read the paper in conference after the student has made the diagnosis on the paper as we have discussed earlier in the chapter. Then the teacher is reading with the writer's vision of the paper in mind. This helps the teacher overlook those twenty or thirty problems that are always present in most drafts, and concentrate on the place where the student is ready to learn.

Teachers may, of course, choose to take the papers home, but they should be disciplined enough to read the papers quickly and to make no written comments on the paper, if possible, so that they will still be able to respond to the student's reaction to the paper and not dominate the conference with the teacher's response.

Most of the time the student will identify a key problem — "It seems to run off in six directions," "I don't know if the reader will understand what I mean," "I think it begins about page three" — and all the teacher needs to do is to scan the piece of writing to confirm the student's identification of the problem before asking the student to suggest some solutions.

We should remind ourselves that we are teaching our students to read their own drafts, and there are papers that do not even need to be read by us. We may need to perform a police function and see that there is a paper, but when a student comes in and says that the paper is dead, that he or she is going to try to do it an entirely different way, and when the account of why the paper has expired and how the student intends to write the next one sounds rational from the teacher's own experience, there may not even be a need to read the text.

If the student asks the teacher to look carefully at a part of the piece of writing or to read the whole draft with line-by-line care, the teacher can agree to pay close attention to the writing if that is what the teacher thinks the student needs. If not, then the teacher should tell the student why that much attention from the teacher at this stage of the learning process is inappropriate.

The closer the paper gets to the end the more careful reading may be needed, and on occasion the teacher may even ask to take the paper home and give it a line-by-line reading. The better the paper and the better the student the more likely the paper deserves close attention. In the traditional composition class we often reverse this priority, hitting the beginning student with a barrage of literary howitzers, and letting the best student — who might be able to handle the barrage and learn from it — simply write on without response.

Most student papers are scanned to confirm the diagnosis of the student and the strategy the student has selected to respond to that diagnosis. It takes training, self-restraint and discipline to read student papers with an appropriate carelessness, concentrating on what is significant in that particular draft and not getting bogged down in all the issues that are not yet significant. But it can be done if the teacher listens to the student, keeps the teacherly pen capped, and reads the paper to confirm or adapt the student's evaluation of the work.

How Fast Should I Read?

Most of us have the illusion that it is virtuous to read slowly. The more slowly we read the more responsible we are. In teaching writing the reverse maybe true. We should train ourselves to read as fast as possible.

But if I read fast I might miss something. Exactly. On most student drafts — and on most professional drafts — there are dozens of problems, ranging from problems of content and structure to problems of syntax and manuscript preparation. It is the job of the writing teacher to help the student deal with the problems that are important at that stage of the writing process.

A helpful way to think of this reading is to imagine the draft as a tapestry woven with threads of many colors. In the conference the student indicates that he or she is concerned with the orange threads, and so you read the piece to see if the orange threads are in their proper places doing their job.

There comes a time, late in the process, when a careful, slow reading is justified, but most of the time the teacher has to be able to read fast, to listen to what the student says, and then to move through the piece quickly to see if that concern is justified, or to look for a new one.

The fast reading is helped by the fact that in the beginning the writer and the teacher are primarily concerned with content, later with structure, and finally with language.

Both the writer and the teacher are also dealing with the same text and the same writer during each reading. The teacher develops a familiarity with the piece of writing and with the writer that helps to make a fast reading effective.

How Long Is a Conference?

Long enough, and no longer. Long enough to achieve closure on one point. Certainly not the fifty-minute hour. Twenty minutes is too long. There's too much time for chitchat, for not getting to the point, for covering too many points. Fifteen minutes — that's the time I choose, even with papers twenty pages long. I don't need fifteen minutes, but it allows time for conversation on other topics, for interruptions from phone calls and colleagues dropping by to stir the political stewpot. Ten minutes is plenty of time for a productive writing conference, but students feel a bit rushed, and six conferences an hour, hour after hour, can be demanding on the teacher. Five minutes is plenty of time to get the central business of the conference done. There's time for the student to talk about the piece, for the teacher to scan and confirm what the student has to say, to make suggestions if necessary, and to respond to the student. Two minutes — amazingly possible. For years I have been running workshops in which I have teachers write and respond to each other's drafts, cutting the conferences at two minutes. After two or three rounds of two-minute conferences I will hear the teachers' voices fall before the two minutes are up. They have achieved a conversation about a piece of writing. Ninety seconds — that's the time I average when I demonstrate conferences in public and have someone else time me. The participants think the conferences are longer, and so do I. But the stopwatch almost always hits ninety seconds on the nose.

Am I arguing for ninety-second writing conferences? Of course not. But I am making the point that conferences can be brief, and should be brief, that the brevity of conferences gives them a productive intensity and limits the agenda in a constructive way. The purpose of the conference is not to lecture or to gossip or visit; the purpose of the conference is to give the writer an opportunity to test the writer's opinion of the most important element in the piece of writing — accomplishment or problem — with an experienced writer.

Of course, the conferences will vary in length in actual practice. There will be times when a long conference is necessary, when an additional conference time needs to be scheduled. But there are many times when the conference will be over in a hurry, when the student is teaching himself or herself and it's obvious to teacher and student that everyone is on the right track.

How Often Should I Confer?

Frequently. I find weekly conferences far more effective than a conference every two weeks, or two or three times a semester, or once a semester.

The student will be better served by an immediate response to each draft than by a more carefully considered response long after the draft is written or by a response to a batch of drafts at one time. The student learns draft by draft, and when students are sick or miss an assignment I usually find it is a waste of their time and mine to have them make up the assignment, coming to conference with two or three drafts. I prefer to have them spend the time they have on one draft and have us respond to that. If they have to make up papers, then I want to have a separate conference after each draft.

How Should I Schedule Conferences?

Conferences must be scheduled in a way that is convenient to both instructor and student. The traditional conference is held outside of class time at the instructor's office. Depending on the disposition of the teacher, the students can simply sign up on the schedule sheet for those slots that are available for that week. Some teachers prefer to assign the students to a regular slot so they appear at the same time each week. Most experienced conference teachers seem to be able to handle a hodge-podge of students from beginning and advanced classes coming in random order, but some teachers prefer to deal with one class on one day, and another class on another day.

Some teachers like to have an hour or two of conferences breaking up the time with the class. This is especially appropriate for teachers in non-residential institutions, so that students can come in before class or stay after class. I prefer to do all my classroom teaching whenever possible on the same days and all my conference teaching on other days. I find it psychologically easier for me to know in the morning I'm going to be a classroom teacher or I'm going to be a conference teacher. I don't mind a whole day of responding to students in conference. In fact, I like that and find it has its own rhythm.

Teachers should be aware that the increased contact time required by conference teaching is compensated for by decreased preparation time. If you add a conference schedule to a regular teaching schedule with extensive preparation time, it's impossible. Remember that most papers are read in conference with the student present.

Most class preparation comes directly from the conferences. The conference teacher knows exactly where every student is, and therefore knows what instruction is appropriate for the class.

Conferences do not need to be held outside of class time. The composition class can be seen as a workshop, in which students write, confer with the instructor, confer with each other, engage in small and large group workshop sessions, and have class meetings on problems of mutual concern.

Some typical conference schedules for out-of-class and in-class conferences follow. There is such a variety of teaching loads across the country that there is no way of establishing a standard. Each teacher has to do his or her own mathematics. The fewer the students, the fewer the courses, the longer the conferences. And the opposite is true. But once you have taught by conference you will see the advantage of the method — its efficiency and effectiveness — and you'll make every effort to schedule the conference time first, giving top priority to the one-on-one contact between student and teacher.

SCHEDULE 1

	MON.	TUES.	WEDS.	THURS.	FRI.
8 A.M.					
8:15					
8:30					
8:45					
9	Comp. Class #1	13	Comp. Class #1	53	
9:15		14		54	
9:30		15		55	
9:45		16		56	
10	1	17	41	57	
10:15	2	18	42	58	
10:30	3	19	43	59	
10:45	4	20	44	60	
11	Comp. Class #2	21	Comp. Class #2	61	
11:15		22		62	
11:30		23		63	
11:45		24		64	
12 noon	Lunch				
1 P.M.	Comp. Class #3	25	Comp. Class #3	65	
1:15		26		66	
1:30		27		67	
1:45		28		68	
2	5	29	45	69	
2:15	6	30	46	70	
2:30	7	31	47	71	
2:45	8	32	48	72	
3	Comp. Class #4	33	Comp. Class #4	73	
3:15		34		74	
3:30		35		75	
3:45		36		76	
4	9	37	49	77	
4:15	10	38	50	78	
4:30	11	39	51	79	
4:45	12	40	52	80	
5					
5:15					
5:30					
5:45					

This schedule is based on twenty students in each composition section, with a teaching load of four sections a term. It is a heavy schedule, with eighty conferences, only a handful more than I had last semester, and it can be done. The classes meet for two hours a week, with the third hour dropped because of the amount of student contact time in this program.

The conferences are fifteen minutes long, with the papers being read in conference. There is very little preparation time, because the intense student contact tells the teacher what needs to be taught or discussed in the classes, and the classes are mostly workshop sessions, in which students are working on one another's work.

If the instructor wants less conference time, then the conferences can be made ten minutes long. That's what I did last semester, but I had to read the papers before conferences, and I find that when I have ten-minute conferences it's more of a problem to handle interruptions.

SCHEDULE 2

	MON.	TUES.	WEDS.	THURS.	FRI.
8 A.M.					
8:15					
8:30					
8:45					
9					
9:15					
9:30					
9:45					
10					
10:15					
10:30					
10:45					
11	Comp. Class #1	9	Comp. Class #1	39	
11:15		10		40	
11:30		11		41	
11:45		12		42	
12 noon			Lunch		
1 P.M.	Comp. Class #2	13	Comp. Class #2	43	
1:15		14		44	
1:30		15		45	
1:45		16		46	
2	1	17	31	47	
2:15	2	18	32	48	
2:30	3	19	33	49	
2:45	4	20	34	50	
3	Comp. Class #3	21	Comp. Class #3	51	
3:15		22		52	
3:30		23		53	
3:45		24		54	
4	5	25	35	55	
4:15	6	26	36	56	
4:30	7	27	37	57	
4:45	8	28	38	58	
5		29		59	
5:15		30		60	
5:30					
5:45					

This is a schedule for three composition sections of twenty students each, with fifteen-minute conferences and two hours of class time. It allows morning hours for the instructor's writing, the best preparation for classes and conferences.

There are obviously many ways to arrange such a schedule. I prefer not to use Friday, since ours is a suitcase college with many students going home to work every week-end. Some people like to teach in the morning. I'd rather write in the morning, and am willing to teach as late in the evening as I have to to make that possible.

I also prefer long runs of conferences. I find I'm more effective when I can get into the role of conference teacher and stay there for a considerable period of time.

SCHEDULE 3

	MON.	TUES.	WEDS.	THURS.	FRI.
8 A.M.					
8:15					
8:30		Lit.		Lit.	
8:45		Class		Class	
9:00		#1		#1	
9:15					
9:30					
9:45					
10		Lit.		Lit.	
10:15		Class		Class	
10:30		#2		#2	
10:45					
11		1		21	
11:15		2		22	
11:30		3		23	
11:45		4		24	
12 noon			Lunch		
1 P.M.		5		25	
1:15	Comp. Class #1	6	Comp. Class #1	26	
1:30		7		27	
1:45		8		28	
2		9		29	
2:15		10		30	
2:30		11		31	
2:45		12		32	
3		13		33	
3:15	Comp. Class #2	14	Comp. Class #2	34	
3:30		15		35	
3:45		16		36	
4		17		37	
4:15		18		38	
4:30		19		39	
4:45		20		40	
5					
5:15					
5:30					
5:45					

This is an example of a schedule for someone who teaches both literature and composition. There are many patterns possible. I've chosen one that would work for me, but the variations are clear, and it would be possible to shift to three literature classes and one composition, or three composition classes and one literature.

SCHEDULE 4

	MON.	TUES.	WEDS.	THURS.	FRI.
8 A.M.					
8:15					
8:30					
8:45					
9					
9:15					
9:30					
9:45					
10					
10:15					
10:30					
10:45					
11		1	25	37	
11:15		2	26	38	
11:30		3	27	39	
11:45		4	28	40	
12 noon			Lunch		
1 P.M.		5	29	41	
1:15		6	30	42	
1:30		7	31	43	
1:45	Comp. Class #1	8	32	44	
2		9	33	45	
2:15		10	34	46	
2:30		11	35	47	
2:45		12	36	48	
3		13		49	
3:15	Mtg.	14	Mtg.	50	
3:30		15		51	
3:45		16		52	
4		17		53	
4:15		18		54	
4:30	Comp. Class #2	19	Comp. Class #3	55	
4:45		20		56	
5		21		57	
5:15		22		58	
5:30		23		59	
5:45		24		60	

We teach our composition classes beyond the freshman level with a single two-hour workshop meeting a week. This would be a typical schedule for me.

SCHEDULE 5

MONDAY	TUESDAY	WEDNESDAY	THURSDAY	FRIDAY
Class Meeting	8	16	Workshop	Students revise and consult in response to workshop
	9	17		
	10	18		
1	11	19		
2	Class Meeting	20		
3		21		
4	12	22		
5	13	23		
6	14	24		
7	15	25		

This is a conference schedule for a secondary teacher who has five 50-minute class meetings a week and twenty-five students. Conference times are five minutes long, more than is probably needed in this situation. This schedule allows the teacher to see every student during the first three days of the week. I've also put in one 15-minute and one 10-minute class meeting. These are times when the teacher can make a presentation or give a demonstration, or encourage students to give testimony on a problem they have solved. These times will move around according to the needs of the instructor.

While the conferences are taking place the students are working on a draft to be published in a Thursday workshop. Friday is free for students to revise their pieces as a result of the workshop and to consult with each other and the instructor.

SCHEDULE 6

	MONDAY
7 P.M.	Class Meeting
7:10	
7:20	1
7:30	2
7:40	3
7:50	4
8	5
8:10	6
8:20	7
8:30	8
8:40	9
8:50	10
9	11
9:10	12
9:20	13

	WEDNESDAY
	14
	15
	16
	17
	18
	19
	20
	Workshop

College instructors may find it helpful to create the same kind of climate by staking out a period of time in which the students do most of their writing and revision in the class while the instructor is holding conferences. This schedule is particularly appropriate for community colleges, in which students are commuting and holding down jobs. They respond especially well to the workshop environment, and the instructor has the advantage of having almost all the work for the course contained within these hours.

How Can I Create a Constructive Conference Climate?

The conference teacher should design an environment in which the teacher is comfortable. It is important for the instructor to feel relaxed and calm, so that all the instructor's attention can be concentrated on the student writer in a natural way.

Some people like busy offices; others like quiet ones. Some are messy; some are neat. Some conference teachers don't like offices at all. One secondary school teacher I worked with chose to use the cafeteria in off-hours for composition classes. He found the environment perfect. People could write by themselves, meet in small or large groups, and he could hold conferences. Other teachers use the library, the student union building, the front lawn in good weather. The most important point is that the instructor is functioning in an environment that makes the instructor comfortable. That comfort will usually be translated to the student.

Most conference teachers like to have students sit beside them to the right if the instructor is right-handed, to the left if the instructor is left-handed, so that the draft can be between them and the instructor can mark on it if it is appropriate. This way of sitting also has the teacher and the student sitting together without a desk between them. I prefer a variation, with the student sitting facing me across the corner of a desk. We can turn to work on the draft if necessary, but I don't like to talk to someone beside me; I like to look directly at them. I'm lucky enough to have a large office, and some students choose to sit with a table between us, others choose to sit in a chair where there is nothing between us. It's their choice.

The geography of the office can make a difference. If I had my conferences in the morning I would have to shift my office furniture, because the sun would blind the student. Everything is arranged to make conference teaching easy. I face the door, because I like to see who is heading my way. Other instructors purposely face away from the door, because they find the people going by in the corridor a distraction. I have a large wall clock I purchased with supermarket stamps positioned where I can see it without the student being aware that I'm keeping track of time. In this way the schedule is followed and each student has an instructor who is reliable and on time.

The best discipline for keeping conferences moving forward, however, are the students themselves. My own conference teacher used to keep us waiting for hours in the corridor, and I don't want to treat my students the same way. I tell them to come to the door and catch my eye when their time is due. If I'm involved in a conference that deserves privacy I can wave them off. Most of the time I nod them in. I've explained in class that we quite often learn more overhearing someone else's conference when our own work isn't on the line than we do in our own conference. Students are not surprised to be invited in, but the student whose paper is up can ask them to leave.

I also encourage teaching assistants and young instructors to observe my conferences, not because I'm a model, but just the opposite. When I write or talk about conferencing it all sounds neater than it is. We should share observations of each other's conferencing to see how it really works. I find that the students are not bothered by these observers, either their classmates or outsiders, but if they are they have the chance to ask me to ask them to leave. And that happens, and I do. And no one seems to worry about it.

Most conference teachers seem to have posters or mottos on the wall to reinforce what they are doing, as well as to create a lively environment. I have the motto *Nulla dies sine linea*, never a day without a line, on the wall where a student can't avoid seeing it. And I have a poster that shows Picasso revising the drawing of a bull, working backwards from the expected complicated vision to a simple drawing.

My fifteen-minute conferences are often interrupted by phone calls, by colleagues, by students wanting adviser cards signed, and so forth. One year I told two classes that I was going to accept no phone calls and allow no interruptions, and both classes rose up to say they liked the interruptions because they gave the students a chance to consider what had been said and to think about what to say next. I come from a city-room background, and I'm comfortable with a fairly high degree of interruptions. My students probably sensed this as well, but I have to be careful that the interruptions do not distract me or my students.

Many conference teachers do not have the luxury of their own office or have a schedule that allows them to have an office by themselves. Officemates need to work out their own relationship with candor and concern for each other, realizing that there is no right environment for the conference, and that if it is important for one person to have a certain condition — for example, no smoking — then that should be respected by the other. It's a tricky situation, and people who share offices suffer many problems: the paranoia that the other instructor is listening and grading the teaching, one instructor interrupting another instructor during the conference, a student appealing to the other instructor — who responds. And, of course, many instructors have not one, but two or three or more officemates. Each instructor must find a way of arranging the tiny territory that is the instructor's own so that the student and the teacher are able to concentrate on listening to each other.

How Does the Professional Conference Teacher — The Editor — Work?

In the conference, the student is an individual and the teacher is able to respond individually, helping the writer see what needs to be done to a text, what can be done, and then sharing in the excitement as the writer's own meaning comes clear in the writer's own voice. Professional editors often work with their authors in much the same way. I asked my editor, Linda Buchanan Allen, to speak directly to you when I realized she was practicing — on me — much of what I was preaching in this text. In the following essay, Ms. Buchanan Allen takes you backstage in the editorial process where she teaches publishing writers how to write more effectively. Note that she writes herself, as composition teachers should, and hones her critical skills on her own copy. It is also significant that she works to help her writers speak in their own voices, which should be the goal of us who teach writing.

AN EDITOR SHOULD BE SEEN AND NOT HEARD
Linda Buchanan Allen

My title at the publishing company is to the point: Editor. I do own a red pencil which I use when reading a manuscript for punctuation and grammar, but that is the final stage of editing. Prior to that, the author and I have worked together for months, sometimes more than a year, to bring about a manuscript that is ready for this final stage of editing. We've covered issues of content, market, and how practical the text will be in the classroom as well as organization, emphasis of topics, and reading level. We've discussed writing style and voice, along with any struggles the author may have had in working on the manuscript.

As an editor, it helps for me to understand the process the author is going through as he or she writes and revises a book; I must also be able to communicate with the author as we take the manuscript through its stages of revision. Thus, I must be able to write — and edit my own writing, even if it is simply a letter to the author. This requires one kind of editing, in which I must be objective, even cruel to myself. The other kind of editing is editing the work of the author; and that requires that I be a clean, clear window through which the reader sees the work of the writer, not the editor. The first type of editing allows me to establish, clarify, strengthen my voice; the second requires that I push my voice away, force its retreat.

Editors are often closet writers, so making the time to write is not so hard; indeed, much of the job involves writing. But editing my own work is harder than writing it; sometimes even harder than facing the blank page. I must be the objective, fresh reader each time I read my own writing. I must choose my words with care, taking more care not to over edit, over write. But I keep in mind that if I can write to discover, then I can also edit to discover. By editing I can clear the haze that hovers around an early draft and find what I did not know I knew, see what it is I wanted to say. It is good to have a mental checklist for editing: organization, clarity, accuracy, authenticity, style, mechanics. All these are things I look for as a reader in a good piece of writing. But I must not leave out serendipity. Editing can bring the delight of the unexpected. By sticking with it, trying different combinations of sounds, rhythms, words, even ideas — I can strengthen my voice, find new ways to speak in writing.

Good editing requires discipline and deftness. And a good exercise for editing one's own work I think is writing poetry; formal poetry. I prefer poems whose lines are defined by the number of syllables they contain rather than by stresses, rhymes, or other definition. This is like tossing the medicine ball around before playing the basketball game; when I return to prose, it seems light, buoyant by comparison. I've tried haiku, sticking to a strict syllable count, but a form that works particularly well in English is the French cinquain. Haiku is intended for a tonal language, and is a conduit for an eastern manner of thinking. The cinquain is intended for western, accentual/syllabic languages and so works quite well. Or I make up my own form: 5 stanzas, for example, with 3 lines per stanza, 7 syllables per line. I stick to the form; I allow myself no departures. By pushing syllables around, sometimes breaking a word from one line to the next (although I try not to do this more than once in a poem), I uncover new ways to say what I thought I wanted to say; and sometimes I discover I really wanted to say something else! Editing, though it requires toughing it out till I find the right combination of sounds, phrases, and sentences, also allows me freedom: I can scrap anything I want, try it from a different angle or three different angles, searching for that one combination that makes everything come clear. In that clarification my writing voice is strengthened, made more precise; thus meaning is more readily conveyed to the reader, and I've gained a bit more insight into the process of writing.

As I read an author's manuscript, whether it is first or final draft I keep in mind the fact that an editor should be seen and not heard. That is the motto of one who edits the work of another person, whether it be teacher to student, book editor to author, city editor to reporter. It is easy to read and edit another person's work for organization, clarity, accuracy, authenticity, style, mechanics, and so forth — that checklist is endless. It is a bit more difficult to edit another person's work without imposing one's own voice on it. A good editor must be able to edit so that the reader will never know the editor was there: the reader must be aware only of the author and a single, seamless voice. I must edit in the author's voice, not my own. I find the antithesis of this (and some bad editing, I think) in several of the national magazines in which every article "sounds the same." The magazine has a voice that is imposed on the writers; the individual voices of the writers are lost.

I must read an author's work with a fresh, critical eye; but with my ear, I must listen for the author's voice. Sometimes this takes several readings, or if I am reading a book manuscript, several chapters. It may take a new author (or beginning composition student) awhile to discover his or her voice; sometimes, a good editor can help an author find that voice. This comes with practice, of course, and the more manuscripts read the better. Reading to listen for an author's voice is a learned skill, but it is also intuitive: it is a matter of tuning one's ear to the voice of another rather than one's own.

Questions, I have found, are the best editing of all: they force the author to reread a sentence or passage and reconsider its meaning, its clarity, its sound. Often, upon rereading in this manner, the author can do the editing alone. Though they may take several forms, specific or general, most of my questions boil down to: "What do you mean?" I write them in the margin of the manuscript, up and down the sides, at the top and bottom of pages as well if necessary. This allows the *author* to discover what he or she wants to say, and how best to say it.

When line editing, I must be especially attuned to the author's voice: I must choose words from the *author's* vocabulary, rhythms from the *author's* sensibilities, syntax that more clearly says what the *author* wants to say. This is the author's piece, not mine; I can always go home later and write my own. As an editor, I must clarify meaning, not change it. If I disagree with the author's point of view or am offended by a particular comment, I simply say so, usually in the form of a question, in the margin. I do not change sentences to change meaning. If a point of view is presented in such a way that it may be misconstrued by readers, then I try to help the author present that point of view more clearly.

Editing really boils down to discovery and voice, just as writing does. As I edit my own writing, I'm on the lookout for anything new to strengthen and clarify my voice. I want to discover more about the process of writing, and I want to communicate well with my authors. When I edit an author's manuscript, I leave my voice behind, tuning my ear to the author's voice so that together we can discover what is to be said and how. We may do this by trying many revisions or only one. We may change a sequence of topics, alter the reading level, send the manuscript out for review, arrange to have it tested in classes. When the author and I reach the red pencil stage, we are both attuned to the manuscript and all the changes it has been through; and usually, agreeing where to place a comma is a breeze.

9 Workshop Teaching: The Group Response

The workshop response naturally evolves from the conference response. Once student writers know how the response of a single reader helps with the writing, they are ready to test drafts with more readers.

Writing is a private act with a public intent, and the student needs to know how to deal with an increasing number of readers who stand at an increasing distance from the writer. At first the readers are close to the writer. They know the writer's intent, the writer's limitations and potential. They are supportive as much as they are critical. The writer needs to move to readers who are less involved, more removed from the writer, but who are still supportive as well as critical. And finally, the writer, facing increasingly distant and critical readers, learns how to reach readers who are not interested in the writer and must be contacted by the writing itself.

The term "workshop" describes a community where writers help each other develop their own meanings and their own voices. It is also a community where apprentices and masters work side by side in the practice of their craft.

Reading Writing in Process

It is important that writing students read drafts — of others as well as their own — in process. Early drafts as well as final drafts, failures as well as successes, varieties of techniques that may work and may not work, all should pass before the eyes of apprentice writers. They need to see writing in the making, significance evolve from a succession of experiments in meaning.

As the students learn how to be constructive readers for others, they will learn how to be constructive readers of their own drafts. They will also learn effective variations in the writing process by seeing fellow writers struggle to make meaning with the symbols of language.

Most students — and many professionals, for that matter — have seen only the finished writing of others. It is important for beginning writers — and experienced writers — to read masterly examples of finished writing. Such writing sets goals, establishes standards, inspires and teaches, but it is just as important for writers to study what takes place before the illusion of ease achieved in the published draft.

To learn a craft you have to observe the oboist shaving a dozen reeds to get one that may be right, to hear the soloist practicing three crucial notes over and over and over again, changing the inflection and rhythm time after time. You have to see the messy palette with all the wrong colors mixed with such false confidence, to observe the failed sketches and inappropriate lines hidden layer after layer underneath the final oil. You have to go to rehearsal night after night to see actors stiffly speaking lines, moving awkwardly, filling the air with unnecessary gestures to comprehend the "naturalness" achieved by opening night.

Students will learn to see the potential in their own drafts only if they have seen potential grow from drafts in which they saw none. In the workshop students have the opportunity and responsibility to help their classmates see the potential in the draft that the writer does not yet see, and when that potential is perceived they have the responsibility and the opportunity to help the writer develop it by solving problems with the writer.

In helping others the writing students help themselves. They are often able to see things in other drafts that they do not have the objectivity necessary to see in their own. The reading of writing in process is a sophisticated kind of reading, but it can be learned as a community of writers share their reading of each others' drafts. Teachers who are not used to reading writing in process will be taught this skill by their students as they work to find the potential in successive drafts.

Publication in all its forms encourages these kinds of readings. The students work simultaneously on their own texts and on the texts of others, learning as they do to read as writers.

Writing to Readers

The writer is the writer's first reader, but not the last. It is the purpose of writing to communicate with other human beings, and it is the magic of writing that communication, transmitted by symbols carved into a rune stone or green words darting across a black electronic screen, can communicate directly with the minds and hearts of other human beings far removed by geography, time, or culture. William Faulkner once said, "The aim of the artist is to arrest motion, which is life. A hundred years later, a stranger looks at it and it moves again."

In the writing workshop the student learns, sometimes slowly and painfully, how to make meaning clear. Students are always surprised that what they think is fully developed and clear to them is so difficult for others to understand. As composition teachers we know that those private visions are often not clearly defined at all. And as the students struggle to make their meanings clear to others, they make them clear to themselves.

In the composition course we are teaching nothing less than critical thinking. The result may appear as poetry or argument, narrative or exposition, essay or report, but every form of writing requires a demanding intellectual discipline and a tough, well-sharpened linguistic craft.

We begin alone with our own observations and our own thoughts, but we need to present them to others, not just to share with others — to persuade, to entertain, to inform — but to find out what we mean. We learn through the interaction between writer and reader.

In conference the student has learned to anticipate the response of an individual reader and begun to develop the skill of conducting an internal dialogue between that part of the writer that is maker and that part of the writer that is receiver. This essential process continues and accelerates in the workshop. The writer begins to be able to internalize through the workshop experience what readers need to know. The writer begins to be able to empathize with readers, to put on the skins of particular readers and therefore to discover how to capture and hold readers.

By observing a workshop in action you can see the essential satisfaction of achieving an audience in the behavior of a student who has been able to create something that is of the student yet apart from the student, a text that stimulates the mind or the emotions of a reader across the room. Many of my students publish beyond the classroom, and I can usually tell when they have achieved such publication by the way they walk down the corridor as they come to my office for conference. They stride with a new confidence, even the shyest carry their heads a bit higher or are quicker to make eye contact, speak in a stronger voice. They have, through publication, reached out of themselves and begun to participate in the world in a significant way.

Diminishing the Authority of the Teacher

Workshop is also important because it begins to diminish the authority of the teacher. The student writer can become dangerously dependent on a response from a teacher. The student can learn to appeal to that one reader and to satisfy that one reader. That's too easy. The student needs to learn to appeal to many individual readers and to handle their contradictory responses. This process forces the student to turn back and decide, individually, what needs to be done to the text. Students can be addicted to a teacher, dependent on that mentor for response, but it is far harder to become addicted and dependent on a changing group of individual readers. The larger the audience the more the student can develop as an individual.

Publication

Publication is a critical, essential step in the development of every writer. The writing act is not completed until the writer has received the response of readers to a draft. At that time connection is made with other human beings who bring their lives, their experience, and their needs into contact with the writer.

Methods of Publication

Teachers too often think of publication as professional publication, when all it really means is that the writer has the opportunity to share a draft with more than one reader.

Publication is achieved when a student reads a draft to two or three other students, when a dittoed draft is shared with a class, when the student publishes in a campus publication.

Arranging for a large number of students to publish frequently can be a difficult logistical problem. In our program we want our students in Freshman English, in the sophomore writing course, and in the poetry, fiction, and non fiction writing courses within the English department to have the opportunity to publish every week if that serves the instructor's educational goals. We have been able through the years to receive support for photocopying equipment and work study students to backstop our secretarial staff.

We have more than 50 sections of Freshman English a semester. The course is a one semester requirement and each class has 26 students, so we need to be able to publish 27 copies of papers that are usually 5 pages long. We have 15 to 20 sections of sophomore composition, and more than 20 sections each semester in advanced writing courses. Publication involved 568 reams of paper at last count, and to fund this publishing operation, we have had to charge a student fee of $5.25, which is paid through the bookstore. We believe strongly that the principal text of the writing course is the student's own writing, and we feel it appropriate that students buy this text as they purchase other texts.

It is not necessary to have such an involved operation. I have taught where copying facilities are not available, and have simply required students to provide copies of their papers for workshop sessions. This can be required in the syllabus on designated dates, and they can make copies for the whole class, or the small groups, according to what is appropriate. I've also said in the syllabus that students will be required to provide workshop copies when asked, and in that case I've been able to have the students come in with enough copies whenever I think they will benefit from publication. Students can absorb this cost. There are many photocopy concerns and machines available, and they find their own way to make copies. I will accept carbon copies, of course, but most of my students have never heard of carbon paper. They print copies from their word processors or use photocopy procedures.

Varieties of Publication

I have focused on publication in one form — the written text provided for each student in the workshop group. There are other forms of publication that are effective. They include:

- *Publishing by overhead projector.* Some teachers publish text by using a projector and allowing the class to suggest changes that can be marked right on the draft by the writer. Usually teachers who have had success with this have modeled it by getting the class to help them edit a draft of their own in front of the workshop.

- *Oral publication.* The student reads the draft to the workshop group. Some writing programs have the draft read by someone else, and some programs discourage "dramatic reading" or a personal style in reading. I do not understand this. I prefer to hear the voice of the writer, so I urge students to read their texts in whatever form is natural to them.

With beginning students in a course, especially in a remedial course, I find it helpful to hear a text from each student before I see a text. These texts may be short, but they allow me and the class to hear the voice of the student before we see the bad penmanship — or bad typemanship — the spelling errors, the garbled syntax that often does not appear before our ears when we hear someone read.

With advanced students it is often helpful to have the students read, even if the audience has a written text in front of them. The reading illuminates the text.

It is not necessary for an entire text to be read. It may be helpful to have the student read just the lead or a section of the text the student thinks works particularly well — or presents a problem.

- *Publishing the original.* The original text can be published by posting it on a class bulletin board, by having it available in a box in the work-shop or in the instructor's office where it can be signed out, or by placing it on reserve in the library. The writers should, of course, have a copy to protect themselves against loss.

- *Computer publication.* As schools become increasingly computerized, students will have the ability to call up a text from another student and read it on their own word processing screen and have a copy printed out if they need hard copy. They will also be able to edit a computer copy of the original text on the screen, and with some software programs students will be able to use a split screen and edit a text so that the writer can see the original version displayed on the left and the edited version displayed on the right.

- *Publication publication.* Whenever possible students should be urged to publish outside the classroom. In many cases their copy will be edited. When it is they should bring the original as well as the edited version to show their classmates in workshop or to the instructor in conference. It's usually productive to discuss what the editor has done to the text. This is true whether it is a positive example of editing or a destructive one.

There is simply no comparison between the artificial, academic situation of classroom publication and the chance to achieve a readership of "real" people. Students feel an extraordinary sense of achievement when they reach an out-of-classroom audience. Some of the forms of publication available for students include:

Student newspapers, magazines, journals, radio and television stations.

Local newspapers, including the Letters to the Editor column.

Special editions of newspapers — vacation, skiing or surfing, auto or food sections.

Hometown newspapers.

Journals in the student's discipline. Nursing, environmental, business, engineering publications are available; in fact, there are few fields that don't have a multitude of regional and national journals.

Publications that cater to the students' hobbies — magazines or newsletters published for computer game freaks, horse owners and breeders, mountain climbers, hunters, bird watchers, and so forth.

Local and regional publications of organizations to which the students belong, such as sororities and fraternities, churches, and political parties.

Book publishers, especially local regional ones. This sounds ridiculous, but I have had students publish in books or write books that have grown out of their work in a composition class.

Newsletters and publications put out by corporations and government agencies for which students work or for which their parents work.

The Workshop Pattern

The workshop pattern should be as familiar as the conference pattern, and should follow the same sequence.

- ○ The writer COMMENTS on the draft.
- ○ The workshop members listen and READ the draft.
- ○ The workshop members RESPOND to the writer's comments and the draft.
- ○ The writer RESPONDS to the workshop members' responses.

That was *not* the workshop pattern used when I was a writing student, and it was not the pattern that I used for many years in my teaching. The normal workshop pattern was a trial by fire, in which the student's draft was subjected to as much criticism as possible by workshop members. The student's work was under attack, and the student was required to keep quiet. The writer could not establish the agenda and certainly could not defend the draft.

I learned how to keep the animals under control, to limit the comments when necessary, and to attempt to make the experience productive for the writer, but I was never comfortable with this form of teaching, although it was the principal activity outside of conferences that I performed. I kept trying to do it better, but I'm embarrassed to say I saw no other alternative to what I had been taught by my teachers, until two things happened that instructed me. I think it is important to share these experiences, because they document a kind of personal, educational research that I think is important for the teacher to understand and practice.

I had a draft of a piece about the writing process I was working on. I planned to submit it to an academic journal, but it wasn't working. The lead — the residue of more than thirty leads I attempted — didn't work, and there were other problems in the text that I could identify but not solve. I submitted it to a faculty group to which I belong, where we share our work in process. They read it ahead of the meeting, and as soon as the meeting opened one person charged in and attacked my lead.

Under attack, I defended myself. For nearly two hours my colleagues tore at the text, and I continued to fight back. They found all my weak spots, and I defended every one of them. At the end of the session I was mad at everybody in the group, angrier still at myself for being such a terrible writer, and totally discouraged with the text.

I got up the next morning to work on the text and could only fantasize tortures for my colleagues. For several days I tried to work on the text, and then I tossed it aside. But I had become more sensitive to how my students must often feel in workshop.

Then I heard two things that I might not have heard if I had not been made more sensitive. I overheard one writing teacher say, "She doesn't have the balls to publish in workshop." I was startled at such a sexist remark, and then realized how much the workshop was a macho test, a walking-on-coals, a trial by fire. And having just been burned, I was ready to be critical of it.

These experiences came together with the conference style I had been evolving. The next time that I had a workshop class I invited the student whose work was being published to speak first, saying, "How can we help you?" The student was startled, but answered, telling us very specifically the doubts she had about the draft and what she thought worked pretty well. She wanted us to tell her if the good parts worked for us and to make suggestions about how the weaker parts might be strengthened. It was the best session I could remember, and that is now the way I start every workshop: "How can we help you?"

The students do know the kind of help they want; they are often more critical than I would be — and more perceptive. They open the door to tough, constructive comments, but they are not threatened or defensive, for the writers themselves have established the agenda and the tone of the workshop session.

Students and teacher can, of course, extend the agenda and add comments on things that work and need work that the student has not mentioned. That happens and should happen, and students do not object to it, for they have had their concerns listened to and responded to. This listening and responding reinforces the constant reading and rereading the writing student must do of his or her text, and this pattern makes the workshop a constructive part of that natural process.

The Spoken Response

The tone of the spoken response to a text in process has been established in the writing conference. It is the tone of fellow writers who are willing to praise successes and share in them, and willing to point out failures and laugh at them. Each teacher will establish his or her own conference voice, and that voice will become the dominant one of the workshop.

It should be relaxed but professional, supportive but critical. There should be room to share the joy and satisfactions of writing, the pain and despair of writing. There should be a place for laughter and for a bit of fire too.

The workshop leader should listen to what is being said and how it is being said. The teacher should make sure by calling on students, if necessary, that a significant number of readers participate. Many times the teacher will know that a particular student doesn't usually participate, but may have special critical skills or a writing experience that will be helpful, and can say, for example, "Jim, you've written on the same subject. Do you have any special counsel for the writer?" Or, "Sheila, you had some problems with making the writing flow. Is there anything that helped you that might help the writer?"

The teacher stands back, but is ever alert, reading the reactions of the writer, reading the reactions of the rest of the class, making sure that no one dominates the discussion, and making sure that it doesn't get off track. Sometimes it's a good idea to sum up what has been said and check that summary with the writer. And I always invite the writer, at the end, to speak. Usually I find students summarizing themselves spontaneously and thanking the class for their help.

The Written Response

Most workshop teachers use only the oral response to a text but I find the written response to be as helpful, often more helpful. It can be a by-product of the oral workshop as I have indicated above, but I think the written workshop response should be a frequent alternative, an integral part of the writing curriculum.

The students are encouraged to comment right on a classmate's text. They can edit line by line, insert, cut, reorder, or make general comments on the back of the pages. All of the class may respond to one text, or small, heterogeneous groups may be brought together; or groups may be formed by common level, common subject, or common writing problem.

The students can give a written response as preparation for class discussion, or the written response can be done in class as a substitute for discussion. One of the most successful things I do is to bring some yellow paper to class and a stapler. I have the students staple several pages to each copy, then I have them respond to the text. In the beginning I usually set the agenda using one of these groups of questions. It may be:

○ What works?
  What needs work?

○ I would publish this because . . .

I would not publish this because . . .

I would publish this if . . .

I urge the students to read fast, the way readers will read. I read too, and add my own comments. People can sign their names, or not, and I keep the papers moving around the classroom. If anyone doesn't have a paper to read I yell out, asking for papers. Some people read slowly, some read fast, and I have to make sure there are no logjams.

At the end of the session I explain that the purpose is to get as many responses as possible. The more contradictory they are the better. It is the writer's piece of writing, and the writer has to decide for himself or herself if the advice is worth paying attention to.

I usually say something about the responses to which I pay the most attention when my own writing is criticized:

○ I pay attention to those responses which cause a shock of recognition. I tried to get away with something, and when the reader catches me I know I have to pay attention.

○ I also pay attention to the comments that seem off the wall, completely unexpected. I reject many of those, but I need to pay attention to those readings that are radically different from what I expected.

○ I pay attention to those suggestions that seem to support and help me to achieve my own purpose.

○ I pay little attention to those responses which seem to reject my purpose. In other words, I may choose to use narrative to make my point, and some readers will say that I'm not allowed to use narrative. A plague on their camels.

○ I pay attention to those points that the readers do not seem to understand. I am not writing to an ideal reader, but to a real reader.

Workshop teaching, like conference teaching, will change according to the needs of the student and the personality and the experience of the instructor. The best rule is to keep experimenting, to try different ways of encouraging responses, to invite your students to participate in designing the responses they want and need, and to invite your students to evaluate the help they get from such responses.

The Non-Student Text

It is often helpful to have workshops of published texts by well known authors. These can be texts from a reader, drafts that you have reproduced, or pieces of writing that students have found particularly effective. In some cases you may have comments that the writer has made about writing or about that particular piece of writing. Such comments are found in the sources indicated in the Appendix or in current newspapers and magazines and they may illuminate the text and take the students into the writer's workroom. They may substitute for the student's statement at the beginning of the workshop session.

In any case, the workshop should subject the published text to the same scrutiny that a draft within the class receives. It is extremely helpful for the students to examine published texts from a writer's point of view. Too often we just worship published texts, when it is more constructive to re-create the choices the writer faced in the making of the text. They should be encouraged to mark up, edit, revise and generally mess around with the text, and you should model this behavior in your own treatment of the text, not to destroy it but to reconstruct it so students will see how they can learn from examples of good writing — or bad. Never forget that the magic of a text, for example, by E. B. White, Joan Didion, or George Orwell may remain a mystery even under the most professional scrutiny, while a failed text by a poor writer may be instructive, for all its potential and the manner in which it was *un*realized is available to the student writer.

The Small Workshop

There are many good reasons to make small group or peer workshops a part of the writing curriculum. Peer workshops:

• Allow students to receive a response from several readers in a short period of time.

• Allow the instructor to schedule workshops without taking a whole class period. Small group workshops need limitations of time in the same way that conferences do. That gives the workshop meeting an intensity that students will know how to use because of the model they have in their conferences. In general I allow five minutes per student, or fifteen minutes if the group has three members, twenty minutes if it has four, twenty-five minutes if it has five. Each teacher will find the length of time most comfortable for the instructor and the students.

• Allow the students to become used to workshop without facing a whole class audience. The student learns to handle the conference, then the small group workshop, and finally the whole class workshop.

• Make it easy for the teacher to bring together students who have common subject matter to deal with or common writing problems.

• Allow the teacher to expand the audience for each writer by moving students into different groups.

- Allow the teacher to develop other teachers in the class. I establish most of my writing groups by picking the four, five or six best students and using them as group leaders, so that each student gets a chance to work with a peer who knows how to write well. I don't announce this, and my ideas of who is good may change during the semester, but I do think that I develop some associate teachers in this way, and some of them can teach a particular student better than I can.

- Allow students to see many drafts at different stages of the writing process. They can also learn to be effective editors so that they can pick up those editorial skills and apply them to their own papers.

- Diminish the authority of the teacher and increase the responsibility of the student.

All of the techniques of the workshop, oral and written, can be used to respond to the concern of the writer. The purpose of every workshop is primarily to help the writer by giving the writer test readers during the writing process.

The students must be educated, through conference model and class discussion, to the importance of workshops in their education. The writer speaks first and sets the agenda. Each writer has a chance to ask for the kind of help he or she needs.

Another technique is to have students pass their drafts to their classmates and have these test readers mark in the margins where the reader:

- Needs to know more.
- Needs to know less.
- Doesn't understand.
- Needs a word or phrase defined.
- Likes the details.
- Feels there are too many details.
- Feels there are too few details.
- Has questions that are not answered.
- Needs an example.
- Has too many examples.
- Likes the genre.
- Thinks a different genre would work better.
- Feels the sequence works.
- Feels another sequence would work better.
- Feels the pace is too fast.
- Feels the pace is too slow.
- Thinks the beginning works.

- ○ Thinks the beginning doesn't work.
- ○ Thinks the ending works.
- ○ Thinks the ending doesn't work.
- ○ Likes the voice.
- ○ Feels the voice falters.
- ○ Doesn't think the voice appropriate.
- ○ Notices incorrect spelling.
- ○ Notices inaccurate details.
- ○ Feels the language isn't used effectively.

Students, certainly in the beginning, will not be able to handle all of these concerns, and will not have the time to do a proper job unless they take the papers home between classes. That may be an interesting exercise, but make sure that they take only copies with them, and that the author has the original.

Students should be encouraged to mark up the drafts, to suggest ways of solving problems or just alternative ways of working with the text. And the writer should be reminded not to take any criticism too seriously. These are not instructions for a revision, just responses from individual readers.

Usually it is better to have the class make a list and to have one or two questions asked during each reading session.

Another way is to have the students read their classmates' drafts, answering the following questions on the back of a draft or on pieces of paper stapled to the top of the sheet.

- ○ What works?
- ○ What needs work?

The teacher can sit in on different workshop groups, but I find that I'm an interference when I do that. The students pay too much attention to me, or I intervene and talk too much, cheating them of their learning. I prefer to monitor the conferences, observing and overhearing, so that after a conference session we can discuss problems, if necessary, and so that I will have some idea of what groups work together well and don't work together well, so I can set up more effective groups next time.

Class Workshops

The class or large group workshop allows the student to reach out to a larger audience, to readers who do not know the writer's purpose, who are not familiar with the writer's subject or the writing history of this particular draft. The workshop provides an essential professional distance, a halfway house between private and public writing.

The writer, of course, should respond to the question, "How can we help you?" And the students should then read the text — or scan it if they've read it before — and respond, first of all, to the writer's agenda. Later they can add further comments. The teacher monitors the comments, times the session, and provides a summing up, if necessary.

I find that half an hour is more than enough time in workshop, even for pieces twenty pages long. There is only so much criticism any writer can handle, and twenty minutes to half an hour gives a writer an adequate serving.

It's important to remind the workshop members that the writer needs to know what works as well as what needs work. Most of us are not at all sure of what we have succeeded in doing well.

I usually publish the best papers in workshop, or I schedule everyone to publish, and let them sign up for a particular date. The point at which the class usually makes a significant breakthrough comes when I publish the best papers. It may be excruciating for me to wait weeks for a paper worthy of workshop publication, but when I get a paper that really works then the class is inspired by what a classmate has done. They begin to see subjects in their own lives and hear voices that are impressive but within their reach.

I always try to publish two or three papers at the same time, and I try to choose papers that are different so the students can share my delight in the diversity that I believe lies at the center of the writing experience. I also choose a variety of papers because most students are too eager to psych out the teacher and discover what he or she wants. I want to confuse my students, to help them see possibilities not a recipe, alternatives not an answer.

When everyone is scheduled to publish in a workshop, then you will have papers that aren't worthy of workshop discussion, and that itself can be helpful for the writer, but it does make it more difficult for the workshop members to respond in a constructive manner.

If you schedule workshops for everyone, then students know that their papers will be published in workshop. If you select certain papers, then I think it's courteous to ask the students for their permission. Another alternative is to make a rule on the syllabus that any paper can be chosen for workshop.

Workshop teaching has its own particular problems, and a few of the most common are:

- *My students won't publish in workshop.* That's not a choice. This is a writing course, and publication is an essential part of the process. An individual student may have a good reason to keep a particular draft confidential, but every student should have the opportunity to publish in a writing course and no one should be allowed to duck that responsibility.

- *The best students won't talk.* Call on them.

- *My worst students talk too much.* Give them a chance to speak. They may be learning — out loud — but make sure that many students are participating in workshop.

It's usually helpful to have the students do some written workshops. More of them are comfortable responding in writing than speaking out in class.

- *Some of my students are really discourteous and destructive.* You establish the tone of the workshop, and if you don't like what's happening you can stop it, or you can speak privately to the ones who are out of line. Usually the most destructive critics are not publishing themselves. It may be a good idea to get them up for a workshop in a hurry so they know how it feels.

- *My students just gossip.* Stop them. Have the writer set the agenda for the draft and hold to it. Keep the discussion on target. If the writer doesn't set a precise goal, set one yourself: "Let's look at the lead to see if it would make you read on. Let's talk about the leads that make you read on, the ones that don't, and why."

- *My students talk about the subject, not the way it was written.* This often happens, particularly when the subject is close to the student. It's your job to let that run for a short while, but then to bring the discussion back to the treatment of the subject, not the subject itself. You have to remember, however, that some discussion of subject is appropriate. It's helpful for the writer and the class to see those topics that attract readers.

The Post-Workshop Conference

It's a good idea to schedule conferences after a student has published in workshop. Students need an opportunity to put the experience in context. What students hear is usually much more critical than what was said, and they need an opportunity to have the instructor's help in interpreting the messages from their readers.

Remember that the writing workshop is a writing community in action. If it is not working well, it is up to the community to confront the problem and work out a solution. The workshop has not been established to satisfy the teacher's ego but to provide an essential service for the workshop members.

10 Solutions to Common Writing and Teaching Problems

Your students will teach you how to teach. Each student will present a particular challenge, and you — and the student when you practice responsive teaching — will solve the problem in front of you and move on to the next one. It will surprise you to discover how fast you develop an inventory of solutions you can draw on. Here is a starter pack of solutions that will soon be replaced by your own.

Problem Writers

Each composition teacher will begin to see a pattern of students and develop a repertoire of techniques to deal with those students. There is a danger, however, in thinking of students as types not individuals, and we must always guard against categorizing a student too quickly and too glibly. But it can be helpful to share some of the ways to respond to those students who present us with familiar challenges.

The Student Who Won't Write

Is dropped from the writing course. If it isn't possible to drop the student, an F minus is awarded — and soon.

I'm constantly amazed at the students who sign up for elective writing courses, yet do not want to write. Other people want to audit writing courses when there is nothing to observe or learn unless the student's own writing is on the line. The teacher also has an obligation to those who are revealing themselves through their writing. There can't be a double standard with some students who ante up and others who don't.

The responsible teacher naturally tries to find out why the student refuses to write and to make clear what writing is — notes and lists and other forms of predraft writing may be accepted in the early stages of the course, but without writing there is no learning and the student who does not write is not taking the course.

The Student Who Demands the Formula

Is the student who, most of all, must be kept from receiving rhetorical patterns that look like formulas and principles or suggestions that the student can turn into rules. The common misconception that writing is a matter of formula, that all the writer has to do is fill in the blanks, is so significant a misconception that it must be attacked in class discussion and conference again and again.

The student must observe, as soon as possible, drafts that are growing, organically, out of what is being said and to whom it is being said. Many of the patterns are familiar, but the patterns are not decided on in the best writing before the subject is discovered and explored. The patterns are found anew in each piece of writing.

The instructor should urge the student to be patient, and you should try to be patient with the student's frustration and desire for a simple formula. The student has been taught by other teachers that such formulas exist, and will be angry at you for holding back what you have to teach. You have to give the student enough support — which may include alternative patterns of development — so that the student can function until the student observes organic patterns evolving in the writing of classmates and the writing under the student's own hand.

The Student Who Hates to Write

Should realize that's a natural reaction, reinforced by an educational system in which writing is used for testing or punishment, or a combination of both. Any piece of writing exposes the student, and it is natural for people to be apprehensive at being revealed on the page. To many students in our society writing is a symbol of an alien authority. Writing is a weapon of government, and our students have learned to be fearful of pieces of paper that make them move out of where they are living, or put them in jail.

I think it's a good idea to fear writing. It is another way of saying that writing is important, that what you say is intimately involved with who you are, and that the message you deliver has power. I don't worry too much if my students hate to write. I hope that I can show them that writing can be fun. But many of my students and my colleagues, who at least say they hate to write, are professional writers. I think it's sad they feel that way, but they are in the majority, and it doesn't keep them from writing.

The Student Who Simply Loves to Write — And Write and Write

I'm more worried about this student, who doesn't feel the terror of the blank page and doesn't understand the importance of writing. The student who writes with a marvelous uncritical delight at what is pouring forth is occasionally charming in the same way that the person who decides to dance on the table at three in the morning may be charming. But such people are not dancers, and we are in the business of producing writers. Innocence, naiveté, and simple uncritical love of self do not make for good writing.

The nature of the writing course will eventually take care of these students, for the conference and the workshop give them readers who do not just delight in what they have said, and soon these students will lose their first love of writing. That is sad, but the love of writing can be rekindled on a firm base of craft by supportive and constructive critics within the writing community.

The Student Who Doesn't Think Writing Is Important

It is conventional to find out the student's career goal — insurance, computer science, politics, engineering, hotel management, whatever — and then bring in reports from that field which show the importance of writing or have the student interview a person in the field who has found that writing is a significant part of the job. Good enough, do it.

I have found, however, that in doing this we diminish the power of writing. It can be helpful to write an accident or nursing report, a sales letter, or a management memo, but the real value of writing is that it allows us to explore our internal and external worlds and then think about what we discover — in writing. I have taught and often directed a general composition course for years that serves business and science students, prelaw and premedical students, those in business administration and sports information, forestry and environmental studies, and the real attraction of the course for most students was not the minor skills required by their respective disciplines, which they did learn, but the power of language to illuminate their world.

Writing does not need to be justified because it can sell insurance. It does that — and much, much more.

The Student Who Won't Revise

May not need to revise. Some composition courses make a myth of the first draft, and do not tolerate revision. In other classes the pendulum swings to the opposite extreme, and revision is made to seem virtuous. The instructor should introduce the skills of revision, have revision demonstrated within the workshop, and encourage it within the assignment structure, but it does not need to be required.

The Student Who Has Another Writing Teacher

They all do. What we have to do is to encourage effective writing teachers and discourage those that are less effective. I urge my students to publish and satisfy editors who may not agree with me. I coach my students on how to respond to the writing demands of other instructors, avoiding the fact that I may disagree with the standards and assignments of other teachers. I emphasize that the writing methods they are learning may be applied to many diverse writing tasks.

Students also have roommates, parents, friends who they use as test readers, and I try not to be threatened by these competing authorities. I urge my students to show their drafts to those test readers who make them want to write. That's my test. I show my drafts to colleagues who are critical but who make me eager to get back to the writing desk, and avoid those whose criticism or praise makes me avoid further writing.

The Student Who Always Overwrites

May need some strict limitations. I make it a game, and encourage the student to say in one page what has been said in fifteen pages. I make the limitations dramatic and excessive — to make a point. And I laugh with the student at the extremity of the assignment. It is a very helpful activity to cut, and the student needs to discover it by cutting.

Students can learn a great deal from an arbitrary assignment as long as it is not an assignment for a grade, and as long as the teacher confesses its arbitrariness and explains its purpose. In teaching newswriting, for example, I will have my students perform a task designed by Professor Andrew Merton, who directs the journalism program of which I am a part. Somewhere after the students have written wordy, discursive news stories — with the best students writing the worst stories — he gives the following instructions for a four- to five-page news story.

- ○ Use only one sentence to a paragraph.
- ○ Use only two commas to a page.

It is amazing what clarity of thought and style evolves. Of course, that is not the way to write effective news style, but it is a dramatic corrective measure, and can be an instructive game.

The Student Who Always Underwrites

After working with such a student in an inductive manner, I may suggest an experiment. I will take the best paragraph or two in a draft and give the student a ridiculous goal, usually twenty-five pages. The student and the teacher can laugh about the assignment, and they will, but I find this the best corrective. In trying to fulfill this assignment the student begins to understand why the professional writer limits the subject much more than the amateur writer. Then the writer has room to develop writing that has depth and density, authority and information.

I rarely give these assignments to a class as an exercise. They are more effective when they are suggested individually. When they work then I often have the students show the class what they've done and share what they learned in doing it. If anyone else wants to try such an experiment that's fine. And if they don't want to, that's just as fine.

The Student Who Cheats

Plagiarism must be defined in the beginning of the course. But once that has been done I have little sympathy for the writer who steals other people's words. I think we have too much understanding of plagiarism by most faculty members, compounded by an administrative fear of lawsuits. I think students who cheat should receive an F and be asked to remove themselves from campus for at least a semester before they are given a second chance.

The Student Who Resists

Should be cherished and used in class as a devil's advocate. There is no one way to write, and at least on my campus the greatest problem is students who are too nice. They swallow whatever we say without the slightest sign of nausea. They do not doubt or question the text, the teacher, their classmates and, worst of all, themselves.

The Student Who Thinks You Are Such a Wonderful Teacher

Is probably inviting you to join a long line of wonderful teachers who have responded with wonderful grades. You will not know what you have taught, and your students will not know what they have learned, until long after the class is over. Simper, say "Aw shucks," blush, do whatever is appropriate when you receive flattery, but don't believe a word of it.

The Student Who Can't Spel, Punctuate and Ain't Got no Gramma

Needs to discover something worth saying and have the experience of an audience who is interested in the subject. It may take weeks to get a student to that stage where there is such a subject and in which you can express legitimate interest. It will take longer to get the student to produce a draft worthy of workshop publication. But those stages are necessary if a student is going to be persuaded that the effort to learn the language is worthwhile.

We must remember that students are not mute. They communicate within their world, and most of them do not see the need to use language correctly to make meaning. They can think, and they can talk, and they can listen. They have not seen language in their own experience as an aid to making meaning.

When they have been taught language in the past it has usually been presented as a matter of learning arbitrary rules, which seem either pointless or a matter of superficial etiquette. Many students will only take language seriously when they see that the traditions of our language can be used as a tool to help them understand their world and to share that understanding with others.

Once the students understand their need for language skills they can move very quickly on their own, using skill sheets, workbooks, or handbooks and applying what they are learning to their own evolving texts.

The Student Who Has a Tin Ear

Is the most difficult student for me to deal with. Some people do not seem to have an ear for language. They do not hear the music in speech, its pace, its rhythm, its inflection. Such students use words interchangeably, as if each word did not have its own denotation and connotation.

I find it is helpful to read at least one or two good pieces of writing in a class that includes some tin ears, because many students have not heard language read well. I point out before and after the reading that it is a kind of music. I may quote Elie Wiesel, for example, who said of the first line in the novel, "The first line sets the tone, the melody. If I hear the tone, the melody, then I have the book."

I urge my students to read aloud, and the more remedial the class the more often I have workshop sessions in which they read their pieces, or parts of their pieces, aloud. I keep reminding them in conference to read aloud, and I have them read to me, or I read their piece to them.

There is hope. Not every tin ear will improve. Some people do not hear language in the same way that some people do not have the coordination to make a tennis racquet meet the tennis ball — or to run through traffic without stumbling — but most people can learn to do both, and many students are simply inexperienced in using oral language to help them with the music of written language. For those students improvement is possible in a short period of time. And a few students make enormous strides in a short period of time. In fact, one teacher recently told me she "had never met a true tin ear, just writers who were scared stiff."

The Student Who Doesn't Care

May be hiding a great deal of caring behind a protective mask of indifference. Or may simply not care. The best way to find out is by challenging the student to find something the student wants to write about, and to respond to the student when the student writes with honesty and vigor, even if the work needs a great deal of improvement.

The Student You Don't Like

I'm lucky; this rarely happens to me. But there are personality conflicts, and I no longer try to blame myself for them. I make an honest and professional effort to like my students, because liking — respecting — is at the basis of the best student-teacher relationship. But I do not expect all my students to like me, and I don't expect myself to like all my students. All I have to do is to be fair and professional.

The Student You Like Too Much

Professional distance is built in between the student that you don't like and yourself. It's harder to achieve that distance when you feel a special identification with a student. I don't think that you have to have an enormous distance between you and the people who are learning with you. I feel that I can be quite close to many students, without our closeness affecting the relationship. This often happens when we are teaching graduate students, who are colleague teachers one hour and colleague students the next. It's a simple matter of professionalism. If you're worried about being too close, step back. You're the teacher. You're in charge.

The Student Who Needs a Therapist

Should get one. You are a writing teacher, not a therapist. You can re-spond to the writing of a student who may have serious personality problems, but you are not qualified to deal with those problems off the page, or to make suggestions of what the student should do about her husband, his mother, her husband's lover, his girlfriend, her childhood, his future. Whenever you see someone you think has serious problems you should take another step back.

This doesn't mean that you show no sympathy when a student writes about a death in the family or the pain of divorce. Of course you can sympathize, but when the student needs more than sympathy and understanding, when the student needs treatment, that's someone else's territory.

The Student Who Isn't Learning

Should have the opportunity to discuss the problem with you. One of the greatest advantages of conference teaching is that both you and the student know what's going on. One of the greatest disadvantages is that you both know when nothing is going on. You shouldn't be surprised. Education is a difficult, complex, individual business. Our students come to us with a great load of intellectual and emotional baggage. We should not be surprised that it is difficult for our students to learn.

In conference teaching, however, we discover that learning isn't tak-ing place early on, while in conventional classes most teachers don't know it until the final exam. The best thing to do is to involve the stu-dent in the situation. "I don't think we're getting anywhere. I seem to be failing you as a teacher, and you seem to be failing me as a student. What are we doing wrong? What's going on? What should be going on?"

The Student Who Writes Better than You Write

There are lots of these in my classes. Get out of the way. Do nothing that interferes with their development as writers.

Many of the best writers do not know they are the best. One reason they are good is that they are extremely critical and therefore they feel inadequate and rarely write to their own excessively high standards. Praise them, support them, encourage them, learn from them, and take credit for what they have learned on their own.

You will develop your own patterns of problem students and your own pattern of response, but never forget that you are dealing with individuals, and begin to worry when your conferences become too easy, when you know what your student will say and what you will respond before anyone has spoken. When that happens, concentrate on what your students are really saying, what the text is saying, and focus on drawing responses from your students. Stop teaching so much. Shut up, sit down and learn from your students and their drafts.

Writing Problems

Each writing problem is discovered by the student in its own context. We should never forget to have the student define the problem and then propose solutions. I am constantly surprised that students in remedial classes will often propose the solutions practiced by professional writers. Those solutions are, however, much more valid when they are suggested by the individual student or by the writing workshop than when they are presented as lessons by the master. If the students propose them, they discover in that process that they can identify, define, and solve writing problems.

When you start to teach, however, you feel a great emptiness. What follows are a few of the solutions taught me by the study of the writing process; by teachers, editors, and colleagues; by myself at my writing desk; and by my students. You will see that most are common sense. Seize on that. You know more about teaching writing than you realized.

Most of these are questions you can ask or suggestions you can make in conference. Remember that it is primarily your students' responsibility to identify their problems and — individually and in groups — to propose solutions. If they do this they will learn problem-identifying and problem-solving techniques they will carry with them all their lives.

Subject

○ What makes you mad?
○ What worries you?
○ What do you know that someone else needs to know?
○ What's your most powerful memory?
○ What would you like to learn?
○ What is important to you?
○ Who is important to you?
○ What would you like to explore?
○ What do you enjoy?
○ What do you keep thinking about?
○ What would you like to know about yourself?
○ What would you like to know about others?
○ What would you like to know about your government?

○ Who would you like to interview?

○ What would you like to observe?

Development

○ Pick the single most important point in the piece, eliminate every-thing else, and develop that point.

○ Imagine that you know nothing about the subject. Write down every question you'd want answered. Answer them.

○ Free-write as fast as you can, for as long as possible, to see what you might have to say about the subject.

○ List all the people, institutions, and resources that might tell you something about the subject. Use them.

Organization

○ Write down the five questions the reader must have answered. Put the questions in the order the reader will ask them. Answer them.

○ If you have a draft, cut it apart, paragraph by paragraph. Spread the paragraphs out on a table, a bed, or the floor and rearrange the paragraphs until they are in an order that takes the reader from be-ginning to end.

○ Write in the margin of a draft how each paragraph advances the meaning. If it doesn't, cut it.

○ Write what the piece means in one sentence. Make sure that each paragraph relates to that sentence.

○ Draw a map of the piece, showing where the reader will start and end.

○ Write down what the reader should conclude at the end. Work back-wards to make sure everything in the piece moves the reader in that direction.

○ Use subheads for the main points in the piece. Order them so they serve the reader the information the reader needs when the reader needs it. Fill in the spaces between subheads. (This is the way most of this chapter was organized and written.)

○ Ask someone else what they would want to know about the subject. Answer their questions.

○ Use a device — a calendar, a clock, a pattern of problem and solu-tion, narrative — to create a skeleton for a draft.

Point of View

○ List the different points of view from which the information can be observed. Choose one.

○ Tell the story from the point of view of the person most responsible for making events happen.

○ Tell the story from the point of view of the person most affected by the events.

○ Be personal. Speak out.

○ Look at the story from the past. From the future. Right now.

Genre

○ Choose the genre or form most often used to make your point. For example, argument for argument, story for story.

○ Choose the opposite genre to make your point. For example, story for argument, argument for story.

○ Study the basic elements of a genre and focus on just one point to get started. For example, in narrative you might focus on character, letting place, plot, theme, and so forth take a back seat. In argument you might focus on structure, not worrying in the beginning about style, documentation, or audience.

Purpose

○ Why should I write this?

○ Why should anyone read it?

○ Why will this serve or help anyone?

○ What should a reader do after reading it?

○ What should a reader think after reading it?

○ What should a reader feel after reading it?

○ What difference will the piece make?

Authority

○ What will make the reader believe what I have to say?

○ Where does the weight of the piece rest?

○ Who is the authority for what is being said? The authorities?

○ What different ways can the authority for the piece be established? First person: "I was there"? Fact? Statistic? Quoted experts? Quoted documents? Reader identification? Authoritative voice? Logical structure?

○ Focus on one authority?

○ Use analogy to reader's own experience?

Commitment

○ Why should I write this?

○ What will I learn by writing this?
○ What will I accomplish by writing this?
○ Whom will I influence by writing this?
○ What may I change by writing this?
○ What will I experience or feel by writing this?

Audience

○ Who needs to know this?
○ Who would like to know it?
○ Who doesn't want to know it, but should?
○ Who is responsible for what I'm writing about?
○ Who is affected by what I'm writing about?
○ Role-play a reader to find out what the reader needs to know.
○ Interview readers to find out what they need to know.
○ Read or show a draft to readers to find out what questions they have. What questions are answered. How they react.

Documentation

○ List all the forms of documentation — quotations, statistics, anecdotes — that might support your case. Choose the ones to use.
○ List all the evidence that makes you believe what you have to say. Include it.
○ List the kinds of evidence that will persuade the unbelieving reader. Use that evidence.
○ List your main points, and then list the different forms of documentation that might be used to support each point.
○ Consider the one that would support the main point to be made.

Distance

○ Imagine you are a photographer. How close can you get to the subject? How far back and still see it? What is the point in between that will help the reader see it most clearly?
○ How distant should the style be? Chatty? Intimate? Conversational? Objective? Professional? Authoritative?
○ List the main points, then decide where the camera should move in close or stand back.
○ Refer to the purpose of the piece and decide what distance will help fulfill that purpose.
○ Decide what the piece means, and then choose a distance that will make that meaning clear to the reader.

Pace

○ Is the reader being rushed? Being confused by too much information? Given too little time to absorb each point?

○ Does the piece evolve so slowly that the reader will be bored? Stop
reading? Think of other things? Forget the last point before the next
one is made?

○ Does the pace change where it should, pulling the reader forward
with energy to a main point, then giving the reader some time to
absorb that point?

○ Are there places where the piece drags?

○ Are there points made so fast the reader will pass right over them?

Proportion

○ Is there an effective portion of information to support each point?

○ Is there an effective and pleasing balance of space given to each section of the piece?

○ Do those points that need space to be developed get it?

○ Are those points that can be developed quickly, developed quickly?

○ Does the amount of space given to each point reflect the importance
of each point?

○ Read the piece backwards to make sure the ending hasn't been
rushed and the first part of the piece overdeveloped.

Superficiality

○ Does the reader have enough information to be satisfied?

○ Is the piece spread too thin? Does it try to cover too much? Should
the piece focus on one part of the subject and dig into it deeply?

○ Is the piece too glib? Does it read too easily, sliding over the surface?

○ Is the piece too simple? Would it be better to reveal the complexity
of the subject?

○ Are complications, complexities, problems, contradictions avoided
or left out?

○ Does the reader see the piece in all its dimensions?

○ Does the reader understand the background of the piece? The impli-
cations of the piece?

○ Is the piece full of jargon, clichés, stereotypes, generalities, abstractions?

Excess

○ Read the piece quickly, putting brackets around anything that could
be cut. Cut.

○ Is the same thing said two, three, or four places in the piece? Say it once, where the reader needs it said, and say it well.

○ Is the something said, then repeated, and repeated? Say it once. Say it well.

○ Is the piece wordy: full of the passive voice; extra words such as "very," "that," "quite"; the verb "to be"; paragraphs that begin with dependent clauses; and meaningless phrases, "more than likely," "in the near future," "at this point in time"?

○ Does the piece start as near the end as possible? Background information can be appreciated by the reader only at that point in the piece when the reader needs it.

Dullness

○ Be more specific.

○ Use quotations.

○ Use dialogue.

○ Put people in the piece.

○ Reveal the people in action.

○ Put the people in a place.

○ Reveal the people interacting with each other in a place. Write in scenes.

○ Use anecdotes.

○ Vary the lengths of paragraphs and sentences, using the shorter ones for points of emphasis.

○ Cut as many adjectives and adverbs as possible.

○ Use concrete nouns.

○ Use active verbs.

○ Use all your senses: make the reader see, hear, touch, taste, smell the subject.

Closure

○ Does the piece get anywhere? Where should it get?

○ Does the reader have a feeling of completeness?

○ What information at the end would give the reader a feeling of completeness?

Teaching Problems

Teaching is a matter of experiment. This isn't heart surgery. Our students have survived a great deal of bad teaching and another experiment that doesn't work won't do them in. Here are some responses I have developed over the years, but I'm continuing to experiment, and by the time you read this I may have another response. Use these comments to spark your own reactions.

My Students Don't Just Have Writing Problems — They Have Problem Problems

If students are allowed to write on subjects that are important to them, they are likely to write on personal subjects or on subjects in which they have a personal investment. And if you are meeting with such students one to one you may wonder if you are playing the role of therapist.

Don't.

We are not trained as therapists, and we should be careful not to assume that role. If you believe a student needs professional help you may be able to find a tactful way to suggest it, or you may be able to turn to a professional to find out how to encourage the student to get help. But you are not in a position to offer that help yourself. You are a writing teacher, and you must maintain an appropriate distance from the student so that you can serve as a teacher of writing.

But.

Writing is therapy. I tried to avoid that issue as a writing teacher, mostly because I had colleagues who accused some of us of using writing as therapy. I can no longer avoid the fact that writing is therapy — for me and for my students. We write because we need to write, and the act of writing rarely solves our problems, but it is a way of dealing with problems and of achieving a momentary distance from them. The act of writing about even the most painful subjects — in my case the death of a daughter — seems both necessary and therapeutic.

I do not encourage my students to use writing as therapy, and I certainly do not assign or encourage personal writing, but neither do I avoid it or prohibit it when it occurs, for I have found that my students learn best when they feel strongly about a subject. Many times the subject they feel strongly about is objective and distant from them. It is not personal, and that is fine too. Some writing courses seem to stack the cards against the student who is unwilling to make public confession. The student who is writing about something personal has to achieve enough distance from the subject to be able to say something significant about it, and this, in a curious way, is exactly what happens to students when they write outside of school. For most of the time the writing problems of professionals are a closeness to the subject, an overabundance of information about a marketing plan, for example, and too personal a commitment to one marketing strategy. The problems that the professional has are remarkably close to the problems of the student with a personal subject. Therefore, I allow my students to use writing as therapy, if not me as a therapist.

As much as possible I concentrate my comments on the writing, and I have one significant thing I keep saying each time they write, "Drop this subject if it's causing you pain. If it feels good to write about this, go ahead, but if it doesn't, stop. You won't be penalized for starting a new subject." The student needs that escape route, but I do find that few need to take it.

My Students Want _Me_ to Teach

It's the only model they have had. They think teaching means military instruction — by the numbers. We are all more comfortable with what is familiar but unpleasant than with what is unfamiliar. Our students need to be told again and again why we are teaching as we are teaching, and we need to have the patience to continue in our method until they have enough experience to feel comfortable with it. For some students that may take most of the course, and some may never feel comfortable about this teaching style. So be it. They'll have plenty of experience with the opposite.

My Students Expect Me to Correct Their Papers

Why not? It makes it a lot easier that way. And you, the teacher, will learn a great deal. The students? Well, they may not learn so much, but they won't have to do any thinking, and they'll be out having a good time while you're sitting in your cloistered cell doing their work for them.

They Don't Have Anything to Say

They don't _think_ they have anything to say. That's a significant difference. We have to make ourselves a reader for whom they will want to write, and we do this by having a sincere interest in them, what they know, what they have experienced, what they can teach us.

It will take some students many weeks to realize they have something to say. You will have to question them about their world, and surround them in workshop with papers from classmates that have been written out of the knowledge and experience of their peers. If you are patient, and if you do not rush in with a premature topic or assignment, they will come to find out that they have something to say. More than that, they will find out that they have something they need to say.

I Care More About the Drafts than My Students Do

Many students have not had pride in their work, and I sometimes feel that I have more investment in my students' papers than they do. Robert Frost allegedly once asked a class after they had passed in poems to him if they wanted him to read them. They were polite or apprehensive and didn't respond. So he tossed the poems away in front of the students, demonstrating that they should have pride in their work. If you sense that your students do not have pride in their work, then you should discuss that problem in conference, and perhaps in class.

They Think Their Draft Is Finished

It may be. Finished for them, if not for you. You should mention areas that may need more work, and even in some cases demand it. But it's usually best if you simply plant the seed of doubt by asking a question or two.

The student who has a "finished" draft that isn't should have the opportunity for publication in small group or whole-class workshop to find out if test readers agree that the piece of writing is finished.

What They Write, They Love

We don't want to make the students hate what they do, and I certainly hope that we don't make students lose the joy of making. But when students have to talk about their writing with an instructor and with classmates, most of them soon gain distance on the text and see that it has both strengths and weaknesses. And when they deal with the weaknesses and the strengths on the page they feel the joy of making again.

I Don't Know What to Say About a Really Good Paper

It may be hard for one trained in critical studies, but it may not be necessary to say anything. You may simply take delight in the paper and share your delight with the student. Few of us would appreciate a detailed critical analysis of dinner by a guest. Praise and gratitude from our guests usually suffice. Yet we feel we have to give the student criticism.

It isn't our job to find something to say about the piece anyway. It's the writer's job. When the writer speaks we may have something to say. I find that my students are often more critical and frequently better critics than I am. They should be. They've worked with the piece closely. But they may not be critical; that's fine. Send it off to get published, pass it in for a grade, do whatever is appropriate, and get going on another piece.

They Think It's All Hopeless

They are sincere; it does seem hopeless to the student — and sometimes to the teacher. The task is to get the student to make just one step, to identify one element that can be worked on. In the beginning that is often something off the page — a topic that interests the student, a message the student wants delivered to the reader, a meaning the student sees in experience, a way of developing the story, an emotion the student feels when confronting the topic. Any of those things, and many more, can give the student a handhold so that the writer can begin to move forward.

I Don't Know What to Say About a Hopeless Paper

You try to draw out of the student what made the student think that the paper had potential in the beginning. You want to work with the student's vision of the paper to find out the potential that is there for the student. Too often as a writer I see a potential the student does not see, and the student keeps trying to satisfy or to deliver my paper to me. I have to keep turning the thing around so that the student is teaching me what may make the paper work.

Some Students Aren't Improving, And I Don't Know What to Do

Discuss it with them. I find that my students usually know they are not learning and can help me find a way I can help them learn.

They Don't Know What I Want

I want to be surprised. That's what I tell my students, and they distrust me — at first. But once they see me demonstrating my delight at surprises — the unexpected phrase, the unexpected meaning, the unexpected insight, the unexpected voice — they begin to trust me. It helps to share a paper from the class that is good — and obviously different from the predictable Freshman English paper on the same subject. Students may be inspired by such a paper and start to trust themselves, to take chances, to do what they think should be done with the piece of writing, not so much second-guessing teacher, but first-guessing themselves in the text.

They Think They Have Different Writing Problems Than I Think They Have

Pay serious attention to what they consider their writing problems — but not overly serious attention. You're the teacher, and they deserve honesty from you. Don't be coy. If you see a different problem than they do, then mention it.

My Colleagues Think I'm Crazy to Teach by Conference

Naturally. It is not the traditional way to teach, and most academics are conservatives. They are the defenders of tradition. This can get confusing for the most traditional English literature professor, because the most traditional of my colleagues admire everything British in education, and that involves a tutorial system that is first cousin — or closer — to conference teaching.

My Colleagues Don't Want to Teach by Conference

I think we have to understand that many teachers are threatened with any change, fearing that it might involve them. And conference teaching is exposed. It brings the teacher into direct, frequent contact with the student. That is absolutely terrifying for many people. We should feel sorry for people who have chosen to be educators and are frightened of personal contact with the students. And we should go our own way, teaching in the way we find best for us without forcing our colleagues to teach the same way, or allowing them to force us into a way of teaching we find inappropriate.

My Administrators Won't Allow Me to Teach by Conference

Try an experiment. Administrators love experiments in education. Experiment sounds progressive, and an experiment gets the administrator off the hook. Propose an experiment in teaching writing: "I've just heard about teaching by conferences, probably the idea of some fat full professor, probably wouldn't work with our students, but I thought I might try it just to see what happens." The administrator doesn't have to make much of a commitment to tolerate that. No huge curriculum change is taking place, no new program is being established. Just a little old experiment.

    If you get results, the administrator will clamber up on the bandwagon. Then, if you want a program, propose an experimental program, a pilot project, just to see what happens . . . Give the administrator an opportunity to take credit for what you have already done, allow the chairperson or dean or vice president or chancellor or provost or president a chance to bet on a sure thing, and brag to the dean or the vice president and so forth so they can brag to the board of trustees or parents or alumni. Keep your administrators busy bowing and bragging and you'll have time to get on with your own teaching and learning.

    How do I know this? I was an administrator.

11 Answers to Questions You May Ask Yourself

Self-doubt is a condition of life for composition teachers. We can never be sure if we have taught and our students have learned. I find my own self-doubt boring, but necessary, and I am always astonished when colleagues are confident they have taught well and their students have learned, and amused when my colleagues are confident they have taught well and it is entirely the students' fault that they have not learned.

We must confront our self-doubt, be honest about it but not paralyzed by it, and this chapter is constructed of questions I have asked myself, with answers I have learned from my own experience and my colleagues' experience and have to tell myself from time to time.

What Do I Do if the Students Rise Up and Charge?

They won't — even when they should. The most serious problem is student passivity, not student action. When I first started to teach I wandered into the wrong class. I was lecturing full speed ahead when a professor from the Spanish department showed up late for his advanced class. Not one student had indicated that it wasn't a section of Freshman English. Don't fear that they will challenge you, worry that they won't.

What if I Don't Know the Answer?

Admit it. See if someone else in the class knows the answer. If they don't, you can promise to look it up. There is nothing that will earn the trust of a class more quickly than a teacher who admits that he or she doesn't know the answer to every question. I worry when my doctor confuses himself with God, and am comforted when he seeks a second or third opinion. The composition teacher is not an authority, but a senior learner, still learning.

Should I Sit, Stand, Perch, or Tap Dance?

Most of us start teaching standing behind a lectern. One of my colleagues used to lug armloads of books to class and build a little fort behind which he could teach. When I started teaching I had to have a lectern. I think I felt I could pick it up and use it for protection the way a lion tamer uses a kitchen chair. Another colleague confessed he took a lectern home and practiced letting go. My problem was the cords on the window shades. I'd stand over by the window lecturing — in a writing course! — and get my right hand all tied up in the cord and then would dismiss the class early so I had privacy in which to untangle myself.

As we become more experienced most of us move out from behind the desk and lean against it. We may even hop up on the desk and dangle our legs — thumpity thrumpity thrump thump our heels keep hitting the desk.

Eventually we teach sitting down, behind the desk at first, beside the desk next, and finally in front of the desk with our students in a circle. This transition from teaching standing up to teaching sitting down is significant. We may all need the superficial trappings of authority at first. We may need to be overprepared, then prepared, and finally underprepared, so that we are able to listen to our students and draw the answers out of them. At first we tell, and then we learn to listen; at first we teach, and at the end we learn how to get out of the way and give the students the opportunity to teach each other and themselves.

Should I Wear Jeans, Cut my Hair, Shave my Beard?

The school will have something to say about this, but within those limitations everything we should do in the classroom and in conference should be a process of becoming ourselves. We should not dress or teach or behave or think like someone else, but find ways that make it possible for us to be natural in the unnatural position of teacher. We may need at first to be performers, but eventually we should integrate our public and private personalities so that we are whatever we are in front of our students.

Now That I've Told Them Everything I Know About Writing What Do I Do with the Next Forty-Five Minutes?

This is the first problem of most writing teachers. They lecture the class on the qualities of good writing, think that most of the hour has passed, and discover that they have used up only five minutes, or six, or four. The normal academic solution is to stretch it out, to say what can be said in five minutes over a whole semester. It is possible to do this. I had the problem in my first classes in journalism, and I learned to inflate a few sentences of advice into more than two hundred hours of lecture over two semesters. I was quite proud of myself, and I was developing a modest reputation as a good lecturer. But some perversity in my personality caused me to give a final exam in May and then give the same final to my beginning students in September. The students in September did not have the benefit of hundreds of hours of lectures, but they did better than the students in May. It gave me pause, and I began to learn how to teach — without lectures.

We do have to develop what we know so that the audience will know it, and we have important things that have to be said, and said again and again. But in the composition course there *is* little that can be said effectively in advance of writing. And what needs to be said will be said in classroom and in conference in response to individual student work. And when it is said by other students and by the writer it will be heard more clearly than if it is said by the teacher.

I Told Them. Why Didn't They Learn?

Learning a skill depends on experience, and there is almost always a delay between knowing what to do and being able to do it. We know how to drive before we can ease a car out of skid. This delay is frustrating for the teacher, but even more frustrating for the student.

I tell my students each semester: "You knew how to ride a bicycle before you rode one. Someone had given you advice, and you had seen other people ride bicycles. It looked easy, if scary, but when you got up on the seat and they got you started and let go, most of you found you couldn't do what you thought you knew how to do. Some of you learned to ride in days, and some took weeks. But it didn't make any difference. Six weeks later everyone was riding bicycles, and you couldn't tell which ones learned right away and which ones took weeks to learn. Some of you will learn to write faster than others, but it won't make any difference. At the end of the semester no one will know who wrote well right away and who took longer to learn."

Why Aren't They Paying Attention?

Most students affect a casual air of indifference. It is a shield against their ignorance, but it is discouraging to the teacher. Don't assume that you can tell who is learning from the look on a face. It is important, however, to involve the students. They should be talking, responding, presenting, discussing, and you should be the best listener in the class-room.

How do you get them involved?

○ They publish their drafts.
○ They respond to their drafts.
○ They read.
○ They respond to what they read.
○ They tell about their experiences with the writing process.
○ They respond to each other's experiences with the writing process.
○ You call on them, and listen.
○ You call on others to respond to them, and listen to them.
○ They respond in writing and share their responses. This is most important. If they won't talk, make them write responses to their papers and share what they have written.

I received very good advice from my colleague, Tom Williams, when I first started to teach: "Wait for an answer to a question. They can't stand silence. They'll break before you do."

I found it was true and so I wait them out, give them time to think and to respond. I have to hold myself back and not rush in, giving my own brilliant response to my own brilliant questions.

What Do I Do with my Hands?

When I first started to teach and speak in public my hands would grow and grow and grow, and I didn't know what to do with them. Finally I saw myself on film, and I found that they fluttered around like great white birds when I spoke, and I had to bring them back home and hold them down, being very careful to use them only when a gesture was necessary to make a point.

Of course teachers are performers, natural performers, I hope, but it takes a while to learn to hold a conversation with a large group. When we teach writing we expect our students to learn one thing at a time. In learning to speak in public the same rule holds true. Work on one thing and then move on to the next. Some of the things I had to learn are:

• *Speak slowly.* Nervousness makes us speak faster, and we think we are speaking normally when we're racing along. One of my students told me in a teaching evaluation that I spoke so fast it gave him a headache.

• *Give the students some room.* My tendency is to cover each point so fast that there's no time for the students to absorb a point and ask questions about it. If you move too fast you'll zip right by them, and if you move too slowly they'll go to sleep. You have to keep reading the class and adjust your pace of presenting to their pace of absorption.

- *Be energetic, but not too energetic.* It's important for the teacher to bring energy to the classroom: commitment, intensity, involvement. At first when I taught, that energy was represented by pacing and moving about. Now I'm able to sit down and let what I have to say and how I say it carry the energy into the classroom.

- *Summarize.* In any classroom, but especially in the responsive classroom, it is the responsibility of the teacher to sum up what has been said and to put it in context. It is often a good idea for the teacher to summarize — or have a student summarize — what has been accomplished at the end of a class or workshop session, and that's good counsel for a conference as well.

- *Prepare.* The teacher should have an agenda for each class, at least a list of what may happen, what may need to be done, what may need to be accomplished, what may need to be said. I have to have this list in front of me. The more experienced I become the more I am able to respond and take advantage of the surprise of what the class says it needs. But I need to have my own agenda in case there are no surprises.

Do not forget that all the writing you do, all the writing you read, all the responses you hear in conference and in workshop are part of your preparation. And as the class evolves all of their experience is part of their preparation. It's your job to weave this experience into a meaningful whole by reminding them of another workshop or a particular paper, or what someone said that reinforces a significant point.

- *Make eye contact.* Make sure that you are seeing each student. Many teachers become focused on one part of the room, the front rows or the back, the left side of the classroom or the right side. You have to keep making individual eye contact with the students in the classroom to keep them involved and to read them, so that you know when to call on them, when to summarize, when to move on, when to repeat, when to start a new activity. This comes with experience. At first you have to do this rather arbitrarily, but as you gain more experience you'll become aware of the significance of what you're seeing as you keep your eyes moving around the classroom.

Should I Encourage Everyone?

Certainly. The encouragement, however, must be on a solid basis. We should not patronize our students by encouraging work that does not deserve encouragement. We do not offer false encouragement, say that bad work is good, speak of potential we do not observe, but our job in beginning writing courses is to encourage our students on the basis of what they have accomplished. If they haven't accomplished anything it's our responsibility to create situations where they can accomplish and earn our justified respect for what they have done.

Do I Have to Cover Everything About Writing?

No. By covering everything we can suffocate our students by covering them with a blanket of superficial information. All you need to teach your students is what they need to know to write the next draft better than the one before.

How Do I Plan a Beginning Composition Course?

There is no one way to plan any course. The plan must depend on your needs, your students' needs, and the limitations of the program in which you function. Here are some guidelines that can help:

- Schedule conference time for each student.
- Schedule deadlines for students to produce drafts.
- Schedule workshop time in which the students will receive peer response to their drafts.
- Consider a writing text or a reader that will support your approach.
- Schedule times for discussion of common writing problems and their solution and discussion of what has been revealed by the students' drafts and any other texts used in the course.

How Do I Plan Special Purpose and Advanced Courses?

All special purpose courses can be built on the same framework in which the emphasis is on the student writing and the class and the teacher responding to that writing.

- *Advanced composition.* The only difference is that the students are advanced. Their papers may be longer, and the problems they face in their writing will be more sophisticated. They should be able to teach themselves more effectively than beginning students.

- *Creative writing.* Every writer I know objects to that term, for it implies a special status for certain forms of writing over others. Because of that students come to the course feeling that poetry and fiction are somehow less disciplined, less demanding, and freer than basic composition. The opposite is true. Poetry is the highest form of writing; it distills truth into a fragment of language; it requires great craft and deserves tough, demanding, critical reading. The standards go up, not down. The same is true of fiction.

- *Writing about literature.* The student needs an introduction to a variety of critical approaches to literature, and then needs the experience of frequent writing, applying those approaches to a text that is known by the instructor and the class, so that the conference and workshop sessions can respond to the particular problems of writing critical prose about a specific piece of literature.

- *Journalism.* Students of journalism need to write frequently about real events under strict limits of time and space. They need to know how to apply the writing process so that they can select the significant from an abundance of insignificant information and order it into a structure that informs the reader. Whenever possible they should have the experience of publishing what they write in campus and off-campus publications, so that they are covering real events for real readers.

- *Business writing.* The instructor should see examples of what the students are expected to write, but the teacher should not be limited to those examples. The danger in business writing is that the students will be taught to fill in the blanks in a few stereotypical forms. What business writers in school and outside need to know is a writing process that is adaptable to many of the tasks demanded of a writer in business. The focus should be on the process, although the student should have experience applying the process to those specific tasks.

- *Science and technical writing.* These are closely related to business writing, in that forms of presentation are often overemphasized and the process of gathering, developing, and clarifying information is ignored. Students need to have a basic process of writing, and they need to have experience applying that process to a variety of specific tasks.

- *Prelaw and premedical writing.* Students in such programs need a basic process that they will be able to use when they face the demands of their professional training. What are those demands? The ability to observe and select significant information from an abundance of insignificant information, and then present it to a reader with specificity, brevity, structure, and clarity.

How Can I Teach Older Students?

More easily than younger students. Older students often come to us with a feeling of insecurity. They believe it is harder to learn when they are older. (Older can mean any age from twenty-five to eighty-five.) This may be true in a ballet class or a class in astrophysics, but I have not found it true in a class in composition. Older students have a decided advantage and they need to know it. They have so much more experience to draw on, experience that is far enough in the past that they have the perspective and distance to make use of it.

How Can I Teach Writing in a Short Summer Course?

I think that the quarter system, with its short term, seriously limits the opportunity students have to learn what they need to know and to practice. When we learn a skill there is a significant delay between the time we know what we need to do and the time when we can actually do it. One of my colleagues, Dr. Thomas Carnicelli, did a study that showed that the students made significant breakthroughs approximately three-quarters of the way through the composition course. This is probably true in every course, no matter how long, but I do think that when we go from 15 weeks to 10 to 8 to 6 to 5 to 4 to 3 to 2 to 1 significant time is lost. I have taught at just about every one of those time limits, and have done many professional workshops that are less than a week long. The shorter terms do allow more time for each class and therefore the intensity of instruction is increased, but there is serious loss in time for reflection between classes.

If you have to teach writing in a short period of time make sure that the majority of the time is spent with the students writing and receiving response to their writing. There is a tendency to try to tell students more whenever a course is made shorter, but they can't absorb it. They have to have time to write, receive response, reflect, and write again. The compromise has to be in the direction of shorter pieces of writing, writing within the class, response within the class, and a chance to write again immediately.

How Can I Teach Special Courses for Corporations and Other Organizations?

I have found that such audiences are exciting. They are motivated, and they are bright. They come ready to work, and they will practice what you preach. The danger is that their employers or the students themselves will think that you should be teaching spelling, grammar, mechanics, usage, specific rhetorical forms, and even graphic presentation first. It is important to get them writing immediately and allow them to experience a writing process that they can then apply to the needs they now have and the needs they do not yet know they will have in the future.

Should I Accept Papers from Other Courses?

This sounds good, and occasionally it's worked for me, but I find it a hazardous enterprise. The assignment from another teacher and the standards of another teacher may be radically different from your own. And if there is a controversy the student suffers. I prefer not to accept papers from other courses, but I am more than willing to consult with my students about how what we are learning in the composition class can be applied to writing tasks outside the class.

How Can I Motivate my Students?

I'm not sure that you can motivate another student, but some of the things I do will, I hope, make writing as exciting for my students as it is for me. Some of those things include:

- Showing an interest in the student's potential when that is justified.
- Showing an interest in the student's accomplishment when that is justified.
- Accepting the student's own writing goals — producing brochures for hotels — as seriously as any other student's goals, and helping that student achieve the goal.
- Sharing my excitement with my own writing.
- Sharing my enthusiasm for things I have read outside of class.
- Sharing my enthusiasm for things I have read within class.
- Connecting the writing process with other processes, such as scientific experimentation, athletic practice, engineering design, theater rehearsal, computer programming.

How Do I Advise a Student Publication?

The adviser of a student publication should not be a censor or an editor. There are guidelines that help support the students without interfering with their learning or without taking on their responsibilities for what is published. The guidelines are:

- Establish regular critique sessions that are held as soon as possible after the publication has come out. All the staff members should attend these sessions, and in the beginning you should give an objective, professional response to the publication. There is no threat of censorship, and you should be direct, tough, demanding, but respond to what works as well as to what doesn't work. Your remarks should encourage discussion, but there should be limited attention given to excuses and apologies. Your focus is on what was published. These sessions are often as educational as a class, but I do not think that you should give academic credit for such meetings. If you give credit you have power and, therefore, authority, and all that adds up to the danger of censorship and editorial responsibility.
- You should be available to the editors of the publication at their initiative. If it's a newspaper, this may mean an occasional call in the middle of the night, but better that than a libel suit later. You

need to be available to the editors and staff members on a regular basis at their initiative, so that when there is a crisis you'll know each other and have a working relationship that allows you to point out problems and alternatives. You should not make their decisions for them.

○ The students should define the problem and propose its solutions. You should monitor these discussions and contribute only when it is absolutely necessary.

Is There a Writing Teacher Profession?

There certainly is, and you should be part of it. It is important for you to know what is going on beyond your own campus and to develop colleagues who are facing problems similar to yours and solving them in different ways.

The teaching of composition is an academic discipline that has expanded and grown extraordinarily in the past two decades. It has developed its own research and scholarship. It has a vigorous group of people who are concerned about students and concerned about writing. I have found this academic community remarkably open and stimulating. It has meant a great deal to me to learn about writing and the teaching of writing with colleagues across the English-speaking world, and sometimes with colleagues from the non-English-speaking world.

Writing teachers should belong to the professional organizations appropriate to what they are teaching. For college teachers this means the Conference on College Composition and Communication (CCCC), a group within the National Council of Teachers of English (NCTE). Secondary school teachers and elementary school teachers have their own groups within the NCTE. Creative-writing-program faculty should belong to Associated Writing Programs (AWP). There are also groups for community college teachers, teachers of technical writing, and teachers of just about any academic specialty in which we are involved.

I think it's also helpful to belong to state and regional organizations and to set up special meetings in an area where colleagues in different institutions can share their common concerns.

Should I Go to Professional Meetings?

I think you should, because you will meet other people who are not trapped within the tunnels of your own institution. You will build a network of colleagues who can share their experience. At every meeting the sessions are uneven, but I find that I learn what is going on, and I need to know what I disagree with as much as what I agree with. I need to confront the devil, and I need reinforcement for my own virtue. It is also at such meetings that we see the materials publishers and other organizations make available for our use.

What's the Role of Research in the Classroom?

I think composition teachers should be carrying on a continual research program in the classroom, trying new things, testing them, evaluating them, and reporting what they discover to their colleagues in their own departments, at professional meetings, and through professional publications. The principal discoveries about how people write effectively and how people learn to write efficiently should come from within the classroom.

Should I Team-Teach?

Yes, as long as you realize that it isn't a time-saver. To team-teach properly means that you have to plan with the other instructor, be in the classroom when the other person is teaching as well as when you are teaching, evaluate what has happened with the other teacher. It is stimulating and educational, but very time-consuming.

How Can I Survive my Colleagues?

And how can my colleagues survive me? Good questions. Our peers will often want us to teach as little as they teach in the way they teach. It may seem that they will not want us to make a greater commitment in time or energy than they do, to challenge tradition, to experiment. The academic world is essentially conservative, and it always surprises me that the public sees us as liberal. Occasionally we may be liberal about social or political issues which do not affect us, but the academy is a very conservative, traditional place.

You have to teach the way you believe is right and try not to worry too much about how your colleagues are teaching. If we go our own way and it works we'll have the support of our students and, eventually, a few colleagues with whom we can share our failures and victories and who may even enlist in our cause. But most of us are in departments where the majority are not composition teachers and there will always be considerable misunderstanding about what we're doing and why.

How Can I Survive Being Supervised?

By taking the initiative and proposing experiments and supporting your proposals with documentation from meetings and from the professional literature. Your case for the experiments should be presented in a professional manner, and should allow the supervisor to share in the credit for what you accomplish.

How Can I Supervise a Composition Staff?

A supervisor should treat the people teaching under his or her supervision the way the supervisor wants the students to be treated. The supervisor is a model teacher and the staff a demonstration class.

The supervisor can provide leadership and put the activities of the staff in its scholarly context. But as much as possible the staff should share in the process of directing the program.

I think it's important to have weekly meetings in which the members of the staff report on what they are doing. The supervisor can share in the delight at the diversity of what is going on. The supervisor should have workshop sessions in which the staff question and state problems and concerns and in which the supervisor participates as one composition teacher of many, attempting to answer the questions, solve the problems, put the concerns into perspective. But most of the talking should be done by the staff in the same way that most of the talking in the composition classroom should be done by the students. It is the challenge of the supervisor to draw out of the staff its own resources, to allow it to discover what it knows so that staff members can teach each other, teach the supervisor, teach themselves, teach their students.

Why Should I Write?

○ To experience and appreciate the craft of writing from the inside, as a maker as well as a user.

○ To prepare yourself to understand what your students are doing and why, and just as important, how they feel and why.

○ To have fun. To fulfill yourself. To understand firsthand the joys and satisfactions of making meaning with words.

Should I Share my Writing with my Students?

Of course. They can teach you, and they can see what is necessary for meaning to be made with language. I think it is an ethical question. We are all revealed on the page, and such exposure is central to our discipline. If we expect our students to expose themselves to us, it seems proper for us to expose ourselves to them and show them our drafts as they show us their drafts.

This does not mean that the teacher should complete every assignment. It simply means that the student should know that the teacher is a dues-paying, voting member of the writing community.

How Can I Find Time to Get my Own Writing Done?

This is the question that plagues writers all their professional lives. No one ever has that perfect Tuesday morning when the writer is rested, there are no interruptions, and there is time to write. Most of us have to make use of small fragments of time, usually on a somewhat regular basis — early in the morning, during a free period, in the evening, late at night. It is amazing how much writing can be done in fifteen minutes, thirty minutes, an hour, if it is on a regular basis.

I find it helpful to have a daybook that is with me at all times so that I can write when I'm waiting for a car at the garage, waiting for a meeting to begin at the university, waiting to pick someone up in a parking lot, riding on an airplane, sitting in a traffic jam, watching television. Writing is a habit and a discipline, and you should be able to find some time to write on a daily or weekly basis. It is, after all, what you're asking your students to do in their own fragmented, harried lives. Both you and your students may find that those moments when you talk to yourself on your page become moments of essential concentration and quiet.

12 Answers to Questions Others May Ask You

Composition is not particle physics, and administrators, colleagues, parents, students, and everyone else over the age of eleven know how writing should be taught — and have no hesitation telling you just how it should be done. I particularly treasure illiterate notes — often from members of the faculty — telling me how to teach my courses in writing.

Each of us must develop our own strategies for dealing with the range of counsel from well-intentioned inanities to arrogant, vicious, personal, public attack. I know of no one who has administered a university writing program who has not been abused, insulted, and sneered at by colleagues from across the university and from within the English department. I have never met another person who is more thin-skinned than I am. I sense a criticism in a slight pause, and rise to my own defense in .04 second, but we have to learn productive ways of responding that fit our personalities and our situation.

My most successful strategy is to offer to meet with the faculty who complain that their students can't write because we don't teach them to write. I tell them I am concerned about the problem, it's part of my job to be concerned, suggest I may be able to help and indicate I'm willing to meet with a department or visit a class to talk about writing. First, I need to see the writing assignments and the papers so that I can diagnose the writing problems of students in that discipline. Most of the time, sadly, that ends it. The faculty say that because their students write so badly they've stopped asking them to write, and they use only short-answer or multiple-choice tests.

When composition teachers in my department have been able to work with other departments or faculty members we have been successful in helping them to understand the writing process and apply it to the tasks appropriate to their discipline. Since we are in a business that attracts Monday morning — and Tuesday through Sunday morning — quarterbacks, it may be helpful to discuss some of the ways we can respond to the questions most frequently asked.

Can Writing Be Taught?

The answer is in the writing folders of the students. Students who explore subjects on which they are authorities or can become authorities, who write frequently — at least once a week or more — who receive individual responses from instructors and classmates on each paper, and who have an opportunity to improve their drafts before a final grade, write better at the end of the writing course than at the beginning, and anyone examining a file drawer of writing folders can see the improvement.

This does not mean that everyone can become a flawless writer or that everyone will write well under every writing condition. Some students work very hard and learn enough to move from F to D or C. Some students write papers about subjects they don't know about or for teachers they don't care about. The results are not good.

Students, however, can experience the writing process and have it on hand to use. They can learn to write better by the end of a writing course than they could on the first day of class.

Where Is the Evidence to Prove They Have Learned to Write?

In the writing folders.

The compulsion to produce statistics to prove that people can write strikes me as absurd. Writing is a profession of self-exposure. The test is the product. It is there for everyone to read.

When Do You Teach Grammar?

Constantly. Students cannot use language effectively to explore their experience and evaluate it — to think critically — without following the traditions of language. Language is not just a matter of courtesy between educated people; it is a reflection of the way we think and a significant aid to thinking clearly. Language helps us to be precise in our thoughts, to create thoughts and to stand back and examine them critically.

As the student writes a sentence and reads that sentence back — an unavoidable and necessary part of the writing process — the student is involved with the question of grammar. As the student's paper is read by the instructor in conference and the classmate in workshop, as it is understood or misunderstood, the issue of language is involved. We cannot teach writing without teaching grammar.

Few composition teachers find that the teaching of grammar in advance of writing does much good. For most students the principles of grammar are abstractions, meaningless until the students are in the process of using language to discover their own meaning. At that time they become meaningful — pun intended — tools of thought. I've often had students who do very well in our grammar courses who cannot write well. They know the principles, but they do not know how to apply them in evolving drafts; they know the tools, but they do not know how to use them. We should know the traditions of our language, but they are best learned within the context of making writing.

How Does Personal Writing Help Students Write Academic Prose?

We do not teach a specific form of writing, for we do not know what writing tasks our students will be asked to complete in school and afterwards. The range of writing within a university or even within an English department can be enormous. One person's high standards is another person's garbage. I cannot tell what my students will be asked to do in their many disciplines, and I certainly cannot tell what they will be asked to write in the years after they leave school. Therefore I try to teach my students a writing process or, better yet, have them develop their own processes of writing they will be able to apply to the tasks that lie ahead of them.

To develop a writing process students usually have to write on a subject on which they are an authority. They have to know the subject well, have an inventory of information, a point of view or opinion, and an audience which can be instructed by a draft. This is exactly the opposite of the experience most of them have had in school, when they have written on subjects of someone else's choosing and on which they have far less information than the reader-teacher. That, unfortunately, is what often happens in academic writing. In writing *writing* the writer is the authority and has an abundance of information, and the problem is to distill that information so that it has meaning for readers who know less about the subject than the writer.

Few of our beginning students have an obsessive and extensive interest in an academic subject. When I was asked to initiate a sophomore writing course shortly after I began teaching I imagined our students writing within their discipline — psychology students would write articles on psychology, chemistry students on chemistry, history majors would write history. I was naive. Our students had had Psychology 1 or Chemistry 2 or a survey of world history in one semester, and few of them were able to write meaningful pieces in their discipline.

The more apprehensive the student is about writing, the more we have to encourage the student to find a subject on which the student is an authority. Most students begin to learn to write in personal papers about subjects that are important to them. Once they have successfully gone through the writing process, taking a subject that is not clear to them and developing and clarifying it so that it is clear to others, they are able to write about increasingly objective subjects, and they can see how to apply the process to a variety of writing tasks, academic and professional as well as personal.

Does the Process Work Only for Creating Writing?

Nope. The process may change according to the writing task, the experience of the writer with that writing task, and the personality or thinking style of the writer. But its similarities are greater than its differences.

Should We Have a Writing Lab?

Much of the best work in the composition field is coming out of writing labs that are run and staffed by bright, dedicated people who have developed constructive ways of dealing with the problems of students with severe academic problems.

I also believe, however, that most writing labs have been set up by departments and institutions that do not commit themselves to composition courses that respond to the needs of the students admitted to the institution. The writing lab is a way of pushing aside those students who most need education. The process of selection types the student, and that in itself confirms and adds to the feeling of inadequacy most students have when they come to a composition class.

It is politically significant that most writing labs are staffed by non-tenure-track faculty, predominantly women, whose salaries are lower than regular faculty and whose status is even lower. It is an exploitive situation at most institutions.

I must admit a prejudice. I was a high school flunk out, and that may make me question the tests we use to separate the poor student from the superior student. I have not seen a test or method of examining writing samples that I trust. When I visit institutions that have remedial programs I have always found that whatever method they use to identify the students who need remedial help, the number of students identified matches the number of sections available to them.

None of the above should be taken as a criticism of my colleagues who work in writing labs and remedial programs. They are often the most effective and most humane teachers of writing on the campus, and the research they have produced plays a leading role in our profession. But I am angry at the fiscal motivation for establishing such programs, and I am angry at the snobbery I observe by the traditional academic community towards their colleagues in such programs. I think the teaching of composition — the teaching of clear thinking in language — should be at the center of the academic structure, and it should be made available to all students who are allowed to enter an academic institution. And the faculty who can teach this central, intellectual discipline should be full members of the academic community.

How Do You Tell Which Students Should Be Exempt from Composition Courses?

This is a political and economic issue. All students can benefit from an experience in writing from an instructor skilled in the teaching of writing. All students should have an opportunity to write at the level of which they are capable and to rise from that point during the semester. At the University of New Hampshire no students are exempt from Freshman English. The student with a verbal SAT score of 790 can learn to write better, and so can the student with a score of 290. Students that are exempt are cheated of a fundamental intellectual experience, central to a college education. There is no one, present company certainly included, who could not benefit from taking a course in basic composition. The professional writer is doing that every day, learning and relearning how to write.

How Can You Help Me Teach Students in my Course to Write Better? I'm Not an English Teacher

Being a teacher of literature, of linguistics, even a writer in residence, does not make one an effective teacher of composition. The faculty member in the English department, or outside of the English department, should write with an experienced composition teacher. And then, when the faculty member has experienced the writing process, that faculty member and the instructor can discuss how to apply the writing process in other disciplines.

Many writing problems are produced by assignments. The experienced composition teacher can help the instructor develop assignments that make good writing possible and help the instructor to design structures within the course which will allow a response to writing in process. For example, most term papers are assigned without guidance, passed in at the end of the course, and piled outside the instructor's door after the course is over. Many instructors are conscientious and mark up the papers. They are appalled when the students do not bother to pick them up. Why should they? It is too late for the students to apply the lessons contained in the teacher's response.

It's possible to work with instructors to show them how a proposal for the paper, perhaps typed on one side of a three-by-five-inch card, can receive a brief but effective response from the instructor and from a group of students in a ten-minute small group session at the beginning of the class. This can be done even in a large lecture class, and the students can learn how to limit their topic and discover what questions the reader will ask about that topic. The students should also have an opportunity to have at least one response to a draft so that they can discover what the instructor and some colleague readers need to know, what they understand, and what they do not understand. This should be done when the students have a chance to respond with a draft for a grade.

The logistics for such a program in a large lecture class are extremely difficult, but not impossible. The term paper topic, for example, can be dealt with in the first two or three weeks of the course, and the students can choose a time when they want to deliver the first draft. That may range from the fifth or sixth week of the course until near the end of the term. This means that the instructor does not have a mountain of papers at one time, but can pace out the reading week by week. A composition teacher can also help the instructor see how it may be important to respond only with reactions to the subject and its focus, or the resources with which that subject can be explored early on. After a first draft the instructor may need to deal only with the structure of development of the text, its logic, and its documentation. In the final draft the instructor may focus on the conventions of scholarly writing and matters of style and clarity.

Professor Melody Graulich is one of several literature teachers in our department who has adapted writing course techniques to a particular literature class. An excerpt from her syllabus reads:

Requirements

Attendance and Participation:

Literature cannot be studied through monologue. In this course you will learn not THE answer but a process through which you can ask questions which will allow you to see multiple "answers," the complexity of possibilities that make up life, the subject of literature. I expect you to attend class regularly, having *finished* the reading assigned on the schedule. Come ready to talk. I may call on you.

Papers

Each Monday you will turn in a short response to the week's reading, approximately 250–300 words. You may write about anything you want, but please be sure to focus or limit your topic so that you don't just generalize randomly. These short papers are a way for you to explore and express your original ideas; they should not be a recounting or paraphrasing of what the text is about, although they should be a response to what the author has to say and how he or she says it. You may turn in two short responses up to one week late; if you exceed this limit, your grade will be affected. Always bring two copies of your short response to class. You will give one to me and exchange the other with a classmate, who will read and comment on your paper, while you read and comment on his or hers. Always sign your comments. Your short responses will not be graded individually, but they will contribute to your final grade.

Two critical essays of approximately 750 words, due March 5 and May 7. These may be revisions of your short papers. I will have more to say about these papers in class.

One personal essay of approximately five typed pages, due April 2. This essay should recount a concrete incident or experience you feel will allow you to convey the values, ethic, or ideology you express through your relationship to the natural world. You will bring to class four copies of this essay. You will give one to me and the others to three classmates, whose papers you will read. You will meet with this group on April 9 to discuss your papers; ATTENDANCE IS REQUIRED AT THIS CLASS. You will then revise your paper, due April 16, and turn in one copy to me.

A "Wilderness Letter," due April 30. This will be your final short response. Be succinct: about 500 words. More on this in class.

What Is the Relationship of Reading to Writing?

Intimate. You can read without writing, but you cannot write, even an X scratched in the dust, without reading. Every writing course is a reading course, a course in reading those writers who establish the tradition or standards in our language, and in reading our drafts and the drafts of others in process so that we can make subsequent drafts more effective.

What Do You Need to Set Up a Writing Program?

A writing program needs a director who has several important qualities. These include:

- ○ Firsthand continuing experience with the writing process. The director of a writing program should write. That does not mean that the director should be a *Writer*; it does mean that he or she should enter into the experience of writing frequently enough to understand the problems and feelings of writing students.
- ○ Awareness of the scholarship that exists within the discipline of composition and familiarity with the resources available in journals and at meetings. I'd add demonstration of participation in that discipline through publication in the journals and participation in the programs of professional organizations.
- ○ A sincere interest in teaching writing to those who do not yet know how to write. This is perhaps the hardest to judge, but in a time of limited academic jobs many opportunists are attracted to this field. We do not need people running writing programs who wish they were doing something else. We need people who are fascinated with the writing process and excited at the prospect of hearing the voices of the students who did not know they had a voice.

13 Why Should I Teach Writing?

You'll have to develop your own answer to that question out of your own experience listening to the writing of your students. My own answers are complicated and personal. But I have found the profession of composition teacher intellectually challenging and spiritually satisfying. It provides me with questions I cannot answer but continually need to ask; it allows me to see human beings finding a way to express their own individuality.

I write, I suppose, because I can never learn to write, only continue to learn writing. If you write, you will find that each day you will go to your writing desk expecting to say one thing and find yourself saying another. Writing is a matter of continuing change and discovery. I have been writing for publication since I was nine years old and published a newspaper on a hectograph in Miss Chapman's room, and as I write this I am fifty-nine years old and more excited, more surprised by what I write than I was when language first ran ahead of me and I began to follow.

I continue to teach writing, because I will never learn to teach writing — even when I write books on how to write and how to teach. I can only continue to experiment with ways of creating an environment in which I can get out of the way of my students and watch — applauding — as they teach themselves the craft none of us can ever learn.

You will, of course, bring new insights to how writing is made to your students. These insights will come from your own experience with the writing process, your own familiarity with the research in composition, and what your students teach you about the way they are writing. Each class will be composed of individuals whose diversity will be a challenge and a delight. The satisfactions of teaching will come as you confront and confirm that diversity, sharing with your students their excitement in hearing the voices they did not know they had rise from the page.

Do not minimize the importance of our calling. We have a vocation, and it is to help our students discover, develop and share their individuality. It makes a difference when a person finds he or she can speak, and it makes a difference to others when they speak. Writing is a way of understanding our world and breaking out of our anonymity and isolation by sharing our diverse understandings.

I grow weary of teaching, I wonder if it is worthwhile, I doubt my ability to listen, to support, to help; I grow angry and impatient with my colleagues. H. L. Mencken reportedly said, "Campus politics are so vicious because the stakes are so low." Some days, coming from meetings in which I have contributed to the pettiness and the meanness, I think I am being bitten to death by ducks, a slow and ridiculous way to go.

But then I return to my office at home and find the face of Michael Biggins staring at me, a copy of his self-portrait scratched in ink on newsprint.

I study that strong face, sensitive, intelligent, and I reread the story of that drawing. It reads:

Portrait of a Failure

Sir Alec Clegg yesterday showed reporters attending the North of England Education Conference at Leeds the self-portrait painted on a sheet of newspaper by a boy of 14. Sir Alec, chief education officer for the West Riding, described it as "the most moving picture I have seen." Sir Alec said the young artist had a low IQ and no formal art training. He had left school at the earliest opportunity, and was now 17. "The last I heard about him was that he had been in some trouble with the police. He had a job as a laborer, but knowing that he lives in Doncaster, I would not be surprised if he was now unemployed," Sir Alec said.

"This picture came from a child who was branded as an educational failure. We have no right to talk about this child in these terms. His fate is a failure for me and for the West Riding. I wrote to his parents to suggest we get him into an art school. We never had a reply."

From the *Guardian*, 5 January 1972. Reprinted by permission.

Michael Biggins reminds me of the importance of what we do, that we make it possible for individuals to realize their potential, demonstrate their individuality, break out of the silence that can imprison all of us, and hear their own voices. Michael Biggins rose out of that silence and spoke in that portrait before he disappeared into silence again. He reminds us of the potential that is there and of our responsibility to help individual students realize their potential. He helps me put the pettiness of the day into perspective.

That drawing reminds me of the debt I owe Bob Hamilton in the sixth grade of the Massachusetts Fields School in Wollaston, Massachusetts; Mort Howell of Tilton Junior College in Tilton, New Hampshire: Gwynne Daggett and Carroll Towle of the University of New Hampshire. They saw in me what I did not see in myself — or perhaps what I saw, secretly, in myself but could not let anyone else see — a vision, a hope, a dream, a possibility.

I listen to my colleagues in the writing programs at the University of New Hampshire as they struggle to learn how to listen to their students and draw out of them what they may become, and I am impressed by their skills and their concern. I attend professional meetings and workshops where I hear other teachers of composition share their caring and their techniques, and I am stimulated, inspired and supported by them.

Most of all, I meet my students in conference and listen to them tell me how they are writing better than they ever hoped to write, saying things that they find important to be said in a voice that they feel is their own. I read their papers and share their surprise in their own diversity with them, and I know that I will never burn out, that I will never lose my excitement at my own and my students' explorations of our world with the writing process.

I hope that your students will teach you — as mine have taught me — why you have to continue to learn to write and teach writing.

Appendix: Reading and Writing as a Professional

The serious teacher of composition will find it satisfying to develop this discipline and to keep this specialty alive through publication and reading.

Publication completes the process of writing, and teachers of composition will find a satisfaction in that completeness. The level of publication is not as important as the experience of publication. The teacher, the teacher's colleagues, and students will all benefit from the increased competence of a teacher who is practicing the craft being taught. We do not expect all our music teachers to play with the New York Philharmonic or our art teachers to be exhibited in the National Gallery, but we do expect them to toot and perform, to paint and exhibit. It keeps them in the game. And composition teachers should put the same demands on themselves.

There is also a significant benefit to those who choose to publish articles and books on composition theory, research, and pedagogy. These composition teachers participate in the profession and influence the direction of our discipline. They contribute to our growing knowledge of how writing is made and how writing is taught.

There is an enormous and continually growing resource of information in our field, and composition teachers should continue to read for inspiration, stimulation, reinforcement, and to keep alive the sense of community we can have with writers and teachers of writing alive and dead. What we read can bring us to our own writing desks and to our classrooms with renewed energy and vision. Reading can help us put what we are observing in perspective and make us observe what has become ordinary with a new insight.

How to Get Published

Writers get published by submitting their manuscript for publication. That sounds too obvious to mention, but as one who teaches students who wish to become professional writers, I believe it is the single distinguishing mark that identifies those students who will become writers. They are often not the most talented, but they are the ones who have the courage, the energy, the naiveté — whatever it is — that makes it possible for them to put their manuscripts in the mail.

What is published is the best — in the editor's view — of what is being submitted. Editors are looking for good stuff, and if you don't like what they are publishing you have the opportunity to submit your drafts and raise the level.

Where to Get Published

In all forms of publication — poems, popular songs, newspaper articles, plays, novels, short stories, essays, composition texts, research articles — there is one important rule: submit to the best. There is no reason not to start at the top, and there is every reason to start at the top. The best publications are often the most open to what is new, contrary to popular opinion; they have the staff to work with beginning writers, and their editors are usually the most skillful. They pay more and reach out to more readers.

To publish a book, go to a librarian and find out who has published the best or the most books in a given field. Then submit a proposal or a draft, if you have it written, to that publisher.

Manuscripts generally get the best reading when they are sent to the top editor. Invest in a phone call and find out who that is. Send it to that person. The top person may not read it, but if it trickles down it will end up higher up than if you just send it in. It will get read at the good places, but it's less likely to trickle up.

The same thing is true for professional journals, magazines, and newspapers. Start with the best, and start with the top person at the best. There are a lot of places I haven't been published, but it hasn't been because they haven't seen my stuff. If they are dumb enough not to realize its value, it's their fault, not mine.

There are other ways for composition teachers to participate in the process of writing. Many publications will hire composition teachers for the summer or for special projects. It is a way for publications to support education, perform a public service, hire relatively inexpensive vacation replacements or extra help when its needed. Composition teachers should seek out such opportunities. The experience of working with professionals who are meeting deadlines may be much more valuable than a summer or an evening graduate course. And it can provide a special kind of satisfaction, and some additional income.

The way to discover such opportunities is to approach those places where such opportunities may exist. Write to the top person, present your case, and see what happens. On a publication you will see how people work with language, and will be able to carry these lessons of publication back to your students.

We need, as teachers of writing, to take the mystery out of writing, to participate in the craft so that we have the authority and the experience of a person who is practicing what we preach.

Reading as a Writer and a Teacher: A Personal Bibliography

There is a constant flow of periodicals about writing and the teaching of writing that passes across my desk. I have a comprehensive membership in the National Council of Teachers of English, which I think is the best professional investment I can make. I receive every one of their periodicals and books as part of this membership. I will list below some of those professional journals which I have found valuable as a reader and which are also available for submission. This list of publications is not definitive, it is just a sample to give you an idea of the resources available.

There is also a lot of information about the writing process that appears in newspapers and magazines, in interviews with writers, book reviews, essays published in book sections, articles about writers and by writers that should be clipped and filed.

Long before I was a teacher of writing I was reading books about writers and by writers to try to understand my craft. When I became a teacher I added books about teaching and volumes of research about the writing process. What follows is a personal list, even an eccentric list, a few selections from my personal library. It could be organized in many ways, but I've chosen a simple alphabetical order by author, so that you can find books easily that you may wish to organize in special lists that serve your own needs.

This is not meant to be a definitive bibliography, but a small sampling to demonstrate the resources available to the teacher of composition. I do not think there is any need to duplicate the continuing bibliographical studies that are being published. There is, however, an extensive resource of information by writers on how they write, and since this source of information on the writing process is not collected in traditional scholarly bibliographies I am listing such books here.

There are some people, writers included, who do not think that the testimony of writers should be taken seriously. They believe that the artist works dumbly, not knowing what he is doing. I believe that the artist is first of all a craftsperson and knows a great deal of what is being done during the act of writing. I think that a careful study of how writers write reveals significant information. Is it the whole story? Of course not. No form of research into the writing process provides the whole story. But the evidence we gather from those who write should be a part of our scholarly resource.

It is worth noting that these resources can provide illumination for the teacher of literature, and that using such evidence in a literature class can take the student behind the scenes in the making of a work of art and provide a bridge between composition and the study of literature.

I have an extensive collection of testimony from artists on their craft, which I believe illuminates the writing process, but I have not included it here. I have also included few examples of writers' bibliographies and autobiographies, collections of letters, published diaries and journals, textbooks by writers on composition or writing a particular journal. All those genres illuminate the writing process, but they are available through traditional library channels. I've also chosen not to list individual articles, because I find that most of the best ones end up in collections.

I have emphasized the collections of interviews with writers because that genre is a rich source of process information from a broad spectrum of writers and it does not seem to appear anywhere else. I have also listed many manuscript facsimile collections because I believe our students should see the masters in process and because I do not think those sources have been used enough to explore the writing and editing processes of experienced writers.

I think a significant area of research in composition would be to study, through protocols, observation and interviews, the writing processes of publishing writers. There has been some work done, but far too little. We need to know how writers write with greater depth and precision if we are to help our students become effective writers.

Periodicals

CEA Forum, Elizabeth Cowan, English Dept., Texas A&M Univ., College Station, TX 77843.

College Composition and Communication, NCTE, 1111 Kenyon Rd., Urbana, IL 61801. The principal journal for the college teacher of composition.

College English, NCTE, 1111 Kenyon Rd., Urbana, IL 61801.

English Education, NCTE, 1111 Kenyon Rd., Urbana, IL 61801.

English Journal, NCTE, 1111 Kenyon Rd., Urbana, IL 61801. The primary journal for secondary school teachers of composition.

Freshman English News, Gary Tate, English Dept., Texas Christian Univ., Fort Worth, TX 76129.

Journal of Advanced Composition, Tim D. P. Lally, Editor, Univ. of South Alabama, Mobile, AL 36688.

Journal of Basic Writing, Sarah G. D'Eloia Fortune, Instructional Resource Center, 535 East 80th St., New York, NY 10012.

Journal of Teaching Writing, 425 Agnes St., Indianapolis, IN 46202,

Language Arts, NCTE, 1111 Kenyon Rd., Urbana, IL 61801.

The National Writing Project Network News Letter, Publications Dept., National Writing Project, School of Education, Univ. of California, Berkeley, CA 94720.

Research in the Teaching of English, NCTE, 1111 Kenyon Rd., Urbana, IL 61801.

Rhetoric Review, Theresa Enos, Dept. of English, Southern Methodist Univ., Dallas, TX 75275.

Teaching in the Two-Year College, Dept. of English, East Carolina Univ., Greenville, NC 27834.

The Writing Center Journal, Lil Brannon, The Writing Center, New York Univ., 269 Mercer St., New York, NY 10003.

The Writing Instructor, The Freshman Writing Program, Univ. of Southern California, Los Angeles, CA 90089-1219.

Written Communication: A Quarterly Journal of Research, Theory, and Applications. The editors are Stephen P. Wittie and John A. Daly, Dept. of English, Parlyn Hall, Univ. of Texas, Austin, TX 78712; Sage Publications, Beverly Hills, CA 90212.

A number of state and regional journals are listed in the Directory published each year by the National Council of Teachers of English (NCTE), 1111 Kenyon Road, Urbana, IL 61801.

Those interested in publishing should also obtain:

Publishing in English Education, edited by Stephen N. Judy, Boynton/Cook, 1982; 206 Claremont Avenue, Montclair, NJ 07042.

A Directory of Publishing Opportunities for Teachers of Writing, edited by William F. Woods, Community Collaborators, 1979, P.O. Box 5429, Charlottesville, VA, 22905.

A Bibliography

Scholarship in the field of composition is multiplying at an enormous rate, and fortunately there are regular literature reviews or bibliographies published in such journals as *College Composition and Communication* and *College English.* In addition there are bibliographical works available to students in the field such as:

The Bedford Bibliography for Teachers of Writing, prepared by Robert M. Gorrell, Patricia Bizzell, and Bruce Herzberg, Bedford Books of St. Martin's Press, New York, 1984.

Teaching Composition: Ten Bibliographical Essays, edited by Gary Tate, Texas Christian Univ. Press, Fort Worth, 1976.

There are a number of anthologies which attempt to survey the general field of composition theory and pedagogy. Reading such books can help a beginner get a feeling for the field and hear many voices of influence within the discipline.

Cooper, Charles R., and Lee Odell, editors, *Research on Composing: Points of Departure*, National Council of Teachers of English, Urbana, IL, 1978.

Donovan, Timothy R., and Ben W. McClelland, editors, *Eight Approaches to Teaching Composition*, National Council of Teachers of English, Urbana, IL, 1980.

Gebhardt, Richard C., editor, *Composition and Its Teaching*, Ohio Council of Teachers of English Language Arts, Findlay, OH, 1979.

Graves, Richard L., editor, *Rhetoric and Composition: A Sourcebook for Teachers and Writers*, Boynton/Cook, Upper Montclair, NJ, 1984.

Stock, Patricia L., editor, *fforum: Essays on Theory and Practice in the Teaching of Writing*, Boynton/Cook, Upper Montclair, NJ, 1983.

Tate, Gary, and Edward P. J. Corbett, editors, *The Writing Teacher's Sourcebook*, Oxford University Press, New York, 1981.

Interviews with writers and books by writers on the process of writing are a great source of information for the composition teacher, both from a teaching and a writing point of view. Below are some of the books that I have found most useful:

Algren, Nelson, *Conversations with Nelson Algren*, edited by H. E. F. Donohue, Berkley, New York, 1965.

Allen, Walter, editor, *Writers on Writing*, Dutton, New York, 1959.

Allott, Miriam, *Novelists on the Novel*, Columbia Univ. Press, New York, 1959.

Autograph Letters and Manuscripts: Major Acquisitions of the Pierpont Morgan Library, 1924–1974, Pierpont Morgan Library, New York, 1974.

Barry, Elaine, *Robert Frost on Writing*, Rutgers Univ. Press, New Brunswick, NJ, 1973.

Bartlett, Phyllis, *Poems in Process*, Oxford Univ. Press, New York, 1951.

Bellamy, Joe David, editor, *The New Fiction: Interviews with Innovative American Writers*, Univ. of Illinois Press, Champaign, 1974.

Bennett, Patrick, *Talking with Texas Writers: Twelve Interviews*, Texas A&M Univ. Press, College Station, 1980.

Bergman, Ingmar, *Bergman on Bergman: Interviews with Ingmar Bergman*, by Stig Bjorkman, Torsten Marms, and Jonas Sima, Touchstone Books, Simon & Schuster, New York, 1973.

Bonnefoy, Claude, *Conversations with Eugene Ionesco*, Holt, Rinehart and Winston, New York, 1971.

Borges, Jorge Luis, *Borges on Writing*, edited by Norman Thomas di Giovanni, Daniel Halpern, and Frank MacShane, Dutton, New York, 1973.

Borges, Jorge Luis, *Conversations with Jorge Luis Borges*, edited by Richard Burgin, Discus/Avon, New York, 1970.

Bowen, Catherine Drinker, *Adventures of a Biographer*, Little Brown, Boston, 1959.

Bowen, Catherine Drinker, *Biography: The Craft and the Calling*, Little Brown, Boston, 1969.

Bowen, Catherine Drinker, *The Writing of Biography*, The Writer, Boston, 1951.

Brady, John, editor, *The Craft of the Screenwriter: Interviews with Six Celebrated Screenwriters,* Simon & Schuster, New York, 1981.

Bruce-Novoa, *Chicano Authors: Inquiry by Interview,* Univ. of Texas Press, Austin, 1980.

Buckler, William E., *Novels in the Making,* Houghton Mifflin, Boston, 1961.

Butt, John, and Kathleen Tillotson, *Dickens at Work,* Essential Books, Fairlawn, NJ, 1958.

Cahoon, Herbert, Thomas V. Lange, and Charles Ryscamp, editors, *American Literary Autographs: From Washington Irving to Henry James,* Dover, New York, 1977.

Cameron, Donald, *Conversations with Canadian Novelists — 1,* Macmillan of Canada, Toronto, 1973.

Cameron, Donald, *Conversations with Canadian Novelists — 2,* Macmillan of Canada, Toronto, 1973.

Cane, Melville, *Making a Poem: An Inquiry into the Creative Process,* Harvest, New York, 1962.

Carr, John C., *Kite Flying and Other Irrational Acts: Conversations with Twelve Southern Writers,* Louisiana State Univ. Press, Baton Rouge, 1972.

Carr, John C., *The Craft of Crime: Conversations with Crime Writers,* Houghton Mifflin, Boston, 1983.

Chandler, Raymond, *Raymond Chandler Speaking,* edited by Dorothy Gardner and Katherine Sorley Walker, Houghton Mifflin, Boston, 1962.

Charlton, James, editor, *The Writer's Quotation Book: A Literary Companion,* Pushcart, New York, 1980.

Clark, Roy Peter, editor, *Best Newspaper Writing 1979,* Modern Media Institute, St. Petersburg, FL. Books have also been published for 1981, 1982, and 1983, and the series is expected to continue. Includes insightful interviews with the winners of the American Society of Newspaper Editors competition.

Corliss, Richard, editor, *The Hollywood Screenwriters: A Film Comment Book,* Discus/Avon, New York, 1972.

Croft, P.J., *Autograph Poetry in the English Language: Facsimiles of Original Manuscripts from the Fourteenth to the Twentieth Century* (2 volumes), McGraw-Hill, New York, 1973.

Dembo, L. S., and Cyrena N. Pondrom, editors, *The Contemporary Writer: Interviews with Sixteen Novelists and Poets,* Univ. of Wisconsin Press, Madison, 1972.

Dembo, L. S., editor, *Interviews with Contemporary Writers,* 2nd Series, 1972–1982, Univ. of Wisconsin Press, Madison, 1983.

Dickey, James, *Night Hurdling: Poems, Essays, Conversations, Commencements, and Afterwords,* Bruccoli Clark, Bloomfield Hills, MI, 1983.

Dickey, James, *Self-Interviews,* Doubleday, Garden City, NY, 1970.

Duerden, Dennis, and Cosmo Pieterse, editors, *African Writers Talking,* Heinemann, London, 1972.

Durrell, Lawrence, *The Big Supposer: A Dialogue with Marc Alyn,* Grove Press, New York, 1974.

Eliot, T. S., *The Wasteland: A Facsimile and Transcript of the Original Drafts, Including the Annotations of Ezra Pound,* edited by Valerie Eliot, Harcourt Brace Jovanovich, New York, 1971.

Faulkner, William, *Faulkner in the University: Class Conferences at the University of Virginia, 1957–1958,* edited by Frederick L. Gwynn and Joseph L. Blotner, Random House, Vintage Books, New York, 1965.

Faulkner, William, *Faulkner's Revision of Absalom, Absalom! A Collation of the*

Manuscript and the Published Book, by Gerald Langford, Univ. of Texas Press, Austin, 1971.

Flaubert, Gustav, *Flaubert and Madame Bovary: A Double Portrait, by* Francis Steegmuller, Random House, Vintage Books, New York, 1939, 1950. An extraordinary account of a writer at work.

Forester, C. S., *The Hornblower Companion: An Atlas and Personal Commentary on the Writing of the Hornblower Saga,* Little Brown, Boston, 1964.

Froug, William, *The Screenwriter Looks at the Screenwriter: Twelve Top Screenwriters Talk About Their Craft, Their Techniques, and Their Vital Role in Shaping a Film,* Macmillan, New York, 1972.

Funke, Lewis, *Playwrights Talk About Writing,* Dramatic Publishing Co., Chicago and Westport, 1975.

Gado, Frank, editor, *First Person: Conversations on Writers and Writing,* Union College Press, Schenectady, NY, 1973.

Gardner, John, *The Art of Fiction: Notes on Craft for Young Writers,* Knopf, New York, 1984.

Gardner, John, *On Becoming a Novelist,* Harper & Row, New York, 1983.

Garrett, George, editor, *The Writer's Voice,* Morrow, New York, 1973.

Gibbons, Reginald, editor, *The Poet's Work,* Houghton Mifflin, Boston, 1979.

Gibson, Graeme, interviewer, *Eleven Canadian Novelists,* Anansi, Toronto, 1972.

Gibson, Walker, *Poems in the Making,* Houghton Mifflin, Boston, 1963.

Golding, William, *Talk: Conversations with William Golding,* edited by Jack I. Biles, Harcourt Brace Jovanovich, New York, 1970.

Greene, Graham, *In Search of a Character: Two African Journals,* Viking, New York, 1962.

Greene, Graham, *The Other Man: Conversations with Marie-Francois Allain,* Simon & Schuster, New York, 1983.

Greene, Graham, *Ways of Escape,* Lester and Orphen Dennys, Canada, 1980.

Guibert, Rita, *Seven Voices: Seven Latin American Writers Talk to Rita Guibert,* Knopf, New York, 1973.

Hale, Nancy, *The Realities of Fiction: A Book About Writing,* Little Brown, Boston, 1962.

Hall, Donald, general editor of a series, *Poets on Poetry,* published by the Univ. of Michigan Press, Ann Arbor, Michigan. This is an important series of books that collects "the articles, interviews, and book reviews by which they have articulated the poetics of a new generation." The poets include Marvin Bell, Robert Bly, Hayden Carruth, Donald Davie, Robert Francis, John Haines, Donald Hall, Donald Justice, David Ignatow, Galway Kinnell, Richard Kostelanetz, Maxine Kumin, John Logan, Alicia Ostriker, Marge Piercy, Louis Simpson, William Stafford, Diane Wakoski, James Wright. I have found the books by Kumin and Stafford particularly helpful.

Hall, Donald, editor, *Claims for Poetry,* Univ. of Michigan Press, Ann Arbor, 1982.

Hayman, Ronald, editor, *Playback,* Davis-Poynter, London, 1973.

Hellman, Lillian, *An Unfinished Woman: A Memoir,* Little Brown, Boston, 1969.

Henry, Marguerite, *Dear Readers and Riders,* Rand McNally, Chicago, 1969.

Hersey, John, *The Writer's Craft,* Knopf, New York, 1974.

Hildick, Wallace, *Word for Word: A Study of Authors' Alterations,* Faber & Faber, London, 1965.

Hildick, Wallace, *Writing with Care,* David White, New York, 1967.

Hopkins, Lee Bennett, editor, *Books Are by People: Interviews with 104 Authors and Illustrators of Books for Young Children,* Citation, New York, 1969.

Hopkins, Lee Bennett, editor, *More Books by More People: Interviews with Sixty-Five Authors of Books for Children,* Citation, New York, 1974.

Horgan, Paul, *Approaches to Writing: Reflections and Notes on the Art of Writing from a Career of Half a Century,* Farrar, Straus & Giroux, New York, 1973.

Housman, A. E., *The Making of "A Shropshire Lad": A Manuscript Variorum,* by Tom Burns Haber, Univ. of Washington Press, Seattle, 1966.

Hugo, Richard, *The Triggering Town: Lectures and Essays on Poetry and Writing,* Norton, New York, 1979.

Hull, Helen, editor, *The Writer's Book,* presented by the Authors Guild, Barnes & Noble, New York, 1956.

Hull, Helen, and Michael Drury, editors, *Writer's Roundtable,* presented by the Authors Guild, Harper & Brothers, New York, 1959.

Janeway, Elizabeth, editor, *The Writer's World,* presented by the Authors Guild, McGraw-Hill, New York, 1972.

Jarrell, Randall, *Jerome: The Biography of a Poem,* Grossman, New York, 1971.

Kantor, MacKinlay, Lawrence Osgood, James Emanuel, How *I Write/2,* Harcourt Brace Jovanovich, New York, 1972.

Keats, John, *The Odes of Keats and Their Earliest Known Manuscripts,* edited by Robert Gittings, Kent State Univ. Press, Kent, OH, 1970.

Kuehl, John, *Creative Writing and Rewriting: Contemporary American Novelists at Work,* Appleton-Century-Crofts, New York, 1967.

Lessing, Doris, *A Small Personal Voice: Essays, Reviews, Interviews,* edited by Paul Schlueter, Random House, Vintage Books, New York, 1975.

Levertov, Denise, *The Poet in the World,* New Directions, New York, 1973.

Lewis, Jenny, editor, *Poetry in the Making: Catalogue of an Exhibition of Poetry Manuscripts in the British Museum,* Turret Books, London, 1967.

MacDonald, Ross, *On Crime Writing,* Capra, Santa Barbara, CA, 1973.

Madden, David, and Richard Powers, *Writers' Revisions: An Annotated Bibliography of Articles and Books About Writers' Revisions and Their Comments on the Creative Process,* Scarecrow Press, Metuchen, NJ, 1981.

Mann, Thomas, *The Story of a Novel: The Genesis of "Dr. Faustus,"* Knopf, New York, 1961.

McCormack, Thomas, editor, *Afterwords: Novelists on Their Novels.* Harper & Row, New York, 1969.

McCrindle, Joseph F., editor, *Behind the Scenes: Theater and Film Interviews from "The Transatlantic Review,"* Pitman Publishing, London, 1971.

McCullough, David W., *McCullough's Brief Lives: Selected "Eye on Books" Interviews,* Book-of-the-Month Club, New York, 1980.

McPhee, John, *The John McPhee Reader,* edited by William Howarth, Random House, Vintage Books, New York, 1977. Includes an extraordinary introduction on the writing method of this master non-fiction writer.

Michener, James A., *In Search of Centennial: A Journey with James A. Michener,* by John Kings, Random House, New York, 1978.

Miller, Henry, *Henry Miller on Writing,* selected by Thomas H. Moore, New Directions, New York, 1964.

Mitford, Jessica, *Poison Penmanship: The Gentle Art of Muckraking,* Knopf, New York, 1979. Includes extensive comments by the author on her pieces.

Nemerov, Howard, editor, *Poets on Poetry,* Basic Books, New York, 1966.

Newquist, Roy, editor, *Conversations,* Rand McNally, Chicago, 1967.

Newquist, Roy, editor, *Counterpoint,* Rand McNally, Chicago, 1964.

Nin, Anais, *Anais Nin Observed, From a Film Portrait of a Woman as Artist,* edited by Robert Snyder, Swallow Press, Chicago, 1976.

Norman, Charles, editor, *Poets on Poetry,* Collier, New York, 1962.

Oates, Joyce Carol, editor, *First Person Singular: Writers on Their Craft,* Ontario Review Press, Princeton, NJ, 1983.

O'Brien, John, editor, *Interviews with Black Writers,* Liveright, New York, 1973.

O'Connor, Flannery, *The Habit of Being: Letters of Flannery O'Connor,* edited by Sally Fitzgerald, Farrar, Straus, & Giroux, New York, 1979.

O'Connor, Flannery, *Mystery and Manners: Occasional Prose,* selected and edited by Sally and Robert Fitzgerald, Farrar, Straus & Giroux, New York, 1969.

Olsen, Tillie, *Silences,* Delacorte Press/Seymour Lawrence, New York, 1978.

Packard, William, editor, *The Craft of Poetry: Interviews from "The New York Quarterly,"* Doubleday, Garden City, NY, 1974.

Phillips, Judson, Lawson Carter, and Robert Hayden, *How I Write/1,* Harcourt Brace Jovanovich, New York, 1972.

Plath, Sylvia, *The Journals of Sylvia Plath,* edited by Ted Hughes and Frances McCullough, Ballantine, New York, 1983.

Pollock, Bruce, editor, *In Their Own Words: Twenty Successful Songwriters Tell How They Write Their Songs,* Collier, New York, 1975.

Ponge, Francis, *The Making of the Pre,* Univ. of Missouri Press, Columbia, 1979.

Rich, Adrienne, *On Lies, Secrets and Silence: Selected Prose, 1966-1978,* Norton, New York, 1979.

Rinehart, Mary Roberts, *Writing Is Work, The Writer,* Boston, 1939.

Roethke, Theodore, *On the Poet and His Craft: Selected Prose of Theodore Roethke,* edited by Ralph J. Mills, Jr., Univ. of Washington Press, Seattle, 1965.

Roussel, Raymond, *How I Wrote Certain of My Books,* Sun, New York, 1977.

Sansom, William, *The Birth of a Story,* Chatto and Windus, London, 1972.

Scott, A. F., *The Poet's Craft,* Cambridge Univ. Press, London, 1957.

Shenker, Israel, *Words and Their Masters,* Doubleday, Garden City, NY, 1974.

Spender, Stephen, *The Making of a Poem,* Norton, New York, 1962.

Steinbeck, John, *A Life in Letters,* edited by Elaine Steinbeck and Robert Wallsten, Penguin, New York, 1976.

Steinbeck, John, *Journal of a Novel: The "East of Eden" Letters,* Viking, New York, 1969.

Sternburg, Janet, editor, *The Writer on Her Work,* Norton, New York, 1980.

Tate, Claudia, editor, *Black Women Writers at Work.* Continuum, New York, 1983.

Taylor, Robert H., *Authors at Work,* Grolier Club, New York, 1957. Includes fascinating facsimiles of manuscripts by famous authors.

Thoreau, Henry David, *H. D. Thoreau: A Writer's Journal,* selected and edited by Laurence Stapleton, Dover, New York, 1960.

Thoreau, Henry David, *The Making of Walden,* by James Lyndon Shanley, Univ. of Chicago Press, Chicago, 1957.

Tooker, Dan, and Roger Hofheins, *Fiction! Interviews with Northern California Novelists,* Series 1, Harcourt Brace Jovanovich/William Kaufman, New York/Los Altos 1976.

Trask, Georgianne, and Charles Burkhart, editors, *Storytellers and Their Art,* Doubleday, Anchor Books, Garden City, NY, 1963.

Turner, Alberta T., editor, *Fifty Contemporary Poets: The Creative Process,* McKay, New York, 1977.

Wager, Walter, editor, *The Playwrights Speak,* Delta, New York, 1967.

Wallenstein, Barry, *Visions and Revisions: An Approach to Poetry,* Crowell, New York, 1971.

Walshe, R.D., editor, *Speaking of Writing . . . : Seventeen Leading Writers of Australian and New Zealand Fiction Answer Questions on Their Craft,* Reed Education, Sydney, Australia, 1975.

Warren, Robert Penn, *Robert Penn Warren Talking: Interviews 1950–1978,* edited by Floyd C. Watkins and John T. Hiers, Random House, New York, 1980.

Webber, Jeannette L., and Joan Grumman, editors, *Woman as Writer,* Houghton Mifflin, Boston, 1978.

Welty, Eudora, *One Writer's Beginnings,* Harvard Univ. Press, Cambridge, 1984.

West, William W., *On Writing, By Writers,* Ginn, Boston, 1966.

White, E. B., *Letters of E. B. White,* collected and edited by Dorothy Lobrano Guth, Harper & Row, New York, 1976.

Williams, William Carlos, *Interviews with William Carlos Williams,* edited by Linda Welshimer Wagner, New Directions, New York, 1976.

Wintle, Justin, and Emma Fisher, editors, *The Pied Pipers: Interviews with the Influential Creators of Children's Literature,* Paddington Press, New York, 1974.

Woolf, Virginia, *A Writer's Diary: Being Extracts from the "Diary of Virginia Woolf,"* edited by Leonard Woolf, with an afterword by Louise Bogan and Josephine Schaefer, New American Library, New York, 1968.

Writers at Work — The Paris Review Interviews:

1st Series, introduction by Malcolm Cowley, edited by Malcolm Cowley, Viking, New York, 1958.

2nd Series, introduction by Van Wyck Brooks, edited by George Plimpton, Viking, New York, 1963.

3rd Series, introduction by Alfred Kazin, edited by George Plimpton, Viking, New York, 1967.

4th Series, edited by George Plimpton, Viking, New York, 1976.

5th Series, introduction by Francine du Plessix Gray, edited by George Plimpton, Viking, New York, 1981.

6th Series, edited by George Plimpton, Viking, New York, 1984.

These books and the ones that should follow, I think, are the single most valuable resource for those who are interested in what the most distinguished writers of our time say about the writing process.

Yeats, W. B., *Vision and Revision in Yeats' Last Poems,* edited by Jon Stallworthy, Oxford Univ. Press, London, 1969.

Yeats, W. B., *Yeats at Work,* by Curtis B. Bradford, Southern Illinois Univ. Press, Carbondale, IL 1965.

Index